From chapter 1 onward, we will explore how climate and environmental drivers can hurl extra fuel onto already-smoldering fires, as per the most widely accepted characterization of climate's contribution to violence, but also how climate change is simultaneously burrowing, termite-like, through the supports that individuals, communities, and nations turn to in times of crisis. What happens, for instance, when drought hobbles a farming village, and its leaders—the ones who used to arbitrate disputes—head for the hills (or, more accurately, the city), leaving the poorest and most vulnerable residents to try and resolve their troubles among themselves? What happens when a person becomes so beaten down by his circumstances that he resorts to behavior that can only be described as wild or deranged?

Many of my interviewees have mused, in seemingly genuine bewilderment, as to why their farmer cousins or pastoralist neighbors took up arms in improbable circumstances. "It's a form of insanity," a young man in Burkina Faso suggested of a nearby village's decision to pick a fight over farmland that it could not hope to win. Amid the dislocation, exhaustion, and sense of powerlessness that climate change can unleash, I think there is something to that.

Crucially, for a book that is meant to be constructive rather than voyeuristic, I will hint at what makes some places more vulnerable to violence than others. As climate security scholars frequently emphasize, climate change need not fuel instability, and in many of the hardest-hit areas it has not. Why, for example, has climate contributed to conflict in Somalia but so far mostly spared the similarly afflicted Somali region of Ethiopia next door?[1] Hint: It has a lot do with governance. Though I yo-yo in my personal assessment of our prospects for avoiding intense climate-related violence, I am heartened by how much can be done to prevent these shocks from spilling into bloodshed, even as temperatures continue to climb. For all its focus on the messy present and potentially

About Island Press

Since 1984, the nonprofit organization Island Press has been stimulating, shaping, and communicating ideas that are essential for solving environmental problems worldwide. With more than 1,000 titles in print and some 30 new releases each year, we are the nation's leading publisher on environmental issues. We identify innovative thinkers and emerging trends in the environmental field. We work with world-renowned experts and authors to develop cross-disciplinary solutions to environmental challenges.

Island Press designs and executes educational campaigns, in conjunction with our authors, to communicate their critical messages in print, in person, and online using the latest technologies, innovative programs, and the media. Our goal is to reach targeted audiences—scientists, policy makers, environmental advocates, urban planners, the media, and concerned citizens—with information that can be used to create the framework for long-term ecological health and human well-being.

Island Press gratefully acknowledges major support from The Bobolink Foundation, Caldera Foundation, The Curtis and Edith Munson Foundation, The Forrest C. and Frances H. Lattner Foundation, The JPB Foundation, The Kresge Foundation, The Summit Charitable Foundation, Inc., and many other generous organizations and individuals.

The opinions expressed in this book are those of the author(s) and do not necessarily reflect the views of our supporters.

The Heat and the Fury

The Heat and the Fury

ON THE FRONTLINES OF CLIMATE VIOLENCE

Peter Schwartzstein

 ISLANDPRESS | Washington | Covelo

Library of Congress Control Number: 2024935673

All Island Press books are printed on environmentally responsible materials.

Manufactured in the United States of America
10 9 8 7 6 5 4 3 2 1

Keywords: Climate change and gender-based violence; Climate change and terrorism; Climate migration; Climate security; Conflict–climate nexus; Drought; Environmental security; Extreme weather; Food security; Grand Ethiopian Renaissance Dam; Land grabs; Resource scarcity; Water security; Water wars

To my parents

Contents

A Note to the Reader Regarding Language and Sources

As with any reporting or research that requires transliteration from different non-Latin alphabets, there is a wide range of possible ways to spell the names and places that appear in many of these chapters. Whenever possible I have plumped for the most common transliteration. In the case of uncommon names and places, I have just chosen the simplest option.

You may also note some unnamed or mostly unnamed sources, certainly more than I would like. However, there is good reason for that. Some of my interviewees only spoke to me on the condition of anonymity—given the potential risks of engaging with a foreign journalist in unfree countries—or, in particularly challenging circumstances, they declined to give their surnames or any names at all. Plenty more did give me their full names, but I have deemed it inappropriate to use them in instances where I feel that their words could come back to bite them. In still others, I spoke to these people in very different guises from that of a journalist or author—for example, as a researcher for a UN agency—and consequently do not feel that they gave informed consent.

INTRODUCTION

The Fundamentals of Climate Violence

Who, where, what, why, how

THE OLD MAN TOOK HIS TIME TO RESPOND. It was late 2014 and I had come to northeastern Syria with one burning question in mind: Was there any evidence that climate change had contributed to the start of that country's civil war? Right from the get-go, reporting went lousily. With ISIS (also known as the ISIL, the Islamic State, or IS) then on the warpath, people were panicked, never more so than when a rumor spread that the jihadists had broken through Kurdish lines, and my colleague and I were roused in the middle of the night to flee. I felt faintly ridiculous asking about drought while fellow journalists reported on—and embedded with—desperately outgunned defenders. Clearly, a few of my interviewees felt the same, and accordingly they fixed me with some very perplexed looks. Then there was the challenge of finding the right people from the right places. Like needles in a stack of needles, the villagers I sought were often indistinguishable from the hundreds of thousands of other refugees, all bundled into rain-sodden camps and swollen towns across a narrow sliver of land along the Turkish border.

1

But then I got lucky. After spotting a group of men ogling a herd of grazing cattle, we pulled to the side of the road and got talking. They were all farmers displaced from other parts of Syria, and they—or more particularly, Talal, the older statesman among them—were keen to tell their tale. For many years in the lead-up to the 2011 revolution against the regime of Bashar al-Assad, he and his family had grappled with governmental corruption, as when officials laced state-provided fertilizers with sawdust and sold some of the genuine product on the private market for personal profit rather than passing it on to the intended recipients. And for about three years preceding the uprising, they had reeled from weak rains, which were debilitating enough in themselves but utterly destructive when fused with regime larceny. The very idea, Talal said, that they were being sabotaged by an unscrupulous state when they most needed its help was a "final indignity." So, when anti-regime protests began, he and his similarly outraged friends and relatives were among the first in their area to join—and a little later, in the case of a few of them, among the first to take up arms. The rest, as they say, is history. "Bad rains, bad government, bad times," Talal told me, withholding his surname. "We could not continue."*

This is the story of climate-related violence, and it is already far more common than you might imagine. In large chunks of Africa and Central

---

* This is a much-simplified version of a complex tale. According to the dominant climate-conflict narrative in Syria, years of drought in the run-up to 2011 had sparked a mass migration of battered villagers to cities, where they struggled to adapt and so were particularly inclined to join anti-regime protests. And that may be at least partly true. But in interviews across several trips to the country's northeast, farmers gave me a slightly different account. That drought hit even harder than it otherwise might because of corruption and state incompetence. If only Damascus had not handicapped them so, perhaps they would have been better placed to cope with both poorly conceived subsidy reforms and a vicious array of climate shocks. Among many other grievances, farmers' sense that the regime was undermining them amid unprecedented hardship was an insult too far.

Asia, climate stresses are fueling fights between farmers and herders. In the Middle East, South Asia, Latin America, and beyond, these changes are intensifying everything from gang warfare in urban neighborhoods, to "old school" piracy in the coastal waters of Bangladesh. Across many of the world's most vulnerable landscapes, climate change and other environmental furies are merging with other, better understood destabilizers, such as corruption, to undermine dozens of countries that can ill-afford additional crises. And that is just the here and the now. As these stresses and shocks come thicker and faster, rapidly changing conditions threaten to apply the kind of pressure that even the richest of places might struggle to withstand.

The Heat and the Fury is an attempt to unpack this "new" violence. Through a range of intensively reported examples, I will try to impress upon you that there are fewer and fewer forms of instability or out-and-out violence that are not at least partly connected to climate or wider environmental woes—and relatively few communities that are not potentially susceptible to warming's violent "entreaties." Because, while climate-related violence is cutting deepest in poor countries, it will, in some form at least, come for "us." As explored in the latter stages of this book, climate is already contributing to everything from increased aggression against women in Europe, to declining military readiness across much of the Western world.

Through an investigation of the muddled, under-the-hood mechanics of this form of violence, I will try to show that climate's contribution to instability can be considerably more complicated—and almost always more nebulous—than is popularly understood. Since the 1990s and especially since the early 2000s, scholars of climate security, as this field is called, have done extraordinary work illuminating the risks that a warming world poses for peace and stability. However, there is still a lot more to uncover.

From chapter 1 onward, we will explore how climate and environmental drivers can hurl extra fuel onto already-smoldering fires, as per the most widely accepted characterization of climate's contribution to violence, but also how climate change is simultaneously burrowing, termite-like, through the supports that individuals, communities, and nations turn to in times of crisis. What happens, for instance, when drought hobbles a farming village, and its leaders—the ones who used to arbitrate disputes—head for the hills (or, more accurately, the city), leaving the poorest and most vulnerable residents to try and resolve their troubles among themselves? What happens when a person becomes so beaten down by his circumstances that he resorts to behavior that can only be described as wild or deranged?

Many of my interviewees have mused, in seemingly genuine bewilderment, as to why their farmer cousins or pastoralist neighbors took up arms in improbable circumstances. "It's a form of insanity," a young man in Burkina Faso suggested of a nearby village's decision to pick a fight over farmland that it could not hope to win. Amid the dislocation, exhaustion, and sense of powerlessness that climate change can unleash, I think there is something to that.

Crucially, for a book that is meant to be constructive rather than voyeuristic, I will hint at what makes some places more vulnerable to violence than others. As climate security scholars frequently emphasize, climate change need not fuel instability, and in many of the hardest-hit areas it has not. Why, for example, has climate contributed to conflict in Somalia but so far mostly spared the similarly afflicted Somali region of Ethiopia next door?[1] Hint: It has a lot do with governance. Though I yo-yo in my personal assessment of our prospects for avoiding intense climate-related violence, I am heartened by how much can be done to prevent these shocks from spilling into bloodshed, even as temperatures continue to climb. For all its focus on the messy present and potentially much messier future, I—and I hope you, too—see this book more as a call to arms than a cheerless requiem for our planet.

***

The Heat and the Fury is grounded in a decade of environmental reporting from over thirty countries, including frequent visits to every place that figures prominently in the book, and countless hours being bounced around the back roads of four continents. The scores of dirt- and sweat-stained notepads that emerged from that work tell the stories of soldiers, scientists, spies, farmers, government officials, and many others who have been kind enough to share their insights over the years. It is through their often-bitter experiences that I have come to understand climate's capacity to wreak havoc. It is largely through them that I will tell this tale.

But throughout this period, I have also depended on the scholars who have cut a long and, until recently, relatively lonely furrow developing the climate security field. Although I like to think that I am on top of my beat now, I did not come to it as a committed, or even half-informed, environmentalist. I grew up between Washington, DC, and the UK and had a love of wilderness, but no more than a superficial interest in its upkeep. It was not until I moved to Egypt at the beginning of 2013 and began to clock both the scale of environmental and climate trouble and how little political or media energy was being devoted to covering (or stifling) the story that I really became invested in the field. Out of an instinct for self-preservation as much as a sense of journalistic fascination, I have been motivated to try to articulate the severity of the climate crisis ever since. And what tells that story most forcefully than the violence it is leaving in its wake?

The journey to produce this book has not always been smooth. Along the way, there have been more bouts of food poisoning than I care to remember—or than you surely would care to hear about—as well as frequent games of cat and mouse with authorities, and a number of the sort of security scares that one might expect of a hands-on exploration of violence. In one instance, while returning from an interview in one of the fast-expanding slum districts of Basra in southern Iraq in 2015, I noticed that the taxi driver whom I had engaged to drive me between meetings that day was behaving oddly. First, he began to nervously finger the gun that he kept lodged by the gearbox. Then he obsessively scanned his wing mirrors. After two men—"cousins who needed a ride," he insisted—jumped into the back seats, I understood what he had in mind. Leaping out of the car at the next traffic jam, I weaved through the backstreets, the "cousins" trailing for the first bit, and sprinted as quickly as I ever did through school and college track and field. That evening, in an interview with the police chief, I learned that a local militia, one that was fittingly chock-full of recent migrants from the countryside, had noted my presence. "They're desperate," he said. "They saw you as money."

Yet through it all, I have had constant reminders of the importance of this subject. One of the most pointed came the day before that terrifying Basra incident. I had traveled about an hour north of the city to one of the region's fast-crumbling farming villages. There, I met an old man, Abu Mohammed, who lay in bed, struggling to breathe. He had no more than a sputtering fan to cool him, despite the humid 110-degree-Fahrenheit heat. Iraq's severe year-round electricity outages are even more pronounced in the summer when air-conditioning demand overloads the grid. And he had had no functioning refrigerator for his many medicines since the family's harvest had failed the previous year, depriving them of the funds to pay for generator fuel. After a brief, uncomfortable chat, I left him in peace. About an hour later, while conducting interviews next door, I heard a great wail from his daughter. He had had a massive, fatal heart attack that the doctor was adamant could have been avoided had he been living in more hospitable conditions.

***

On some level, it could be tempting to question what is new about climate- and environment-related violence. After all, conflict connected to water is as old as civilization itself, with some of the first recorded clashes fought between Sumerian city-states around 4,500 years ago, only miles from where Abu Mohammed took his last breath. I read a lot of environmental history, and natural landscapes have figured prominently as drivers, as victims, and as weapons of war over the millennia. According to one prominent theory, ancient Rome's rise owed a lot to a centuries-long period of warmer, rainier, and hence prime crop-growing conditions, which allowed the empire to produce much more food for its tens of millions of people than the period's farming techniques would otherwise have allowed. The violent famine- and plague-ridden fall of the empire's western portion may have turned in part on the end of that climactic idyll a few hundred years later.[2] According to another, rich rains may have facilitated the advance of Genghis Khan's Mongol horde across the steppe to Europe in the thirteenth century, the pasture lush enough to support unprecedented numbers of horses and the troops they carried.[3]

But while the parallels with past perils are clear, I hope readers will emerge with the sense that we are now up against a different beast, or at least one that is striking in different ways with more complex ramifications across a more challenging political landscape. Decades of progressively fiercer warming means that more people have less access to resources, or at least less consistent access to them, while at the same time they must confront rampant extreme weather-fueled disasters, such as floods and fires. These cascading risks are merging with other day-to-day challenges to overtax coping mechanisms and fuel poverty of a sort that is hardly conducive to happy, well-ordered societies. "In the past, summer was summer, and winter was winter, but now everything's mixed up," said Awad Hawran, who grows mangoes, sugarcane, dates, and watermelons on a one-and-a-half-acre plot alongside the Nile in Sudan. "It's hard to continue farming when even the desert and weather are against you."[4]

None of that immiseration necessarily leads to violence, but climate change is desperately unequal in its application of pressure. In my experience, troubles are more likely to emerge in places where some people are suffering mightily from climate-related stress, such as farmers or villagers in general, at the same time as others are getting by just fine or even prospering. It is that relative disparity in fortunes and government responses, a mirror of wider inequalities, that, much more than the poverty itself, can fuel dangerous degrees of resentment. "*We* suffer the most. *They* get all the help," I have frequently heard communities and individuals say of another. Mohammed Atiyeh, a farmer and activist in a dangerously parched part of Jordan, perhaps put it best. "In a country that might run out of water," he said, "there is regulation only for the weak and poor." His own crops, already ailing from weak rains and feeble river flow, had been withered by the water hoarding of a politically connected neighbor.[5]

All the while, a half century or more of intense environmental degradation has combined with prolific population growth to maximize the impacts of these stresses. Climate-induced drought is a challenge. Climate-induced drought is significantly more challenging when it strikes communities that are already reeling from pollution, groundwater depletion, and other very "prosaic" ills. In these instances, minor manifestations of climate change can be enough to pitch struggling people into violence—particularly if they feel that corruption or other forms of state action or inaction are hobbling them at their time of greatest need, à la Syria. "Even a mosquito can make a lion's eye bleed," an Arab proverb goes.

It is no coincidence that many of the worst climate-related security crises are unfolding in precisely the places that are also battling severe non-climate-related environmental woes. Nor is it an accident that I have chosen to mention plenty of the latter in this book, many of which are either overlooked despite their often greater significance, or incorrectly lumped under the banner of climate change. Climate change is often considered "sexier" by donors and hence talked up by aid recipients too. Sometimes, the distinction between the two is seemingly lost on scientifically illiterate elites.

(Though not necessarily a challenge in absolute "Malthusian" terms, given that we seemingly do have the capacity to provide for eight billion people and counting, booming populations are reducing many communities' and states' margin for error—and sometimes sparking aggressive or erratic behavior from authoritarian governments who fear that climate change could compromise their sourcing of sufficient food and water in the future. As a measure of just how swiftly the global population has mushroomed, the number of people who could be displaced by climate change by 2050 is roughly equal to the total who lived on Earth around the time of Jesus' birth—about 200 million.)

Vitally, climate change is not playing out in a political vacuum, and the world that spawned it and that is, in turn, now suffering from its fallout is arguably more geopolitically complex than at any time in recent history. After a peaceful-ish hiatus through the 1990s and early 2000s, the number of armed conflicts of any sort is at its highest since the Cold War and the number of intra-state conflicts in particular is possibly at its highest since World War II, while the quantity and quality of democracies has wavered badly across the board.[6,7] There are more displaced and hungry people now than at any time since 1945. There is more state mismanagement, or more accurately perhaps, there are more complex issues for more states to mismanage. Almost like a faceless, nameless cartoon villain, climate change is stealing into communities where people are already divided, institutions weak and discredited, and officials reviled, and stomping its metaphorical boot on wounds that often need little encouragement to widen or reopen.

***

There is a good deal new about this book too. Because while *The Heat and the Fury* owes an enormous debt to the academic and security communities that have dominated the climate security space since its inception, it is also written as something of a reaction to the not-always-accessible fare they have often produced over the years. At the same time, some media have been guilty of hyper-sensationalizing accounts of budding water wars and other supposedly inevitable disasters. In attempting to walk the line between the scholarly and the simplistic, I have put together something that I hope will appeal to a wider audience than the climate security field has previously enjoyed.

I have also heard frequent suggestions that we need more real-world illustrations of how you go from X climate stress or shock to Y violence. By writing a book based almost entirely on original reporting, I have tried to fill part of that gap. And by venturing into places and subjects that are less frequently covered, I have sought to expand the web of climate-conflict examples beyond the most-documented. Through the so-called Streetlight Effect, there can be a tendency for researchers to focus on the safest, most accessible, and linguistically familiar locations.[8] In this regard, I hope there is still plenty to interest those who have been in this field for significantly longer than I have.

Above all, this is one of the first books of its kind—if not *the* first—to explain on a very granular level how climate change interacts with and sometimes intensifies *other* drivers of conflict. Indeed, if you are new to this subject but have already heard about climate and conflict, your knowledge is likely related to Syria—and the discussion with which

I began this introduction. Almost since that conflict began, there has been an energetic back-and-forth in academia about the precise nature of climate's role in triggering the initial revolution. That is all highly worthy in light of the policy implications, and important, given the tendency of leaders from Assad himself to former Nigerian president Muhammadu Buhari to use climate change as a convenient means of explaining away violence that is often of their own creation. But, to my mind, the "death by a thousand cuts" nature of climate change and the overlapping "polycrises" with which so many communities are now wrestling renders that something of a red herring.

For example, climate can help push long-standing public anger over issues such as state brutality or inequality and corruption into violence—and all in ways that can make it impossible to gauge where one stressor ends and another begins. To that end, *The Heat and the Fury* does not attempt to quantify the magnitude of climate change's contribution to violence (nor, of course, to attribute to climate shocks all, or even most, of the chaos described in this book), but merely to show that it is almost always part of the mix. Again, I feel that a decade-plus of relevant ground-based reporting has given me the capacity to do just that. Ultimately, this book is as much about poor governance and the messy mosaic of other destabilizers as it is about climate change itself.

***

Climate security can seem like the most intractably insoluble—and hence depressing—of topics. For one, we know that good governance is pivotal in preventing climate stresses from spilling into bloodshed, as you will read throughout the book. Yet those very same stresses are also kneecapping governments' capacity to govern well, thereby reducing states' ability to act when their services are most desperately required. You want to help the victims of widespread flooding in Pakistan—and ignore mounting popular fury in the process? Try doing that when those waters have also washed away the very roads and bridges that you need in order to distribute aid, as happened when up to a third of that country was inundated in late 2022.

You want to "climate-proof" farming communities, whose livelihoods are among the most vulnerable to climate change and whose prevalence can be one of the clearest markers of possible climate-related violence?* Good luck with that when technical innovations tend to kill farm jobs and accelerate migration to the cities, which can itself unleash new security challenges. For example, police in Kathmandu already report more frequent fistfights among competing day laborers on construction sites. Officers do not relish the prospect of more turmoil as displaced rural Nepalis continue to pour into the city.

Even well-intentioned attempts to address climate change can prompt as much trouble than the initial challenges, if not more—a concept called *backdraft*. It is clear that large-scale electrification will be pivotal to weaning our economies off oil and gas. But that will require an awful lot of new mining for battery components in troubled countries such as the Democratic Republic of the Congo, which is tricky to envisage without considerable violence. It is possible, too, that we will eventually need to turn to exciting, if still very unproven, carbon-capture technologies to rein in warming. Can we do that without opening a whole new Pandora's box of trouble? At a TED climate summit in Scotland in 2021, an exercise dedicated to gaming out the possible ramifications of

---

* Scholars Josh Busby and Nina Von Uexkull have identified three characteristics that they deem particularly likely to contribute to climate-related conflict. In addition to a large percentage of the population engaged in agriculture, they noted that places with histories of recent or ongoing conflict (and so with plenty of existing cleavages for climate stresses to exacerbate) and exclusive political systems (which are frequently unresponsive to climate-related crises) are uniquely vulnerable to this form of violence.

countries using cloud seeding and other forms of geoengineering rapidly descended into war.

There is a deep unfairness to much of this as well, one that goes beyond the fact that it is those who contributed least to climate change who are most vulnerable to its violence. In the long run, some of the most significant climate chaos might emerge from climate-battered states failing to meet citizens' expectations. Those mismatches can undermine authorities' perceived legitimacy and fuel anti-statism, even if the lost or reduced services—regular water supply, superior roads, and so on—are largely a product of recent developmental advances. In other words, climate might punish with violence states that have enjoyed some success in raising living standards, while sparing those that have failed to progress.

Nevertheless, there is still a big question mark as to how much violence climate change will eventually fuel. And a lot of that, beyond issues of governance, boils down to the as-yet-unknowable extent to which the planet actually warms. For every incremental shift toward higher temperatures or more extreme rainfall, some regions could see a 14 percent increase in group-on-group violence, according to one (very contested) study.[9] The amount of warming will determine whether one billion or possibly even three billion people live outside the "human climate niche," the range of conditions that have served us so well, according to another.[10] For all the complications inherent in decarbonization (which I will also get into), there is little doubt that meaningful climate action—and meaningful climate action alone—can stifle the worst of this form of violence. As faint a hopeful note as that might initially seem, the grand reality is that most of this remains in our hands.

***

The Heat and the Fury is ambitious and wide-ranging and, I hope, very readable. But there are plenty of things it is not. For one, this book is more a series of snapshots of the violence that climate change is leaving in its wake than a systematic exploration of the climate security field—and most certainly not of the climate domain in general. There are plenty of key stories that are not told or not told in any depth, such as the instability that could emerge from the prolific mining of rare-earth elements, or the tussle for resources and strategic positioning in a thawing Arctic. There are plenty that are overrepresented. You will read a lot about water, which, as scientist Jay Famiglietti says, "is the stealthy messenger that delivers the bad news about climate change to your town, to your neighborhood, and to your front door."[11] Since 2001, about three-quarters of all natural hazards have been water-related.[12] I will repeatedly revisit the uncertainty that climate change brings, a complication that may be generating more violence than does absolute scarcity, despite the latter's greater celebrity.

You may note a limit to the geographic range of these stories. Having been based in Cairo for almost six years and then Athens, Greece, for six and counting, my reporting has naturally been centered on the Middle East as well as North, East, and West Africa, with frequent forays into South Asia and Eastern Europe. I have not worked in other current or potentially climate-violence-heavy hotspots, such as Latin America, Southeast Asia, and Southern and Central Africa. Adamant as I have been about basing everything on my own research, these other regions remain largely untouched in this book. Fortunately, in reporting terms, climate-related violence is even less equitably distributed than "regular" climate change impacts. In their grimly perfect marriage of severe climate stresses and dreadful governance, I have had a lot to work with on my doorstep.

Progressing through these chapters, you may also perceive an occasionally blinkered-looking focus on *physical* security at the expense of other, arguably more-serious forms of climate-related fallout—that is, spotlighting violence among some Sahelian herders and pastoralists at a time when many more people there are going without sufficient food for similarly climate-related reasons. But there are two explanations for that. The first is that this book would have bloated into an unmanageable mess without a relatively tight focal point. The second is that most books about climate change have explored the subject through the prism of food access, justice, human rights, migration, and so on. And so they should. (Insofar as those subjects relate to security, they come up plenty.) However, I am trying to tell a slightly different kind of story that may appeal to a slightly different readership, which requires a slightly different framing. As Jonathan Franzen writes, "The paradox of nature writing is that to succeed as evangelism, it can't only be about nature."[13] Sometimes it has got to be about violence and war.

Finally, in an attempt to produce something that is compelling for a wide audience, I have also excised a lot of jargon and alphabet-soup-like acronyms, kept statistics to a relative minimum, and trimmed a bunch of country-level context. In doing so while simultaneously deploying frequent anecdotal evidence rather than important contextual studies, this book could come across as somewhat lightweight. The plural of anecdote is not data, after all. But I have almost always taken whatever studies exist into account. Owing to my fixation on un- or under-covered research angles, there often have not been any to cite. Additionally, I argue that the messy interplay between climate change and other drivers of conflict is generally impervious to quantitative study, requiring instead the kind of very "human" stories that I have tried to deploy throughout. For more-detailed, nuts-and-bolts descriptions of climate security, I have provided a list of relevant books and papers in a bibliography at the end.

***

This brings us to the journey that you are about to begin! These chapters could be read in isolation, each effectively a standalone investigation with its own "cast of characters" and plot, but there is a narrative arc throughout, and I would love for you to follow it. Just as climate change builds on other challenges to complicate the lives of millions, so I have tried to sequence these chapters in such a way as to show the cascading nature of climate-related security risks. For lack of a better, less-grim way of putting it, I want the sense of violence to close in on you. Each chapter explains how varying manifestations of climate change are combining with very different socio-economic-political contexts to fuel different forms of violence. More practically, I have tried to fold in relevant science along the way—and generally try not to repeat myself.

Chapter 1 is a years-long investigation in Iraq, where water shortages formed a rich backdrop for ISIS to recruit and conduct its terror operations. Chapter 2 takes you to Bangladesh. There, merciless pirates are making fat profits by kidnapping displaced farmers and holding them for ransom—or worse. Then on to the Nile basin (chapter 3), the scene of a possible conflict between Egypt and Ethiopia centered on a mega-dam, and Nepal (chapter 4), where the state's inability to keep the taps flowing in a water-rich nation may spell its downfall. Chapter 5 is set in Africa's Sahel. Based on reporting across a half-dozen countries, this chapter delves into violence between farmers and herders, who are attacking one another across a drier, less predictable landscape. From there, we will begin to explore some of the violence arising out of *responses* to climate change.

Struggling villagers in Jordan have traditionally leaned on the government for army jobs during lean farming times. But as conditions worsen and public coffers empty, that quick fix is crumbling, with dangers big and small for the country (chapter 6). Chapter 7 is located in Sudan, where drought-wary foreign nations are buying up farmland to secure their food future—at local people's expense. Chapter 8 makes clear that the West is neither safe from direct climate violence, particularly against women, nor invulnerable to the possible fallout from our attempts to mitigate and adapt to warming temperatures. Finally, this book will culminate with a hopeful chapter 9. Because even though climate change is tearing plenty of states and communities apart, it can also in certain circumstances help bring them back together. Through a whirlwind tour of environmental peacebuilding successes, many in the countries that we will have visited beforehand, I will emphasize that there is some reason for optimism.

Turkey

Tel Afar
Sinjar
Sahaji
Mosul
Erbil
Shirqat
Hawija
Tigris
Tikrit
Huiesh
Samarra
Syria
Euphrates
Iran
Ramadi
Fallujah
Baghdad
Abu Ghraib

Iraq

Tigris

Euphrates

Tigris

Euphrates
The Marshes
Basra

Saudi Arabia

CHAPTER 1

Cultivating Terror[1]

How did water crises fuel ISIS? A years-long investigation reveals the environmental roots of Iraqi extremism.

WHEN IRAQI SECURITY FORCES FINALLY ROUTED ISIS from the west bank of the Tigris near Samarra in the early months of 2015, advancing troops were stunned by how little the jihadists had left for them to liberate.

In the riverside village of Huiesh, ISIS had stolen every single water pump, leaving the village—some three thousand people and more than two thousand animals—high and dry for perhaps the first time in its history. Just to its west, beyond a now bombed-out military installation, they punctured the country's main north–south oil pipeline, coating acres of farmland in sticky black crude in their zeal to tap its contents. Throughout the area, ISIS fighters had unearthed dozens of painstakingly laid farm watering grids. That, an army explosives expert explained, was a trick the group sometimes pulled to mold makeshift projectiles from pipes and compensate for a shortage of munitions when cut off from reinforcements. But in other instances, where the jihadists had also pockmarked the pipes with bullet holes, this sabotage seemingly served no purpose other than to impoverish returnees. "What dogs," the expert said of the culprits as he levered a defused device into a flatbed truck.

The rot only intensified along the Watban Way, the road that extends out into the desert from Huiesh and which was named after Saddam Hussein's half-brother. ISIS (the Islamic State) had not been in quite as much of a hurry to retreat here, which meant more time to empty the two dozen or so roadside agricultural goods shops of their fertilizer—and more time to repurpose that explosive mix into a web of booby traps across the army's line of advance. In this at least, they would eventually grant de-miners an accidental assist. By the time the area was fully secured, many of these farming products had seeped out of their equally make-do canisters, sprouting vegetation in neat, easily identifiable patterns.

Worse was to come, though. Progressing a few more miles into the arid periphery of the Tigris valley, Iraqi troops encountered barely anyone living or anything intact. The jihadists had killed whatever livestock they had not been able to cart away, throwing at least one sheep down a well. They had cannibalized the area's all-important mechanized irrigation systems for anything of value, committing the owners to paying their monthly installments for years after the costly equipment had rusted into unusable hulks. With few people and no means of making the land grow, it did not seem like it would be long before this area returned to the desert from which it had been painstakingly carved. Indeed, a thin layer of sand had already begun to settle across fields that had been almost impossibly lush only a year earlier.

"They have sent us back to the stone age," said my companion, a man who I will call Abbas and who accompanied me throughout the first few of a number of visits to the area between 2015 and 2017. "They have killed our communities."

With Us or Against Us

A paunchy, chain-smoking parody of a mid-level career policeman, Abbas had worked across the Samarra area of central Iraq for seven years before ISIS arrived in the summer of 2014. He had been proud of his role in helping to restore a veneer of calm to an area that had been roiled by sectarian Sunni–Shia violence in the years following the US-led invasion in 2003. And so, when the order came for some state employees to return to the west bank of the Tigris after its liberation, Abbas was among the first to heed the call. Initially, he seemed delighted by the opportunity to reconnect with the agrarian communities he had come to know and like—and whose troubles he could well appreciate. Coming from a farming family himself, he certainly seemed to have a more natural rapport with the locals than did his more urban peers, some of whom saw handling rural grievances as practically a punishment posting.

But as Abbas began to piece together what had happened before and during the jihadi surge, his warmth for the area slowly began to ebb. These villages had bowed far too meekly to ISIS, he soon concluded. Many of their residents were more accessories to the destruction than victims of it. Now, in tandem with district agricultural officials and an internal security agent dispatched from Baghdad, he resolved to help identify which locals had sided with the jihadists. "They fucked us," he said, momentarily losing his poise. "Our approach was: We're going to find out who was with us and who was against us."

Over the following months, Abbas and his colleagues sifted through whatever records had not been torched or stolen during the fighting. They questioned many of those who had stayed behind after the ISIS occupation began, and—though he never explicitly said so—forcibly interrogated others with the assistance of Saraya al-Salam, one of the largest of the pro-government militias and the dominant security force in the Samarra area. (I was pretty sure I heard muffled screams coming from the basement on a visit to one of the group's bases.) Through discussions with community leaders, many of whom knew which of their kin had displayed extremist sympathies in the past, and the examination of scarce and dangerously shot bits of cellphone footage from within the "caliphate," they soon formed a partial picture of which locals had most enthusiastically abetted ISIS.

What they concluded largely matched my own reporting both there and in other parts of Iraq and neighboring Syria. In the villages close to the river, like Huiesh, where most farmers had regular access to the Tigris waters and hence tolerably strong crop yields, few residents had thrown in their lot with the jihadists. "They had good irrigation. They got good harvests," Abbas said. But in the more peripheral communities beyond the river—and the canals that emanated from it, it was a very different story. For the farmers and pastoralists here, almost all of whom shared the same Sunni Arab ethno-religious profile as their riverside peers, the past decade had been one of bitter financial and emotional struggle.

The rains on which they partly relied to sustain their crops had repeatedly failed, shrinking or sometimes wholly extinguishing their harvests. The groundwater that they usually turned to as a substitute at times of drought was disappearing because of the frequency with which they were now having to exploit it—and moreover was often prohibitively expensive to access because of the amount of diesel required to power their generators and extract groundwater from the depths. On one trip, Abbas waxed so enthusiastically about how green these wastelands once were that he completely missed spotting the IED trip wires that jihadist remnants had run across the road the previous night. We later found out that the explosives had already been defused, but we resolved to drive in silence from there on out.

Most infuriatingly, as far as residents were concerned, big Baghdad and Samarra businessmen had snapped up swathes of communal land and then enclosed it with fences to guard their quarter-mile-wide, water-guzzling irrigation pivots. That had put further strain on the aquifer, while simultaneously reducing the space available for grazing the livestock that many locals had acquired to pad their incomes. "Life was hard. People were angry," said a local tribal leader. He, like many others, preferred to speak anonymously for fear of being deemed an ISIS sympathizer, a charge that was thrown around willy-nilly during and after the war. "And angry people can do crazy things." It is no coincidence, several interviewees suggested, that those mechanized irrigation systems were singled out for particularly rigorous jihadi sabotage.

As the drought dragged on longer than locals had ever experienced before, their meager savings vanished, to be replaced, in many instances, by fierce resentment. And, by this time, outsiders were paying attention. Al-Qaeda had previously lavished attention on this area, enticing to them in part by its proximity to Baghdad, some seventy miles to the south, and Samarra, a city with sites holy to Shiite Muslims and one that the Sunni extremist group had successfully attacked on a number of occasions. Now, as ISIS set about trying to build something significantly bigger and more ambitious than its jihadi forebear, the group's recruiters began to pull out all the stops.

Swooping into these villages in the winter of 2013–14, they dangled salaries—of up to $1,000 a month—that broke, desperate residents could otherwise only imagine. Recruiters most energetically targeted families who had lost the most to drought—and those whose small, unproductive fields bordered some of the bigger, more bountiful ones. There is nothing quite like desperation and envy to arouse the worst demons of our nature, the extremists seemingly reasoned. Seizing upon the sectarianism that had flourished after the US-led invasion, they pointed out how little the Shia-led government was doing to help Sunni farmers at their time of greatest need. That was only partly true, with few Shia farmers any better off, but for people who had had less inclination and capacity to visit Shia majority villages since 2003, this narrative resonated. "Farmers are suffering everywhere, but these people were clever," Abbas said of ISIS. "They preyed on the ignorance."

Though relevant statistics are few and inexact, pastoralists and farmers within semiarid tracts of Tharthar district seemingly joined ISIS at roughly three times the rate of their riparian counterparts, according to Abbas and the local tribal leader. A full two-thirds of those held as suspected jihadists in Saraya al-Salem's Samarra jail were farmers, a media officer for the militia said, a cohort so big that discussion of cattle breeds and seed types reportedly rivaled professions of innocence as cellblock conversation topics. Initially skeptical of my climate-conflict fixation, Abbas too came to accept the link. "The less the water, the more the jihadists. And the countryside is dying," he said. "This is a security nightmare."

Weaponizing Misery

You may well know the meat and potatoes of ISIS's emergence: The seizure and occupation of a chunk of Iraq and Syria the size of Great Britain for varying periods between 2013 and 2019. The group's almost cartoonishly graphic, made-for-camera brutality—and success in recruiting into terrorism misfit youngsters from London to Los Angeles and across the Middle East itself. You may even have read up on the toxic combination of religious fanaticism, avarice, and grievances of various stripes that underlay its triumphant exploitation of preexisting chaos, first in civil-war-ridden Syria, and then across the border in post-invasion Iraq.

But you are unlikely to have heard much about the bleak environmental circumstances that turbocharged ISIS's rise and, arguably, aided in its initial success against the anti-jihadi coalition. Many years of accumulating climate and other environmental woes had thrust both countries' agricultural heartlands into deep economic downturns. Even longer periods of mismanagement and marginalization had fueled tremendous rural fury against the Iraqi and Syrian states, which many villagers held responsible for their reduced circumstances. Like hyenas feasting on a sickly zebra, the jihadists expertly took advantage of that poverty and pent-up rancor to swell their ranks into a force of roughly sixty-thousand fighters at one point.*

National data about ISIS's composition are as limited as those available around Samarra. But what we do know is telling. In Tel Afar, a northern Iraqi town notorious for its vastly disproportionate cohort of native-born ISIS sons, almost a third of respondents in a UN study reported knowing someone who had a joined an armed group for reasons related to climate changes over the war—likely the jihadists, in most instances.[2] In northeastern Syria, ISIS attracted at least a third of its local recruits from pastoralist communities, which accounted for no more than 2 or 3 percent of the country's prewar population and whose already difficult lives had deteriorated in lockstep with the quantity of vegetation in the semiarid *badia*, a Syrian Kurdish security source told me. Over seven years of intermittent reporting across afflicted parts of both countries, I found that the path from water-deprived farming community to armed-group recruitment frequently resembled a well-greased conveyor belt, a highway to hell transporting a frankly stunning number of resentful rural left-behinds.

"These kinds of countryside people ticked all the boxes," Husham al-Hashimi, a top scholar of terrorism, told me over tea in a chic Baghdad hotel a few years ago. "They were poor, they felt they had less power than they deserved, they felt that they were forgotten, they felt that they had all these rich resources that Baghdad was stealing. That was a bad mixture." Having rubbed shoulders with plenty of these men

---

* Unhelpfully, estimates of ISIS's peak fighting strength in Iraq and Syria ranged from 9,000 to 200,000. The latter number seems improbably high (unless one considers all of its "support staff" and assorted hangers-on). The former is certainly far too low, with an estimated six to seven thousand ISIS militants killed or captured in the Syrian town of Baghouz alone, where the group made its final stand as a coherent military force in 2019.

during his own youthful flirtation with jihadism, Hashimi had a better understanding of what propelled people into extremism than most of his peers. That might have contributed to his undoing too, as he soon focused his fine mind and deep connections on the influence of Iraq's powerful Iran-aligned militia groups, at least one of which was seemingly responsible for his assassination in 2020.

In some ways, the black-flag-waving jihadists were in good historic and contemporary company in appealing to the poor and prospectless. Through the eighteenth and nineteenth centuries, European commanders ransacked villages for "sluggards, rakes, debauchees, rioters, undutiful sons, and the like," as the Prussian king, Frederick the Great, referred to his men.[3] A little later on, in the immediate aftermath of World War II, the French Foreign Legion took on an inordinately large number of battered-looking men with strong German accents and suspiciously impressive aptitudes for fighting. Modern militaries from Jordan (which, as we will explore in chapter 6, enlists villagers as something of a safety valve at a time of climate-induced job losses) to the US (which has at times concentrated recruitment in deprived urban areas) have stacked their forces with men who often lack attractive alternatives. In pursuit of cannon fodder for its war in Ukraine, Moscow has partly relied on the most "old school" of tactics, forcibly snaffling poorer, unempowered ethnic minorities like a latter-day Royal Navy pressgang.[4]

I found that this dependence on the poorest of the rural poor is also partly true of the anti-ISIS coalition. The largely Shiite militias, like Saraya al-Salam, that assembled across Iraq to defend Baghdad and other areas as the hollowed out Iraqi army collapsed in the face of the jihadi charge, drew an inordinate share of their men from impoverished, waterless stretches of the southern marshes.[5] So, too, Iraq's Federal Police and the Syrian Democratic Forces (SDF), the umbrella grouping of mostly Kurdish fighters that controls the northeast of that country. These forces have enlisted many villagers whose lands have been lost to drought—or the oil industry.

In Suwaydiyah, a small Syrian village that is surrounded by leaky, crop-killing refineries, some 40 percent of its young men and women joined the SDF, the mayor told me, a figure many times that of more agriculturally viable communities in the area.[6] In Turk Alan, just outside the Iraqi city of Kirkuk, a tribal leader disclosed that no fewer than four hundred of the community's roughly six thousand inhabitants had found work with the police or militias after the jihadi surge. At the entrance to the village, pictures of the roughly twenty of them who had died in combat stare out against a backdrop of flaring oil wells and crude-pocked fields.

Yet there the comparison ends. For, in its weaponization of rural misery and repurposing of it to the grimmest of ends, ISIS transformed common recruiting practices into a dark, hideously effective art. They targeted the most destitute farmers and pastoralists, who were often at their drought-hobbled nadir. They harnessed long-standing political and social grievances to present environmental and climate ills as signs of a government that was out to get them, rather than the unfortunate byproduct of extreme mismanagement and increasingly inhospitable global conditions. With a bevy of former intelligence operatives from Saddam Hussein's notoriously effective security apparatus among its senior leadership, ISIS knew a thing or two about manipulating weakness. A fast-deteriorating natural landscape gave them an ideal setting to do just that.

"This beast [ISIS] has many causes," said Omar, a former agriculture ministry administrator from Mosul, who fled as the jihadists seized his city and who wished to withhold his surname for security reasons. "But in the countryside these new problems just pushed people over the edge."

Dotted with date palms, the Balad area, just north of Baghdad, was once a rich agricultural area. But as water access deteriorates, many farmers from families like this one have traded in their hoes for assault rifles in the service of militias. (Photo by Emily Garthwaite)

A Countryside Primed to Blow

In retrospect, we could—or perhaps should—have seen some sort of trouble brewing. Over the past half century, rural Iraq has been trapped in a long, sad decline that still shows few signs of reversing. Beginning with the surge in global oil prices from the early 1970s, Baghdad slowly lost interest in agriculture, the source of most village livelihoods and previously a nationally significant economic sector. In the fifty years until 2022, farming's share of national GDP fell sixfold to about 3 percent.[7] With that drop went much of the interest of a state now flush with tens of billions of dollars of monthly fossil fuel revenues.

Then came conflict. Following his seizure of power in 1979, Saddam Hussein quickly sucked Iraq into a number of wars—both abroad against Iran and Kuwait, and at home versus his own people in Kurdistan and the far south—that struck farmers particularly hard. During the eight-year Iran–Iraq War, the dictator forced tens of thousands of them into uniform. He trashed tracts of prime farmland, even destroying millions of southern Iraq's prized date palms for fear that Iranian saboteurs might use them as cover to attack oil facilities. In doing so, he transformed once idyllic stretches of river valley into uncultivable and, on the Faw Peninsula where the far south meets the sea, near-uninhabitable badlands. And not just there. Abbas was always at pains to point out the tree stumps along the road from Baghdad to Kirkuk, victims of Saddam's fear of assassination as he motored between his many palaces.

In the meantime, Iraq launched a series of ill-starred agricultural initiatives, all part of its drive for regime-buffering food self-sufficiency, which were abandoned after the dictator's toppling. Under international sanctions after invading Kuwait in 1990, the state granted farmers most of their seeds and fertilizer for free or at discounted rates in a bid to drive up grain production. In turn, it then purchased much of their crop for up to three times the international price. But that costly system has wobbled badly since 2003, with inputs erratically distributed or of poor quality, and payments for crops often delayed. Having been reared on this "cradle-to-grave" support system, many rural Iraqis have struggled as it has waned. By 2007, some 39 percent of people in rural areas were living in poverty, two and a half times the country's urban rate.[8] Hundreds of thousands of villagers had abandoned their fields altogether, turning instead to the slum districts of Baghdad and other cities.

Yet still the blows kept coming, and off the back of worsening insecurity, rural discontent was starting to crest in the years prior to ISIS's surge. Water shortages, seldom previously a problem in the Fertile Crescent, began to bite due to deepening droughts—and upstream dam construction. Since World War II, Turkey has built dozens of large dams within the Tigris and Euphrates basins, the two river systems on which

Iraq has historically relied, while Iran has dammed, diverted, or cut off every one of the roughly thirty Tigris tributaries that flow west from its territory. Officials have been either powerless, or in the eyes of experts, too incompetent and focused on lining their pockets to stymie the damage. "The only thing ministers care about water is the water they put into their whiskey," said Talib Murad Elam, at the time an adviser to the prime minister of the Kurdistan Regional Government (KRG) in northern Iraq, smiling the smile of a man who knows he has just said something eminently quotable.[9]

Infrastructural neglect, which had already begun under the sanctions, worsened. What water Iraqi farmers did receive was so tainted with pollution as to be unusable, or so salty from backwashed agricultural wastewater as to corrode water-treatment plants faster than their operators could source spare parts.[10] The system, leaky and susceptible to evaporation, also loses Iraq billions of cubic meters of water that it can no longer afford to squander. In this unvirtuous circle, Iraq may lack the personnel to right these wrongs, even though it once produced perhaps the region's largest class of capable professionals. "We used to produce scientists like they grow on trees. But now they've fled," Jafar Dia Jafar, the father of Iraq's nuclear program, told me from the foreign city that he, too, now calls home. "We don't have the people to fix our problems anymore." Irrespective of whether his take is wholly fair, Iraq has indeed bled talent, the venal political class that US administrators promoted following the toppling of Saddam's Baath regime frittering away the skills of the brilliant individuals that it does still have at its disposal.

Enter more intense climate change stage right. Creeping into this already noxious mix like a vengeful ex-lover, both rapid and slow-moving stresses have barreled across Iraq, imposing an additional challenge that citizens feel woefully ill-placed to handle. Over the past few years, the country has experienced what can feel like an elaborate laundry list of climate disasters. There is that ever-intensifying drought, felt both directly at home with weaker rains, and indirectly through Iran's and Turkey's retention of extra water upstream to compensate for their own dearth of rainfall. That, many Iraqis feel, is a hostile ploy to deprive them of their hydro birthright. And there *may* be an underlying element of strategic brinkmanship. However, both Iran and Turkey are populous and boast vast agricultural sectors. If others must suffer for them to quench their thirst, so be it. This is a classic "the strong do as they can, the weak suffer as they must" setup. According to a 2023 study, the drought that has ripped through the Euphrates-Tigris basins for three years since 2020 has been made twenty-five times more likely by climate change.[11]

There is the heat, sometimes peaking around 130 degrees Fahrenheit, which has occasionally forced my colleagues and me to cool our misfiring phones in supermarket freezers while out reporting, and, in a grimly cyclical manner, maximized water requirements for parched crops. With insufficient electricity generation to power home AC units much of the time, Baghdad parents have been known to drive their kids around the city during temperature spikes.[12] Then there are the other extreme weather events. There is perhaps nothing quite like the sand-stormy conditions that now envelop parts of the country for months of the year and occasionally even coat the country's highest snow-covered twelve-thousand-foot peak with sand, to bring home the apocalyptic nature of climate shocks. Iraq, as a friend reminded me, is the land where agriculture as we know it was born. It is now doing a very good impression of a place where it has gone to die.

Meeting me in his Baghdad office back in 2016, with charts of Iraq's elaborate hydraulic network arrayed along the walls, Hassan al-Janabi, the minister of water resources from 2016 until 2018, seemed tired and overworked. A well-regarded hydrologist who had spent much of Saddam's latter years in exile—and has the flicker of an Australian accent to prove it—he seemed to be one of the few senior officials who understood the magnitude of Iraq's environmental collapse. He had few resources with which to combat it. His budget for renewing the country's crumbling infrastructure had been sundered by falling global oil prices. He struggled to command his colleagues' attention, the agricultural ministry bluntly ignoring an agreement to reduce cultivable land for want of water. Now, here was ISIS and the multi-billion-dollar water-system repair bill that it would inevitably leave. In an unguarded moment, he seemed almost bowled over by the challenge. "The disappearance of our water and environment has been unstoppable in places," he said. "And there's just not enough assistance to make a difference."

Exploiting Grievances

Even by the often sorry standards of rural northwestern Iraq, the village of Sahaji is a desperately unhappy-looking place. The streets, most of which are unpaved, bleed dust through the summer, and then crumble into sodden messes in the winter. The concrete and mud-brick houses are in various states of disrepair. Among the few locals who are obligated or brave or foolish enough to venture out in the afternoon heat, there is scarcely a welcoming look among any of them. "We'll drive on," an Iraqi journalist colleague said when we first passed through in late 2017. Like most communities of its kind, Sahaji suffered a great deal during the campaign to defeat the jihadists. But you would not necessarily know it to see the place. Already poor and neglected, it and its small but all-important farms had settled into a drought-plagued death spiral in the years prior to ISIS's arrival. The village was, by all accounts, an unhappy tinderbox almost waiting for a spark.

None of this meant that ISIS was predestined to absorb as many of Sahaji's menfolk as locally based tribal figures and security services say it did. Poverty is no clear-cut recipe for extremism. That decades-long catalogue of intense environmental and climate woes has hit many villages elsewhere in the country even harder, and they have not, for the most part, taken up arms in pursuit of brutal causes. But unfortunately for villagers and particularly the people that were to suffer from the horrors they abetted, the jihadists were well-practiced in the exploitation of grievances. They and their local contacts and ex–intel operatives knew precisely which buttons to push to entice some of these people to take up their cause. (One of ISIS's senior commanders, Izzat al-Douri, who had previously served as Saddam's deputy and was known as the "red devil" for his ginger hair and brutal record, developed a Houdini-esque reputation for surviving airstrikes. I attended one of his Baghdad "funerals" in 2015, the streets of part of the capital brought to a stand-still with a Roman-style triumph of his supposed body. Some Iraqi journalists went to at least three such events.)

In the case of Sahaji and many like-minded surrounding villages, at least some of its ISIS enthusiasm was seemingly grounded in a parade of very petty human jealousies. For years, residents had noticed an ever-increasing disparity between their fortunes and those of the nearby city of Mosul, some twelve miles to their east. They had seen their yields and incomes vaporize. They had seen Mosul residents prospering, or at least appear to be. By hammering agrarian communities, whose liveli-hoods are generally much more bound up with the health of the natural landscape than those of urbanites, climate shocks have accentuated the gap—or the perceived gap—between the "haves" and the "have nots."[13]

But three things made this divergence all the more intolerable. The first was the state's superior service provision in the city. Although Mosul schools and roads and wastewater disposal failed to meet most of its resi-dents' idea of satisfactory, they were a great deal better than anything in impoverished Sahaji. "There was a feeling that they were suffering the most but that they were getting nothing," said Najim al-Jubouri, when we met at his heavily guarded headquarters laden with US special forces on Mosul's east bank in 2018. Jubouri led the operation to retake the city and then served as governor of Nineveh, the governorate around Mosul, from 2020 to 2023.

Officials around Huiesh also hinted at the consequence of inequality as an ISIS-animating force. As the rains weakened in the years prior to 2014, farmers there turned to wells as an alternative source of irrigation, only to find that, with limited mains electricity and insufficient funds to power their pumps with increasingly costly diesel fuel, this was no longer an option that most could afford. "People were having to spend more and more on their generators," said Ahmed al-Thaer Abbas, director of the Tharthar Agricultural Office, which was responsible for Samarra's west bank. "It's not sustainable." By his calculation, area farmers needed to spend $6,000 on fuel a year to irrigate twelve acres of fields, a sum beyond most smallholders' means.

The second gripe centered on big-city arrogance, or perhaps more accurately again, villagers' perception of it, according to Mosul residents. Whenever they visited Mosul, Sahajis were reminded of their "country bumpkin" ways. They were ridiculed for their accents and unfashionable clothing. They were disturbed by the city's slightly less conservative mores—and by its multitude of Christians and Yazidis and other non-Sunni Muslim groups. Coming at a time when those declining farming fortunes were casting the rural–urban economic divide into even sharper relief, angry opportunistic villagers were out for revenge. Indeed, it is no coincidence that ISIS appears to have won over a particularly large share of peri-urban villagers, the cross-section of the agrarian poor that are most likely to have interacted with city dwellers.[14]

And to hear how Abbas's police colleagues, all urbanites, discussed the locals, I thought it no wonder that many of them had struggled to gel with those under their authority. One of them, Mohammed, possessed an almost inexhaustible reservoir of jokes about countryfolk in which the punchline always seemed to be some variation of "they're so dumb."

The third, a contributor to instability whom I will return to elsewhere in the book, may have been pivotal in Sahaji. When villages shed inhabitants at times of stress, it is often those with agency who leave. They are the ones who are more likely to have the means to set themselves up elsewhere, and they are, by dint of their generally greater ambitions, more likely to take the chance. Migrating generally requires money. It always requires boldness. As Sahaji plunged deeper into immiseration, its smartest and most esteemed citizens were among the first to migrate. In their absence, local conflict-resolution mechanisms broke down, according to the one local who ultimately agreed to talk to me on a subsequent trip, and the social fabric fragmented. The village that ISIS found, he said, was less a community than a cluster of climate-battered individuals riven with disputes big and small.

More than One Way to Skin a Cat

Reporting across liberated swathes of Iraq and Syria, I heard as many motivations for jihadi recruiting success as one might expect of a wildly diverse landscape. But even among the most ostensibly political or economic of grievances, there was almost always an environmental angle.

Around the oil-rich city of Kirkuk, a roughly two-hour drive southeast of Mosul, farmers and pastoralists had long struggled with corruption. There were the daily demands for kickbacks as they passed through highway checkpoints on their way to market. There were the requests for "administrative fees" to complete run-of-the-mill business at state agricultural offices, if indeed there was anyone there at all. Some farmers allege that these agencies had "ghost employees" of the same sort as those who contributed to the Iraqi army's 2014 collapse, workers who never came to the office and whose salaries were collected by their bosses in exchange for a cut. If Hassan, a farmer from near Tuz Khurmatu managed to complete his rounds of government offices without shelling out more than a few dollars' worth of dinars, then he, like so many others in the country, considered it a job well done. "They are thieves," he said. "May God damn them."

But, as the impact of drought worsened through the late aughts and earnings bottomed out, so too did local tolerance of corruption. At various points in 2013, livestock vendors in Kirkuk say they had to hike beef prices up to 30 percent to account for financial appetites at the checkpoints that ring the city. Having lost his entire crop, one farmer told me he could barely buy enough food for his family, let alone meet an agricultural bank manager's demand for cash before he would even consider his loan application. Among rural communities, who are poorer than most city dwellers and yet simultaneously more subject to corruption due to their regular exposure to the most bribe-seeking institutions, like checkpoints, this predation appears to have been a bridge too far for many. To paraphrase Sarah Chayes in *Thieves of State*, her exploration of corruption in post-2001 Afghanistan and its contribution to the Taliban's ultimate triumph, "People think: if government steals from you, why not give the self-described moral ascetics a try?"

Around Tikrit, about halfway between Kirkuk and Samarra, locals had wrestled with their diminished status since the downfall of Saddam Hussein, a native son. Under his rule, many of them had enjoyed privileged access to security-sector roles and other positions of authority. But since 2003, when politicians from the previously marginalized Shia majority had come to dominate government, they had faced both genuine discrimination in the form of worse-quality seeds and reduced delivery of the basic food basket that most families receive from the state, among other abuses—and, in some instances, the whiplash that can accompany lost standing. In this, ISIS with its ex-Baathist personnel were to find to plenty of environmental levers with which to rally angry, Saddam-nostalgic, and now water-impoverished people to their cause.

In the run-up to the group's surge in 2014, one farmer recalled an ISIS-affiliated preacher saying that the rains were failing because of cloud seeding in neighboring (and mostly Shia) Iran. Other recruiters suggested that irrigation canals were not flowing as they used to because the "Sunni haters" in Baghdad were redirecting water to farmers of their own sect. Even the delayed crop payments and intensifying dust storms, another argument went, were a deliberate government ploy to impoverish the Sunni heartland. Whether people truly believed these outlandish explanations scarcely mattered. With mounting desperation, many were only too willing to direct their fury at a familiar foe. "We said just wait until the next harvest, life will get better, life will become easier," said Saleh Mohammed al-Jabouri, a tribal sheikh from Shirqat, roughly halfway between Mosul and Kirkuk along the Tigris, who watched for years as suspicious, bearded outsiders circled his community like vultures. "But things just weren't getting better. There was always another disaster."

And around Ramadi, the capital of Anbar governorate, a sprawling and mostly arid province that stretches from Baghdad's western suburbs to the Saudi border, I heard consistent suggestions that mental illness had contributed to ISIS success. Much of this hinged on the decade of near-constant instability and insecurity that Iraq had by that point experienced. But as climate stresses set in, some interviewees spoke of the psychological dislocation that unrecognizable agrarian conditions had also unleashed. Though life had seldom been easy, farmers, fishermen, and pastoralists say that at least there was a drab predictability to many of their past struggles. No longer. Droughts are more frequent and more severe, giving an unfamiliar hue to age-old troubles. Temperatures and seasonal variations are often horribly out of whack. Together, this disconnect seems to be fueling what can only be described as a devil-may-care attitude in which family, community, and tribal structures are even less likely to keep people in check.[15]

In some war-ravaged communities, residents appear genuinely mystified as to how their friends or family could ever have been foolish enough to join ISIS. It is madness, they suggest, temporary insanity brought on by desperation and the loss of their lives' few constants. Sometimes these people might be genuinely unwell. Up to one in five of the residents in war zones may suffer from a mental health condition, according to the World Health Organization; well over a third of residents polled in Tel Afar had lost a loved one to violence or abduction in the years leading up to the ISIS takeover.[16] The fact that government in Iraq (and Syria) appeared to be offering less or worse-quality support, even as these individuals confronted unprecedented difficulties, swelled anti-statist sentiments.[17] Because why, interviewees sometimes implied, would one bother toeing the line when everything is going to hell anyway?*

Yet no matter where they were within their as-yet-undeclared "caliphate," or whatever local grievances they identified and dined off to maximize their advantage, ISIS fighters were thoroughly consistent in targeting the most deprived individuals in the most battered communities. They enjoyed a compelling advantage as the environmental situation worsened by the year. I heard frequent reports of extremists preying on the most ragged-looking men at agricultural goods markets, as well as those selling their cattle at livestock markets for depressingly low prices at times of drought, as in different parts of Kirkuk governorate. With hundreds of pastoralists looking to offload their animals while the scrawny, ill-fed beasts were still fit for slaughter, wholesalers could

---

* Admittedly, not everyone was buying this possibility. When I broached it with Peshmerga Colonel Jemil Mohammed as he and his unit took a break from patrolling Nineveh villages that had long made a living smuggling goods back and forth across the nearby Syrian border, his response was as pithy as it was unambiguous. "They're jihadi scumbags, they've always been jihadi scumbags, and they always will be jihadi scumbags" (Schwartzstein, "The perfect recipe for making jihadis was developed in this small Iraqi town," *Quartz*, 2016).

buy cows for as little as $30 a pop. "They just watched us. We were like food on the table to them," said Abbas Luay Essawi, a herder from near Hawija, about the ISIS recruiters.

I heard at least two reports of ISIS making particularly forceful approaches to farmers whom they knew to have defaulted on agricultural bank loans that, like the Kirkuki man, they had apparently taken out to replant after failed harvests. Recruiters are known to have distributed cash or food to families just as their harvests failed.[18] Ever mindful of intercommunal tensions, the group made special efforts to win over Arab and Turkmen families who had lost land around Kirkuk as Kurdish regional authorities flexed their newfound muscle in disputed areas following the fall of Saddam—and, conversely, special efforts with some Kurdish families who had been displaced in similar circumstances in Syria in the decades before the revolution. It was a pattern of unremitting pressure and opportunity that, come the summer of 2014, yielded dreadful results across the country.

According to a joke that Abbas the policeman told me on several occasions as we bounded between destroyed villages, "God will never send any Iraqi to hell because they had their share in this life." Pointedly, neither he nor others around us ever seemed to laugh during or after the telling.

ISIS Weather

The interview was over only minutes after it had begun. Mohannad al-Azawy had been in a foul mood all morning, and having given much of his twenties—and his left eye—fighting the Americans, I cannot imagine that my presence much improved it. But, in this instance, it was the weather, not the annoying Westerner with his relentless questions, that had him on edge. As one of the Saraya al-Salam militia's most-senior operatives in the Samarra area, he was charged with helping maintain security along the western approaches to the city, beyond Huiesh. The fast-moving sandstorm that had threatened all morning and just ful-filled its promise consequently meant nothing but bad news. "Get up. All of you," he said, barking rapid-fire instructions into a walkie-talkie. "I don't want to see anyone sleeping." His men, who had only moments before been lounging around the barracks, drinking sickly sweet tea and trading darkly comic stories, leapt to their feet. There they would remain for most of the rest of the day, their rifles trained across a Tigris River that, though only about half a football field away, had very quickly fallen from view.

No sooner had the jihadists announced themselves to the world through their stunning early success, than Iraqi commanders learned that poor visibility was "ISIS weather." By timing many of their attacks during periods of fog, fierce rain, and, crucially, sun-choking sand-storms, the jihadists were able to deploy their favored smash-and-grab tactics to grim effect. And by maximizing operations during periods when the American and other air forces were less able to support troops on the ground, they could partially counteract the coalition's single biggest advantage. The United States alone conducted tens of thou-sands of strikes against ISIS—though notably fewer when visibility was low and targets could not be properly identified, a spokesperson confirmed. For all the assistance that climate and environmental phe-nomena provided in terms of recruitment, their impact on the group's successful early campaigning might have been every bit as profound. "I hate this weather," Azawy said, the last words I would get out of him for many hours.

From 2014 onward, Iraqi troops battled frequent assaults on their positions under the cover of sand and dust. The jihadists harnessed those conditions to storm army lines to the south of Kirkuk soon after they had seized Mosul, and then, in similarly murky light, hurled men at the Peshmerga—Iraqi Kurdish forces—during their ultimately unsuccessful bid to capture Erbil, the Iraqi Kurdish capital. They repeatedly used sandstorms to bring suicide car bombs to within meters of unsuspecting soldiers before detonating them, all part of their efforts to sow confusion and shatter morale along what was at one point a nearly a thousand-mile-long frontline. If nature did not oblige, ISIS was even known to create its own storms of sorts.

Around Qayyarah, just to the south of Mosul, its fighters torched scores of oil wells to cover their retreat in 2016 and 2017, an environmentally debilitating duplication of Saddam's withdrawal from Kuwait in 1991, and one that was made all the worse because the group then laid strategically placed mines to slow efforts to extinguish the fires. Even now, tracts of surrounding farmland still glisten with so much crude that I had to borrow a flick knife to scrape some of the muck from my shoes after a 2022 visit, all in an ultimately futile attempt to look presentable for a meeting with a local bigwig later that day. "When you're fighting in nice weather, there are few surprises," Ebbas Mohammed, an officer in the Syrian Kurdish YPG militia told me soon after his unit had beaten back a nighttime ISIS raid near the northeastern Syrian city of Qamishli, in late 2014. "But when it's raining, when you can't see, anything can happen."[19]

Very quickly, frontline soldiers learned to adapt, to dig trenches, to build rings of earth berms to prevent the bombers from propelling deadly loads onto their laps. But through it all, ISIS enjoyed the kind of helping hand that the coalition could do little to combat. Although sandstorms are a thoroughly natural beast, it is far from normal for them to strike with this regularity or intensity. Years of deforestation, poor water management, and bad agricultural policy, which incentivizes the cultivation of marginal, easily scoured land, have left Iraq primed for worse sandstorms. High winds and climate-induced drought have done the rest. Iraqis know all about the most in-your-face consequences of these storms—hospital emergency rooms jammed with suffocating asthmatics for much of the year, and homemakers and restaurants alike struggling to prevent their food from tasting grainy during the thickest hazes. But few people, Abbas added in another reflective moment, seem to grasp how much blood the sandstorms have cost the country too.

In Pursuit of Water

Having weathered several ISIS attempts to catch his positions unawares over the previous year, Azawy remained jumpy and monosyllabic until the air cleared around sunset that day. But when he finally relaxed enough to talk, I found the militiaman keener to discuss a very different form of environmental warfare. This one was centered on the river that lapped, all too meekly, near where we sat.

As with poor weather conditions, the jihadists displayed a consistent interest in water. At their peak, they controlled at least five of the large dams and barrages that regulate the Tigris's and Euphrates' flow, and, by my calculation, at least three thousand miles of the irrigation canals that extend out from the rivers in lattice-like formations. They knew how to wield some of this infrastructure too. With technical experts within their ranks who ranged from Sudanese water engineers (one of whom was entrusted with running the Fallujah barrage) to hydrologists (another of whom presided over the Mosul dam during ISIS's twelve-day-long occupation there), they showed a greater facility in administering these structures than even some sovereign states might have managed.[20] Azawy, continuing to loosen up, though no less willing or able to disguise his disregard for me, offered grudging praise for his foe. "They know what they are doing."

Much of this focus was an extension of the millennia-old use of water as a weapon. Control of upstream infrastructure on both sides of the Syria–Iraq border allowed ISIS to alternately flood the fields of downstream farmers and deprive them of water. In doing so, they could punish Shiites whom they deemed heretical, while also showcasing the impotence of the Iraqi state to would-be new Sunni recruits. The release of large volumes of water, as at Syria's Tabqa Dam near Raqqa, sometimes enabled them to slow the anti-ISIS coalition's advance, a textbook historic maneuver practiced by everyone from the seventeenth-century Dutch to the twentieth-century Chinese. When Iraqi, Iraqi Kurdish, and Syrian Kurdish forces began to roll the group back, as started to happen from late summer 2014, the jihadists knew precisely what to do then as well. By blowing up the barrages at Fallujah and Ramadi, on the Euphrates, they condemned tens of thousands of farmers to absolute penury.

Around Abu Ghraib, a town to the west of Baghdad notorious as the site of the American prison abuses, I met despondent men whose fields were among the thousands that had been rendered useless by the retreating jihadists' sabotage at Fallujah. With no means of diverting or controlling river flow into their canals until the damage was fixed, they had lost both the crop that they had planted and, given the lost income and hence insufficient means to buy seeds, perhaps the next one too.[21] For Azawy, the fear that ISIS might inflict similar damage with comparable consequences to "his" barrage over the Tigris appeared to weigh on him heavily. "They come up through the reeds," he said, gesturing at the dense thicket of vegetation on either side of the barrage. "We must be on guard at all times."

Leading me down to the river's edge, Azawy pointed out the bed of broken reeds where his men had recently seized an "ISIS scout." The man had binoculars, army-issue boots, and several days' worth of food. When I asked what had become of him, Azawy scowled and then led me a little further along the river. Here, he said, they had previously pulled bodies from the water, some seemingly victims of the jihadists' massacre of 1,700 Shia army recruits at a base thirty miles upstream. None of the troops, one of Azawy's aides added, eat nonfarmed fish anymore. After later stumbling on a bloated carcass, which looked like that of a middle-aged man but which was far too decomposed to say with total certainty, a few steps away from a fisherman just north of Baghdad, nor do I, in Iraq.

But in prioritizing the seizure of water resources, ISIS was also signaling ambitions that went beyond mere military expedience. ISIS commanders cannot have missed the role that water shortages played in fueling their own rise. Nor, as natives of some of the driest, most battered pockets of Iraq (as roughly three-quarters of the group's entire upper echelon were), can they have overlooked the fact that there was increasingly little rain or river to go around. Husham al-Hashimi wondered whether all that time shuttling back and forth across the Syrian desert planning ISIS's rise might have given senior jihadists a more acute sense of what it would take to keep agriculture-dependent communities content. As a group with long-term designs on the land and an awareness that hostile neighbors would do it few favors, ISIS's pursuit of these resources was above all a bid to acquire the critical resources of a living, breathing state while it still could. (In this, they were merely following local autarkic precedent. Assad's Syria, postrevolutionary Iran, and of course Saddam-era Iraq previously prioritized or continue to privilege food self-sufficiency as a means of partly insulating their regimes from external pressure.)

Initially, the jihadists were to enjoy an unfair burst of good fortune. For just as the half decade leading up to the ISIS surge was marked by mostly low rainfall, the year of and the year after its massive expansion into Iraq was characterized by bountiful precipitation. In 2014, they took over Iraq's Nineveh governorate shortly before its wheat crop, one of the richest in years and the bedrock of the country's domestic supply, was due for harvest. In 2015, they once more benefitted from bumper rains. Together with their capture of seed-laden government storehouses in 2014, they were for a time able to provide the kinds of services and abundant water supply that Baghdad had struggled to deliver of late.

And that, as scholars have pointed out, can be as symbolically important as it is popular. In places where security is weak and livelihoods
uncertain, perceived legitimacy can come down to the provision of basic
services alone. In its early "charm" offensive, ISIS was essentially staking
a claim to areas where some residents felt the Iraqi state had all but abandoned its own. To this suggestion, which I presented to Azawy shortly
before I said my goodbyes, he only snorted in derision.

Attuned as it was to the crumbling natural landscape, ISIS might
sound like a kind of desert-dwelling Viet Cong, an adversary that knew
how and when to exploit the environment to its own brutally effective ends. In its emergence and early campaigning, as recounted in this
chapter, that was partly true. But once the group had secured a measure
of control, that "green savvy" was rapidly discarded in favor of human-
and environment-wrecking terror. Nowhere was this more devastatingly
illustrated than among the Yazidis, adherents of a small pre-Abrahamic
faith group who were largely clustered in villages near Sinjar, about
ninety minutes' drive due west of Mosul.

After killing many local men, at least three thousand of whom were
dumped in mass graves, ISIS fighters proceeded to sell into slavery
whatever Yazidi women they could capture. They turned the main town
silo into a den of horrors, having first, true to form, shipped much of
its wheat to Mosul to keep residents of their biggest capture and crown
jewel fed and more compliant. The smell and sight of spent condoms,
ripped women's clothes, and abandoned, bloodstained shoes almost
made me vomit when I visited soon after the area's liberation from ISIS
control. Then, turning to the surrounding countryside, they torched
orchards, laced wells with diesel, and boobytrapped farm buildings with
devilishly hard-to-find explosives. There was no strategic environmental
imperative here. Only a desire to eviscerate the landscape in such ways
that any Yazidi who escaped their clutches might never again make a
living in his or her ancestral homeland.

For years after ISIS's defeat, Tigris fishermen such as Omar would stumble on the corpses of jihadi victims and jihadi fighters. Even now, with downed bridges and oil spills, the river tells the story of a war. (Photo by Emily Garthwaite)

Hope?

For a man who had just lost a presidency that he had fought tooth and nail to retain, Barham Salih cut a remarkably relaxed figure when we met at his well-guarded Kurdish mountaintop retreat in late 2022. Over the previous four years, he had used his largely ceremonial role as head of the Iraqi state to try to elevate climate and water within Iraqi politicians' consciousness. Despite his energetic efforts and rhetorical talent, that bid was widely perceived as having failed to move the governing class to action.

Seated in his sun-drenched drawing room with his wife, Sarbagh, a botanist, at his side, Salih acknowledged the lack of progress, the corruption that ails the state from parliament on down to provincial agricultural offices, the time lost to everything from conflict to misplaced priorities and incompetence. But on the apparent impossibility of ever persuading the powers-that-be to take environmental issues seriously, he forcefully disagreed. "When I first became president, the delegations I received were all about security, about car bombs," he said. "But more recently they were all about water, water, water. The reality is that MPs need to reflect the interests of constituents. In the end, they will act on climate change because they have no choice." Besides, he continued, many of the power brokers, including the current prime minister, are from the south. "They feel this issue themselves. They see fights over water."

His was one of the more bullish and quietly optimistic readings of Iraq's environmental future—and, as self-interested as it was, Salih was not wrong to say that there was something of a change in tenor over the course of his tenure. Seemingly rattled by the country's most recent brush with chaos, at least some officials are finally taking climate's destabilizing potential seriously. Iraq co-sponsored a United Nations resolution on the environmental impacts of conflict. Ministries have tightened up regulations on the importation and use of chemicals, intent on ensuring that non-state armed groups can never again use fertilizers and pesticides for the production of explosives. "Terrorist groups used simple chemicals to hurt my country and our people," said Jassim al-Falahi, deputy minister of health and environment. "That's why we need changes."[22] As low a benchmark as this might be, I think the days of being laughed out of the room for broaching climate's contribution to conflict, as happened with a police general in Baghdad in 2015, are over.

More significantly, some rural Iraqis are quietly but surely adapting to their less hospitable surroundings. I met a shepherd near Mosul who, having lost his sheep to drought, restocked with goats for the first time, a practice that, as we shall see in the Sahel (chapter 5), is increasingly deployed the world over. They are less hungry, he said—and more sure-footed, which is vital in the drought- and mine-riddled plains around the city. I have met savvy young men, like Hamid and Ali Mohsen, who moved to Baghdad's southern periphery after losing their jobs as agricultural laborers in the waterless south. The brothers quickly noticed that there was nowhere to buy fish among these fast-expanding suburbs. They now visit a nearby fish farm every week, and then go door-to-door selling their ice-packed wares from the trunk of rickety old Lada.[23] If the country is to survive, it will likely be through their energy, adaptive capacities, and enterprise.

Then there is the youth, the bands of tweens, teens, and twenty-somethings who make up well over half the population and in whom older generations of environmentalists in Iraq and so many other countries place their hopes. These activists have had some success in carving out more protected areas—on paper at least, and in campaigning for superior transboundary water cooperation. It is they, more than any official or scholar, who have succeeded in elevating international awareness of Iraq's environmental woes. It is they who, even at their preachiest moments, can dispel what I thought were unshakeable levels of cynicism. In 2019, I attended the first Mesopotamian Water Forum in the city of Sulaymaniyah, a gathering of activists and conservationists from across the Tigris and Euphrates basin states. I realized almost as soon as I arrived that this was not my usual scene. There were declarations of solidarity with this jailed figure and denunciations of that empire. A lot of their politics were "out there." But as I got talking to the participants, my mood began to lift. Many had endured trying, if not outright dangerous, experiences to get there, fearful in a few instances of detention as they crossed borders. Almost all had weathered extraordinary levels of state "fuckery," as one of them put it, as they went about their hard, thankless, poorly paid work. And yet here they were, excited to share ideas on how to salvage their shared natural patrimony. All of a sudden, positive change felt very possible.

ISIS 2.0

Yet, in other crucial respects, the years since ISIS's territorial defeat have brought nothing but a continuation, or even acceleration, of the unsustainable status quo. The country's water deficit is projected to near eleven billion cubic meters by 2035, according to the World Bank, a total that is roughly equal to ten times next-door Jordan's current annual water consumption and one that could make current shortages seem paltry by comparison.[24] However, little is being done to begin transforming Iraq from a culture of water plenty to one of relative scarcity. The work of talented individuals such as the Mohsen brothers is worthwhile, but ultimately their efforts are either not replicable by the wider population or are mere rounding errors in a big, bulbous state-dominated economy. "With the environment, it's like the pre-2003 times," said Hassan al-Janabi, the former water minister, hearkening back to the days of Saddam. "There are a lot of big mouths, but nothing is being done." In his retirement, he too has repeatedly run up against corruption. After settling on his farm in southern Iraq, he tried to expand it through a loan from the central bank's agricultural program. But despite meeting all the conditions, he was denied. "It was because I refused to pay the inspectors," he said. "I will not play that game."

Other forms of environmental degradation are only worsening by the year too. Since 2003, Baghdad has lost most of its tree cover, those sandstorm and heat-absorbing green lungs disappearing under mounds of concrete that only aggravate both troubles. Illegal logging and wildfires continue to claim tranches of the highland woodland and river valley palm groves that remain. While accompanying an Iraqi forest police patrol in the Kurdish mountains along the Iranian border in 2018, I frequently encountered signs of illicit deforestation, even overhearing the telltale whine of chainsaws in the distance. But with limited fuel for their vehicles—and an unstated fear of running up against loggers with political ties, the rangers were powerless to do more than lope through the wintery valleys, picking flowers and sharing gossip. It was a telling insight into a country awash with gasoline but so deficient in environmental chops, at a state level at least, that these men had to get by on twenty liters a month. "We are few, and the problems are many," said Aram Ismail, the lead ranger. "God willing, we'll protect the trees. It's our identity. Our homeland. But we need more help."[25]

Among many other enduring gripes, rural Iraqis are still wrestling with agricultural policies that almost seem calculated to complicate their lives. Payments for crops remain unpunctual and supplies of inputs are inconsistent, sometimes willfully so. Those new anti-bomb-making chemical regulations have inadvertently limited fertilizer access for farmers in areas that were occupied by ISIS. With fewer means of making a living amid climate-, environment-, and policy-induced stress, unprecedented numbers of villagers are migrating to the cities. There, up to four million of them are living in slums, fueling an employment, services, and possibly a security crunch for which the state appears to have no plan. "A lot of them come here with nothing and they struggle," Zekra Alwach, the then-mayor of Baghdad told me a few years ago. "So, of course we fear more crime and more armed groups. This is the natural conclusion."

Right now, Iraq is at something of an inflection point, a period in which rural and wider environmental concerns could help "heal" the country—or possibly fuel even fiercer discontent down the line. Because while ISIS 2.0—a revived, reinvigorated jihadi organization—remains weak, its cells scattered and capable "only" of perpetrating about a fifth of the attacks in Ramadan 2023 as it did the previous year, it is not hard to see how it—or a successor—could one day wreak renewed havoc.[26]

For its part, the group is doing everything it can to create the conditions for future jihadi prosperity. By waging localized but consistent campaigns of intimidation and sabotage, it is stifling NGO and aid organization efforts to help the most battered and isolated villages, a demonstration in miniature of the difficulties that states in conflict face in adapting to climate change. ISIS cells have reportedly laced agricultural land around Sinjar and Tel Afar with new explosives, only months after mine clearance organizations had given the "all clear." They have damaged wells in places like Baaj and Hawija, thereby maximizing natural water shortages. In their bid to keep communities extra poor, doubly resentful, and hence potentially amenable to non-state alternatives in the future, its cells are most actively targeting anything that resembles promise. It might be working in places. In late 2018, while I conducted interviews in villages around Hawija, an elderly woman quietly noted that ISIS fighters had passed by her family farm demanding food that very morning. My colleagues and I quickly made our excuses and retreated to the relative safety of the villages closer to Kirkuk city.

Legislators are repeating several long-standing mistakes as well. First, there is their chronic economic short-sightedness. At the time of writing, the country is flush with the sort of money it needs to begin "climate-proofing" its water networks, gird farmers for even trickier growing conditions to come, and start building the green economy that a post-fossil-fuels age will ultimately require. "Again, we'll have no choice but to act," Barham Salih said. "Oil will not be as pricey by 2030. And if countries much, much poorer than Iraq are managing to transition, then we have no excuse." But previous oil-price booms have yielded so few lasting improvements that even the most optimistic Iraq watchers struggle to see where the vision for economic diversification would come from. On a 2023 visit to Iraqi Kurdistan, I tried to meet the region's newly appointed environment chief. I messaged on WhatsApp and Twitter (now X). I tried to call. It was only when I checked LinkedIn that I understood why he would not answer. After a short period in office, he had jumped ship and joined an oil company.

Moreover, there is the state's treatment of some war-torn rural areas. Though sectarianism has lost a good deal of its potency, officials can make it all too easy for ISIS-like ideologues to construe its actions as those of a vengeful Shia bloc. On the Tigris, to the north of Tikrit, the state is trying to build the Makhoul Dam, an ill-conceived structure that conservationists say is in too hot and too geologically porous a place to avoid mega water losses—and whose construction anti-corruption campaigners see as a purely money-making scheme by militia-affiliated contractors. "This is like a poor man building a massive safe," one top Iraqi environmentalist said of the wisdom of building new reservoirs at a time when Iraq can scarcely fill its existing ones. But local chatter has it that Makhoul is being erected to flood troublesome Sunni villages—and only Sunni villages. Resentment is mounting.

Likewise, in the Tigris valley villages near Samarra where ISIS enjoyed recruitment success, Saraya al-Salam leadership has seemingly judged everyone guilty by association with those who did join the jihadists. Since liberation, militiamen have prevented most its people from return-ing to the fast-desertifying area, which has fueled widespread anger and sparked local protests against the loss of their land. Abbas, my minder and sometime guide in the area, feels it is a mistake, an invitation for future trouble. But he and his police colleagues are not the power in these parts. He knows when to bite his tongue. "We can forgive or for-get, but you must allow these wounds to heal," he said.

Shortly before we parted ways for what turned out to be the final time, Abbas decided that he wanted to provide a bit of a counterpoint to the destruction we had documented together, a more optimistic foil to many months of "disaster porn." Bundling me into his car, he first took me to a restaurant that specialized in *pacha*, a regional delicacy of sheep organs and offcuts which I tried very hard to pretend I enjoyed. Then we went to the Qasr al-Ashiq, a monumental ninth-century palace that was built during Iraq's Abbasid-era heyday and that stands on a low rise along the Tigris near Huiesh. The intended takeaway seemed clear: "Look what we are capable of!" Finally, amid the soft "golden hour" light that my photographer colleagues swear by, he pulled a few warm Tuborg beers from his bag and began to wax lyrical about, of all things, palm trees, many of which he had grown up tending. "They have their feet in the water and their heads in the fire of the sky," he said. "They are beautiful but they are difficult. They are a bit like Iraq."

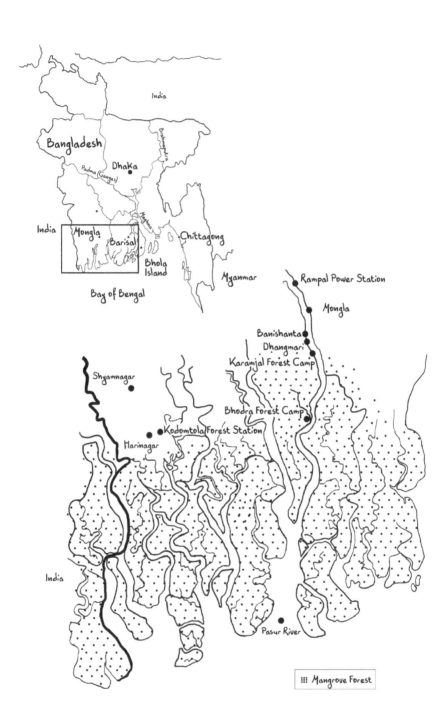

CHAPTER 2

Bandit Fodder

Along a Bangladeshi coastline battered by sea level rise,
the pirates are king.

I AM NOT SURE WHAT I THOUGHT a modern pirate would look like. No peg leg or talking parrot, of course. Nor did I expect my interviewee to arrive blood-dripping cutlass in hand. But, on balance, I expected someone a little more menacing-looking than Rafikul Mali. Heavyset and with a calm, almost apologetic demeanor, he spoke so softly that my interpreter friend had to lean uncomfortably close to hear his muttered responses to our questions. When a very squishable bug landed on his hand, Mali carefully and slightly ostentatiously ushered it away, as if to say: "Look, I'm a changed man. I wouldn't hurt a fly."

And yet for two years before I first met him in 2018, Mali had engaged in precisely the kind of misdeeds that might have made even Blackbeard blush. Throughout that period, he and the others in his pirate band had marauded through the inland waterways of coastal southern Bangladesh. They had kidnapped untold numbers of jungle honey collectors, holding them for ransom, and sometimes chopping off the unfortunate men's fingers to focus slow-paying family members' minds. They had robbed fishermen blind. On occasions when they were not fighting among themselves, the roughly dozen different pirate groups cooperated to build a smuggling network so wide-ranging that there were very few goods that they could not—or would not—fence.

"The pirate thinking is to make money wherever—from people, from tigers, it doesn't matter," Mali said, a hint of something that sounded an awful lot like pride creeping into his voice. "There's nothing that a pirate won't touch."[1]

Mali adamantly insists he never hurt anyone. Indeed, he would not have been eligible for the government amnesty that he ultimately received if officials suspected that he had. But in their passion for pillage and plunder, the pirates have collectively racked up quite the kill count. In the five years until 2017, pirates murdered more than four hundred fishermen in Bangladesh's eastern waters, according to a local fishing association. They reportedly killed at least forty-five more around there in 2011 and 2012.[2] Though fatalities appear to have declined somewhat since then, these groups still appear to have few inhibitions about dispensing with those who get in their way. In Mongla, Bangladesh's second-busiest port, powerful floodlights keep the docks aglow from dusk to dawn, scanning the darkness for threats, and perhaps offering some succor to ships in an area that has suffered at least four different fatal attacks since the summer of 2022.[3]

Now back in his home village on the periphery of the Sundarbans, the world's largest contiguous mangrove forest and the principal pirate lair, Mali is trying to readapt to law-abiding life. But every day is a struggle. He is still haunted by the conditions he experienced in the jungle—the crocodiles who turned every wash into a nerve-shredding ordeal, the venomous snakes whose bites were potential death sentences so many miles from medical attention, the stomach parasites that, years on, still have him bouncing up and down to the toilet throughout our interview. Above all, he remembers the tigers. Many nights, their roars kept Mali and his peers awake and searching the undergrowth with their rifles for signs of movement.[4] They still plague his dreams, he says.

He has not been forgiven by his neighbors. Many of them are so swamped with the debt they have taken on to pay pirate ransoms that they have had to part with their furniture to buy food; others still display the telltale marks of the *dhama* and the *kirich*, the bamboo sticks and homemade machetes with which most pirate bands begin their attacks, hoping to cow their quarry into submission before they have a chance to fight back. Although the village mayor insists that Mali will not meet the same fate as other amnestied pirates, a number of whom have reportedly been lynched soon after their return, few locals appear to want anything to do with him. As Mali walked us back to the boat landing after concluding our chat, passers-by treated him like something of a leper, selling him cigarettes in a wordless transaction and pointedly ignoring him when he asked about fish prices.

Most important, Mali says, are enduring reminders of the temptations that led him to piracy in the first place. Most of the *jaladoshyu*, as the "water brigands" are referred to locally, appear to have been drawn to banditry by the same mixture of craven greed and luckless circumstance that characterize so much criminality. But here, in an area where climate change is leaving few slices of life untouched, water and wider environmental factors have figured prominently too. With agriculture less viable than ever for reasons that include sea level rise and diminishing river flows, more farmers are trying their hand as fishermen or honey collectors, among the few alternative local livelihoods around the Sundarbans. And with more people consequently venturing into these traditionally lawless waters and forests, the pirates have had unprecedented potential human loot sailing, defenseless and desperate, into their domains.

For men like Mali, struggling to earn a living from the land and already facing prison on illegal gun-possession charges, this promise of bounty proved impossible to resist. Tellingly, with the Sundarbans even more flush with "prey" than when he first took to the water, he implies that it might yet prove his undoing. "I know how horrible the conditions are. I know that it is wrong," he said. "But I make no money like this. It has you thinking: is this the life?"

And not just him, for that matter. Later that day, as my colleague and I sat down for an evening beer in Mongla, a large mustachioed man, no more than a drink or two from collapse, staggered over to our table. Shouting to make himself heard over the raucous crowd, he insistently and annoyingly demanded to know what had brought us to his corner of the country. Trying to get him to go away, we leveled with him. He took a moment to process the nature of our reporting trip, and then roared with laughter. "Pirates?" he slurred, lifting his shirt to flash a pistol in his pant belt. "Pirates? Everyone in this bar is a pirate."

A Modern Twist on Piracy

When we talk about climate security, we often talk about conflict, about ISIS and other terrorist groups, about the instances in which climate change contributes to globally significant violence in ways large and small. But a lot of the time, the stakes are lower and the insecurity more localized, even if the consequences are no less punishing for those in the eye of the storm. The pirates of the Sundarbans are a potent case in point.

For years now, these groups have reduced many coastal communities to poorer, more tormented versions of their former selves. Residents say that the financial shakedowns have robbed them of the resources they need to educate their children, rebuild or fortify homes in the face of intense climate-fueled cyclones, and even feed themselves, among other deprivations. Pirates raked in about $1.3 million in ransoms from two coastal communities alone between 2011 and the end of 2012, a king's fortune in a country where rural incomes average around $2,000 a year.[5] They say that the psychological strain of sailing, time and again, into danger is pushing some to suicide. Up to a quarter of Bangladeshi fishermen have been directly affected by piracy, according to a 2017 report, some of them kidnapped more than five times.[6]

Despite frequent anguished appeals for state intervention, these men as well as a few women have not had much recourse to justice, either. By cleverly focusing their attentions on isolated, politically unconnected constituencies, the pirates have (until relatively recently, at least) shielded themselves from the kind of blowback that would almost certainly follow attacks on foreigners or "well-dressed" Bangladeshi visitors to the Sundarbans. The state, villagers say, simply does not care about poor people. "This is why you are safe here and I am not," one fisherman pointed out.

As bleak as the picture painted by available statistics might seem, the reality is likely much worse. Most pirate attacks go unreported because victims see little value in bringing them to the attention of potentially corrupt police—or because they were attacked in areas where they lacked the permits required to work. For their part, international organizations, such as the Malaysia-based Piracy Reporting Centre of the International Maritime Bureau mostly focus on the high seas, which means that a lot of Bangladesh's river-centric violence passes them by. Certainly, local media cannot help much. Indian newspapers devote an average of 0.6 percent of their front pages to rural coverage.[7] Bangladeshi journalists say the situation is no better on their side of the border.

Piracy is very far from a uniquely Bangladeshi phenomenon, of course. Between about 2007 and 2012, Somali gangs seized so many ships in East African waters that they prompted unprecedented—and ultimately very effective—joint US–Chinese–European naval action. Off the coast of West Africa, raiders from the Niger Delta have turned the Gulf of Guinea into a kind of "pirates' alley," a gauntlet which oil tankers and other ships must run at tremendous personal risk. These groups kidnapped at least 180 seafarers within that area between 2020 and 2022 alone.[8] From the Straits of Malacca, through which about 40 percent of global trade passes, to the port anchorages of financially stricken Venezuela and Peru, waterborne raiders of various stripes have kidnapped, killed, and burgled their way through thousands of ships in recent years alone. Faint consolation though it may be, fishermen in the Sundarbans are at least in a better position than some of their Filipino and Indonesian counterparts. Abu Sayyaf, an ISIS-affiliated group in the southern Philippines, targets fishermen as a means of financing its terrorism.

Again, maritime experts suggest that global piracy is probably more prolific than the data indicate. Some captains do not welcome careful inspection of their vessels and so do not report assaults, while owners may fear increased insurance premiums and lost sailing time.

This iteration of Bangladeshi piracy is also but the latest in a centuries-long catalog of banditry in and around the Bay of Bengal. As far back as records extend, pirates in what is now Bangladesh and neighboring India and Myanmar harnessed one of the world's greatest webs of navigable rivers to plague communities well beyond the coastline. They kidnapped locals with the same abandon as their Mediterranean peers snatched the likes of Julius Caesar and Miguel de Cervantes many centuries earlier. They slowed the development of Dhaka, the current capital, by sacking it during a seventeenth-century raid. When the European powers arrived in earnest, their navies and trading companies soon established a form of state-licensed privateering so voracious that one of the old Bengali words for pirate, *olandaj*, is a corruption of "Holland."[9] To this day, some Bangladeshi pirates use a variation of the same "protection" racket that the Portuguese, Dutch, and British introduced, demanding payments in advance in exchange for safe passage.[10]

So far, so "ordinary." But in form and possible consequence, the sort of piracy that Rafikul Mali embraced is arguably a thing unto itself. By transforming the Sundarbans into more of an anarchic free-for-all, these groups threaten its Bengal tiger population, one of the greatest remaining concentrations of big cats in the world—and, even more importantly, the forest on whose fortunes the existence of the country might be said to rest. By rendering life for coastal peoples that bit less tolerable, pirates are contributing to already sky-high levels of rural-to-urban migration. Dhaka's population has mushroomed from around one million in 1960 to over twenty times that today. If nothing else, these pirate bands illustrate the changing incentive structures that climate and environmental challenges can unleash. Where once-meager state policing efforts were enough to stifle most Sundarbans banditry, increasing deprivation has ensured that that is no longer the case. Think of this as a thoroughly modern twist on one of the world's oldest professions.

A Landscape Fighting to Survive

It was a little after eight in the morning by the time we reached Bhodra Forest Department camp, and after two hours of boating through the punishingly humid heat, I was struggling to differentiate air from water. The ink in my note pads was so smudged as to be borderline illegible; the pages were littered with squashed bugs. At one point, with the plaintive self-pity of someone more used to reporting in places with too little water as opposed to too much, I appear to have scrawled something along the lines of, "I have sweat all my sweat. Send aid."

And yet I was captivated. Because almost alone among global landscapes, the Sundarbans are a place where "geological processes that usually unfold in deep time appear to occur at a speed where they can be followed from week to week and month to month," as novelist and climate commentator Amitav Ghosh puts it.[11] The rivers shape-shift so swiftly that maps lose some of their accuracy almost as soon as they are printed. The (ostensibly) uninhabited forest stands out all the more in a country the size of Illinois but with roughly 170 million people—and where, as a consequence, you are practically never alone. Here, within this chunk of deltaic lushness, some of the planet's greatest rivers finally meet the sea with the kind of splendor that their thousand-plus-mile descents from the Himalayas surely warrant.

I had ventured into the Sundarbans themselves to try to better understand why so many locals felt compelled to chance life and financial solvency within these pirate-infested waters. It did not take long for the penny to drop. Because while the Sundarbans are accustomed to dramatic change, they—and, most particularly, the surrounding agricultural areas that depend on the mangroves' good health—are not well placed to withstand the kind of assault that man, nature, and upstream powers have inflicted of late.

The forest, which once covered almost the entirety of the Bangladeshi coastline, has been brutally sheared, pared back now to the southwestern corner of the country. Although most of that destruction came before or during the British colonial era, it continues to this day in places, despite a near-total moratorium on tree cutting within the Sundarbans since the early 2000s. Barely concealing his distress and perhaps embarrassment, Jannatul Azad, my Forest Department guide, pointed out the clearings where dense, interwoven clumps of mangroves had stood until relatively recently. In the process, loggers have eaten away at vegetation that is both a vital carbon sink (given the capacity of mangrove swamps to sequester up to four times more carbon than rainforests)—and, crucially as far as locals are concerned, a shield without which their communities simply could not exist. By blunting the impact of the cyclones that roll in off the Bay of Bengal, the mangroves enable life in places which would otherwise stand little chance.

The freshwater flows from the north are increasingly insufficient too. Mangroves, particularly the *sundari,* the dominant species after which the forest is named, thrive in brackish coastal waters. Yet, as upstream countries siphon off more river for their own booming populations' needs, the Sundarbans are receiving less of the fresh water needed to maintain an optimal mix. As we barreled deeper into the Sundarbans,

Azad identified the telltale signs of excessive salinity—the thin, sickly-looking saplings, the changing plant life. "This is a landscape that is having to fight to survive," he said. This problem is particularly acute in the western portion of the Bangladeshi Sundarbans, which lost much of its freshwater access after India built the Farakka Barrage on the Ganges (known as the Padma in Bangladesh). It threatens to get much worse if China pushes ahead with an enormous dam-construction program planned for the Tibetan headwaters of the Brahmaputra. (I'll add much more about climate change's contribution to transboundary water disputes in the next chapter. Suffice it to say that little good will emerge out of it, particularly for downstream parties.)

All the while, climate change is bearing down on Bangladesh, cleaving the country in ways that the Sundarbans area, one of its most vulnerable parts, is extra hard-pressed to resist. As a low-lying nation, in which more than half its people live less than five meters above sea level, and through which the roughly 700 rivers that crisscross its territory drain a basin more than ten times larger, Bangladesh is precariously poised between rising sea and Himalayan meltwater. Even small changes can wreak havoc. Those cyclones are seemingly getting stronger, roaring into the depleted, thinned-out Sundarbans. Sea level rise is adding to the freshwater deficit among the mangroves. Here, too, Azad, now on much more comfortable ground, says the signs are all too apparent. "Without this kind of effort, the tigers would die of dehydration," he said, gesturing at a metallic tub about twice the size of a kid's paddling pool on the shoreline. "The cyclones salinize their drinking sources, so we have to fill these to keep them alive after the storms."

Among a rash of other climate-related ills, the monsoon season—the "real finance minister of South Asia," as it is frequently and only somewhat jocularly called—is unprecedently erratic. That can mean intense drought. More usually, in Bangladesh's case, it means downpours so fierce that parts of the country can receive eleven meters of rain a year.

In 1998, an especially monstrous flood inundated about 70 percent of its landmass. It is no wonder, I finally understood, that some farmers refer to their country as a kind of divine prank. The soil is fantastically fertile, but you are forever in danger of getting washed away.[12]

Trapped by the actions of their predecessors, those of neighboring countries, and climatic forces beyond their control, Bangladeshi authorities insist they are doing all they can to fortify the Sundarbans "shield." However, that is not how it feels to nearby communities, many of whom see the state's hand—or, more accurately, the lack of it—in their struggle. They are angry about water pollution, which is so overwhelming in urban areas that some rivers, like the Buriganga that flows through Dhaka, have been declared "technically dead," almost totally devoid of life. It is bad enough in the south that many fishermen steer as far out into the rivers as possible to avoid the filth.

They are angry about sand mining. As Jannatul Azad and I made our way back and forth along the Passur River searching in vain for traces of tiger presence, we stumbled on a dozen or so barges, all greedily gobbling up sand with power hoses for construction in the fast-expanding cities. These theoretically regulated but generally unmonitored practices tend to deepen and narrow the riverbeds, speeding up flow and thereby exacerbating flooding and riverbank erosion.

Above all, the local communities are furious about the shrimp industry. Since the 1980s, big-city businessmen have carved out hundreds of thousands of acres of prawn aquaculture. Initially encouraged by the World Bank and other international financial institutions, which felt that already-salinizing coastal Bangladesh was perfectly placed to cater to and benefit from the world's growing appetite for costly shellfish, these operations have transformed swathes of the Sundarbans into vegetationless monocultures. They offer absolutely no protection from cyclones—and very little sustenance for birds, few of whom still appear in these parts to fulfill their historic pest-eating duties for farmers.

The greatest impacts center on the region's flood defenses, though. Many shrimp farmers have burrowed illegal water channels under the protective embankments to fill their fields with prawn-appropriate brackish water. In doing so, they have both undermined structures that were built from the 1960s onward to safeguard much of the south's agriculture—and inadvertently (or sometimes not so inadvertently) contaminated their neighbors' crops with salt, leaving many with no choice but to sell out to the shrimp syndicates.[13] When cyclones strike, many of the weakened embankments have proved particularly susceptible to collapse. Men like Shihab Bishash have become pirate fodder as a consequence.

Bangladeshi authorities are trying to stop or at least slow intensifying erosion along the country's rivers, such as the Meghna (pictured). Flood defenses are rarely sufficient, though. Every year thousands of people are losing their homes, and tens of thousands of farmers are losing their land. For those along the periphery of the Sundarbans, fishing among the pirate-infested forests can feel like one of their few alternatives. (Photo by Sohan Rahat)

For over thirty years, he grew rice and vegetables on a small plot in Banishanta, a short hop by boat over the Passur from Mongla. Amid rising soil salinity due to sea level rise, those upstream dams, and poor embankment management, his yields had been steadily declining for some time. But it was the expansion of the local shrimp industry—and the impact on local flood defenses that came with it—that spelled the end of his farming career. Since Cyclone Aila eviscerated his fields in 2009, he and most of his neighbors have made their living within the Sundarbans for want of alternative options. The dangers, illegality, and grim conditions be damned. "Tell me this," he half said, half asked. "What choice do I have?"

Pirate Heaven

Shivapada Mondol became a doctor because he wanted to help people like his arthritic grandparents. Little did he suspect how much of his time would be consumed treating everything from gunshot wounds to injuries sustained during torture. As one of the few medical professionals in the southern Shyamnagar area, he is frequently called upon to help those at the receiving end of pirate violence. During weeks like the one when we met in 2018, he has time for little else.

Two honey collectors had limped in that morning with deep machete gashes sustained during run-ins with the "Master Bahini," one of the largest of the pirate crews. They were soon followed by a man who had been assaulted by pirates and then confined to his boat with cuts so infected that Mondol quietly confided that he would likely lose at least one hand, if not both. By the time the mayor of a nearby village called, demanding help for a man who had just been released after ten days of *jaladoshyu* captivity, the doctor seemed resigned to yet another night with little sleep. "These pirates have no mercy," he said. "None."[14]

Perched on the western edge of Bangladesh's portion of the Sundarbans and just shy of the shuttered Indian frontier, this area knows more about piracy than perhaps any other in the country. Residents are at their wits' end. Their salt-saturated fields are as incapable as Banishanta's of producing much other than shrimp these days. That industry is frequently uninviting because the shrimp kingpins allegedly collude among themselves to keep payments low, irrespective of global prices. With the plentiful fish, honey, and timber stocks of the Sundarbans literally on their doorstep, villagers here have felt particularly powerless to resist the area's call. They have consequently developed a deep, if horribly hard-won, grasp of what makes their nemeses tick.

In some ways, community leaders say, the pirates are as much victims of the degrading environment as they are. Some of them were also farmers, men whose yields had plumbed the same intolerable new lows. Others were fishermen whose livelihoods had been destroyed by pollution, especially those plying inland waters near major industry and cities. In Dhaka's Buriganga-side shipyards, I met "Master" Shihab, a ship's first mate, as he presided over the cleaning of his vessel's barnacle-encrusted hull. In 2020, he and his crew were attacked while anchored off Chandpur, at the confluence of the Padma and Meghna rivers. He recognized some of the raiders as fishermen from his home village, all of whom had abandoned their nets due to toxic runoff from nearby garment factories, many producing clothing for Western "fast fashion" brands. "We did what they told us do, because if we didn't they'd beat the hell out of us," he said.

Plenty of pirates appear to be villagers running away from the debts that they had incurred to make up for poor harvests or unsatisfactory catches, but that they stood little hope of repaying when those conditions replicated themselves the following year. For example, on Bhola Island I heard several stories of fishermen taking out over $5,000 in agricultural bank loans and then fleeing when repayments were due. Those men appear to have sought sanctuary among the relative anonymity of

Dhaka's sprawling slums. Plenty of their peers, having already broken the law, have opted to go a step further.

For the most part, though, pirate victims insist that this is a tale of avarice and opportunism, much more than one of poor, misbegotten individuals resorting to desperate measures. Some of these pirate bands are composed of longtime criminals, including fugitives on the lam from prison, who can recognize a rich money-making possibility when they see it. As with some of their jihadi peers in Iraq and Syria, they have not been inclined to pass this one up.

The setting is perfect. How, after all, are you to police an area this big, this carpeted with dense vegetation, and this laced with handy boat-concealing inlets? The Sundarbans, as my government interviewees correctly, if self-interestedly, pointed out, has long been a den of ne'er-do-wells and rebels. Why do I suppose that they could fully control the forest when the British Empire at its peak could not? Having initially decided to quit piracy after his first month, Rafikul Mali says he was persuaded to stay on by his confederates, who talked up the ease of evading capture.

The pirates' adversary is, or at least was, ideal. For years prior to the amnesty, authorities appeared uninterested in taking on these gangs, or at best insufficiently equipped to make much of a dent in their operations. With about 120 patrol posts and stations spread across the Sundarbans, the Forest Department has primary responsibility for the area. But during my time with them they only sported World War II–era Lee–Enfield rifles, no match for the pirates' trove of automatic weapons, and, in a grim mirror of their Iraqi counterparts' experience, they did not seem to have enough boat fuel to do their jobs. On occasions when the department has made arrests, coordination with other security forces or disputes over jurisdiction has sometimes undermined their good work. In at least two instances in 2017, suspected pirates went free because the Forest Department and local police could not agree over who would be responsible for feeding and transporting the men to prison, officers told me.[15]

And what of the pirates' quarry? Perfect, from a *jaladoshyu* perspective. When I asked Khogan Shana, a fisherman from the western village of Munshiganj, why the pirate crews were able to operate with relative impunity, he reeled off the usual reasons—villagers' lack of political heft, the state's disinterest in their plight. But then he paused. "Many of us are breaking the law, and the pirates know it." To enter the Sundarbans legally, you need a permit, which, at around $2.50 for seven days, can be out of reach for villagers, who frequently go without as a consequence.[16] Many fishermen also use banned nets, ones with tiny holes that trap small fry and hence jeopardize future hauls. In these circumstances, ever fewer locals are inclined to report pirate run-ins. The pirate bands, with their keen sense of danger, know that as well.

Through it all, the people of the Sundarbans might at least hope for help from a landscape that they know and treasure. Here, too, though, conditions have become more pirate-friendly by the year. Most fishermen in the Sundarbans pursue hilsa, a herring-like fish that is much prized by Bangladeshis and their neighbors over the border in the Indian state of West Bengal. But those stocks are fluctuating due to overfishing and warming waters, among other reasons, forcing fishermen to travel deeper into cleaner, less populated waters to catch what remains. There the pirates await, often attacking them on their return journey when they are heavily laden and so are less likely to be able to escape—and all the more attractive with that cargo of increasingly scarce and thus pricier hilsa.

Honey collectors, crab catchers, and gatherers of *golpata* leaves (for use in roofing) can make life every bit as easy for the pirates. Their work is often centered on identifiable locations and particular seasons—three to four months in spring when the bees are most busily collecting pollen, in the case of the honey collectors.[17] As a consequence, their movements can be very predictable, not least when they are quite literally betraying their whereabouts. Over time, many of these forest extractors have developed a habit of blowing horns to signal their positions to their colleagues and avoid getting lost in the dense undergrowth. It is music to the ears of the ransom-hungry bands on their trail.

Though the nature of these attacks varies enormously, the pirates typically beat and restrain their victims before transferring their belongings—fish, fuel, nets, and anything else of value—onto their own vessels. Sometimes they filch the boat itself if it is better than their own, though that is rare. Many of the fishing boats I saw were repurposed ship's lifeboats of dubious seaworthiness. If the pirates elect to kidnap the fishermen, they typically release one or more of the crew to inform the families and begin the painful process of hitting up friends, distant family, and money lenders for cash. The ransoms of $50 to $2,000 per person are often transferred via cell phone, using app-based services such as bKash, with higher sums charged for captains and boat owners.[18] Then and only then might the battered, hungry, and often traumatized men be released. (According to survivor testimony, beatings from some of the few female pirates are often worse, intent as they seemingly are, on warding off the impression of weakness.)

Unlike some of their upriver peers, who suffer fewer attacks and so are less aware of the pirate threat, those who work the Sundarbans are acutely conscious of what they are up against. But that is scant consolation when they feel trapped in a bind from which there are few escapes. Escalating climate shocks are pushing more farmers out onto the water, the numbers of fishing and crabbing boats in the Shyamnagar area surging from around three hundred to over two thousand in the decade to 2018.[19] More fishermen generally means more danger. Indeed, the concentration of pirates appears closely tied related to the amount of available lucre. Attacks are most prevalent in the western Sundarbans, where salinity and farming conditions are worst. This, in turn, has led to more kidnappings for which the only solution at most locals' disposal is to venture back out, like pigs to the slaughter, into the Sundarbans as soon as possible to repay the cost of ransoms and lost earnings.

Meeting outside Banishanta's notorious—and, by the look of its revolving door of visiting johns, highly successful—riverside brothel, "Mujib" appeared painfully contrite as he recounted his contribution to that suffering. An ex-pirate who agreed to speak on the condition that I not use his real name, he said he had worked hard to make up for the three years he plagued Sundarbans-area villagers. But, like Rafikul Mali, he suggested that he, too, had felt powerless to resist the riches on offer. "Sometimes people paid us in advance. We didn't have to do anything," he said, referring to a system whereby some of the bigger pirate bands would issue "pirate permits"—guarantees of safe passage in exchange for smaller prepayments. "This was the kind of easy money I could not imagine."

Like their counterparts in the Sundarbans, fishermen off Bhola Island must run a gauntlet of pirate bands to ply their trade. This uncle-nephew duo still bear the scars from an earlier attack. (Photo by Sohan Rahat)

The Consequences for Man and Beast

Even without prolific piracy, the village of Harinagar would likely be very poor—positioned, as it is, at the end of a long, bumpy, dead-end road and subject to weather events so extreme that, most decades, it has to rebuild itself. With the piracy, it is about as deprived a place as you will find in southwestern Bangladesh. Much of the money that locals do earn out on the water, in the mangrove forest, or among the few remaining non-shrimp-producing fields finds its way into pirate pockets. The ramifications are writ large on the lifestyles of the district's residents.

Mohammed Ruhol Amin was once considered a rich man by local standards. But then Cyclone Aila took his house. Shrimp farms and sea level rise claimed his previously profitable vegetable patches. When he, like so many others, made the ultimately fateful decision to turn to fishing, the pirates plundered pretty much everything else he had left. Ushering my interpreter friend and me into his new home—a ramshackle bamboo-and-sheet-metal structure in the shadow of the embankment, Amin was at pains to show how his life had changed since his third and most recent kidnapping.

He had almost no belongings, with most of what he had been able to salvage from the cyclone now gone to partially repay the money lender. His children looked hungry. The daughter in particular displayed the stunted growth, vacant expression, and other signs of malnutrition that primarily afflict girls because boys are often prioritized at mealtimes. Maksud, Amin's brother, was laid up on a flimsy mattress in the corner, suffering from injuries inflicted by pirates during his own encounter with them the previous year—and a later snake bite to his lower leg, which had gone green and slightly gangrenous, and gave off a rank stench akin to slightly spoiled chicken. The family simply could not afford medical attention. "Just imagine. I once had money," Amin mumbled. "I was once a man."

Amin's example might sound like an extreme one. And insofar as most other victims do not have quite as far to fall, it is. But in the most pirate-afflicted villages, few families have survived this banditry unharmed financially. In the market, no vendor could break a 1,000 taka note (roughly equal to $10), such are their lowly takings. Among the carpenters, the tradesmen who can usually be most assured of work in cyclone-afflicted communities, there is not enough work to go around. That bodes ill for the next mega-cyclone, which will strike poorly prepared families in particular. (There is a grim circularity to much of this. One climate-related disaster can leave people unable to confront others.) For a population for whom food and the ritual around it has traditionally provided reassurance at times of scant alternative comforts, there might be worse in store. "Fish and rice make a Bengali," goes a regional saying. Yet, increasingly, the indebted Sundarbanis who catch so much of the former must subsist mostly on the latter.

This brings us to the big cats. I had come to the Sundarbans intent on avoiding writing about tigers. These animals, an estimated two hundred of which roam across the Bangladeshi and Indian portions of the forest, have received most of the meager media coverage centered on this area. I thought it was churlish, inappropriate perhaps, to focus on their fate when there was an even less known human story to report. Only after I arrived did I come to understand that there was no disentangling the two—and certainly no separating them from the pirate onslaught.

Keen to minimize exposure to the *jaladoshyu* out on the rivers, more Sundarbans-area farmers are heading into the forests to collect honey and other resources. But there they are running headlong into a tiger population that appears more enamored of human flesh that any other in the world. In the Bangladeshi part of the forest alone, the man-eaters might be killing up to 170 people a year, only a fraction of which are reported.[20] Most of those casualties have come in the same western reaches of the mangroves where the pirates hold greatest sway—and for some of the same reasons. With higher levels of salinity in and around this part of the forest, there are more intruding people and perhaps less alternative prey traipsing through the tiger habitat. According to one particularly morbid theory, centuries or more of monster cyclones may even have given this type of tiger an unusual taste for humans that it is in no hurry to forget.[21]

One might therefore suspect, amid this big-cat bloodbath of sorts, that villagers might quietly welcome the pirates' targeting of tigers. Not one bit, said the widow of a tiger victim when I asked her just that. Although Sundarbanis live in terror of tigers, often praying for protection to Bonbibi, a forest-dwelling deity sacred to both local Hindus and Muslims, most people seem to have a strong awareness of the stakes. By actively pursuing tigers for their parts and pelts, mostly for use in Chinese traditional medicine, the pirates are jeopardizing the forest and its protective properties. Locals suspect that it is only the fear of meeting a tiger on its own turf that keeps most would-be loggers at bay. And by killing at least half of the twenty tigers known to have died by human hands between 2003 and 2014, these men threaten the very identity of a country where the animals are emblazoned on everything from election posters to cricket team jerseys. As Cambodians have found to their dismay, it is only when the big cats are dead and gone, with the last tiger spotted there in 2007, that you realize what you have lost. Ultimately, in a shape-shifting region experiencing innumerable dizzying transformations, it could just be that the tigers represent one of the few remaining constants.

That last insight was one that Azad Kobir, the officer in charge of the Karamjal ranger station, ventured on one of my final evenings in the Sundarbans area. I had mentioned to him that I wanted to get more of a sense of what the jungle was really like, to better understand the fear that so many of my interviewees had evinced and that I, on my daytime boat trips through the mangroves, had not quite grasped. So it was that a few hours later I accompanied him on his early-evening rounds. First, he checked on the deer, a few of whom were kept caged as a kind of mewing early-warning system in case any tigers approached.[22] Then he rattled the iron-barred doors, giving each an aggressive shake. Finally, with the last of the natural light fading and Mongla port, just a few miles over the water, now wholly obscured by the darkness, he tested his phone. "Do you see now?" he said. "We are so close to the city, but from here it seems so far."

Fleeing Pirates and Tigers

Battered by bandits, big cats, and the climate challenges that are aggravating both those menaces and causing considerable damage in their own right, the people of the Sundarbans have experienced an awful lot of hardship. For the most part, they endure it with the uncomplaining stoicism of those who know they have little choice. Yet, for a growing number among them, circumstances have become untenable, and they are seeking safety and fortune elsewhere.*

Some Sundarbanis have followed millions of their countryfolk and South Asian neighbors in migrating to Dubai and other Gulf Arab cities. There is no mistaking the houses of those who have spent years earning superior foreign salaries, their big, often gaudy multistory mansions standing out like flashing neon dollar signs in the otherwise monochrome, low-rise villages. Nor, with the departure of this predominantly male cohort, is there any escaping the impact in now

---

* In some ways, international migration is only becoming trickier, with tighter border controls and visa regimes. But in other ways it is considerably simpler than it was a few years back. Many migrants or would-be migrants have an improved understanding of their migration prospects due to social media and pointers from those who have migrated before them, as well as more chances to make good on those prospects thanks to remittances and "better-greased" and hence cheaper migration pathways.

largely female-dominated villages. Much of this is positive, with women able to assume more leadership roles, including replanting cleared or cyclone-mangled mangrove patches; some of it is not, with the dearth of marriageable young men fueling social unease.[23]

Ironically, a select few have even turned to the very pirates they are fleeing for help in migrating. For a time, the *jaladoshyu* supplemented their kidnapping and tiger-killing by ferrying locals and some of the roughly one million Rohingya refugees who have fled Myanmar through the warren of waterways to the Indian border. New Delhi has fenced off all 2,500 miles of it, but the portion of the Sundarbans to the south of Kolkata is as impervious to total state control as the Bangladeshi bit. Kaamil Ahmed, author of *I Feel No Peace* about the Rohingya crisis, writes of tragic-absurd situations in which refugees have gone in both directions at once, almost crossing paths (though mostly along Bangladesh's northern frontier). Some hope for better prospects in India without having heard about its changing political climate. At the same time, others are returning to Bangladesh having decided that even camp life is preferable to repression.

But, as with most global migrants, the large majority of wantaway Sundarbanis are gravitating to other parts of their own country. In Barisal, a roughly half-million-person city about six hours by boat from Dhaka, real estate prices have almost tripled over the past four years, a broker told me. In Khulna, the closest major settlement to the Sundarbans, whole villages have effectively transplanted themselves to cramped cityscapes. In plain language, one resident there laid out why he had traded in his airy farmhouse near Banishanta for a stifling windowless room there: "Once I could grow forty *muns* of rice in a season [a *mun* is about ninety pounds]. Now, because of the conditions I get less than ten. I cannot survive on this." In Dhaka, which has grown faster than any other megacity on Earth, rural migrants account for much of its fivefold surge in population to about 25 million since 1990.

Plenty of these people have moved for the superior services and education and economic opportunities that cities offer. Plenty more appear to be there for reasons beyond their control. The capital has received at least 400,000 new rural arrivals a year over the past decade, according to one study, more than 80 percent of whom list environmental drivers as causes of displacement. As I followed Tazara Begum from Bhola Island to the Dhaka slum she now calls home after losing her coastal village home to river erosion, she rhapsodized in her quiet understated way about the big skies, big breezes, and fresh food she was leaving behind. The very idea that she might not see her village again was almost enough to bring her to tears. "We tried everything to stay. Everything. But in the end we found it impossible."[24]

I, for one, struggled to understand how she and her neighbors endured their oppressively hot subterranean rooms, with only a few tired, spluttering fans to cool them, and no gust to dispel the stench from the adjacent sewage canal. I certainly could not fathom how, amid influxes of rats and other rodents of an indeterminate nature, they kept their spaces spotlessly clean and community relations relatively friendly.

Though some scholars quibble with headline-grabbing migration projections, there is a strong chance that these past and present movements will pale in comparison to future ones. The World Bank suggests Bangladesh could have 19 million internal "climate migrants" by 2050, about half the South Asian total (and the biggest per capita displacement of any non-island state).[25] None of that need be a bad thing, as global migration advocates frequently point out. More, it will be an essential coping mechanism as climate change levies a fiercer toll on low-lying agrarian communities. But, as in Baghdad and so many other swelling metropolises, migration also presents a serious headache for officials, a rural security crisis helping to give rise to an urban one. Authorities in Dhaka have at times lost their grip on the city's slums, the warrens of densely packed shanties proving hospitable surroundings for gangs.

Officials admitted to me in off-the-record conversations that they fear a replication of those conditions. "These places are like paradises for bad guys," one said. "We couldn't drive a tank into one even if we wanted."

The Future

As of 2018, the pirates of Bangladesh are officially no more. Under the terms of a 2016–17 amnesty that was brokered by Mohsin-ul Hakim, a TV journalist who only came to learn about the pirate threat after reporting on the destruction from Cyclone Sidr a decade before, anyone not accused of rape or murder was allowed to return home if they laid down their arms. At least 100 pirates, Rafikul Mali and "Mujib" among them, accepted the offer, collectively handing over 250 guns and tens of thousands of rounds of ammunition in the process.[26] "Our law enforcement agencies have caught and killed many of them," said Habibul Haque Khan, director of the Khulna area's environment office, insisted to me in a 2018 interview. "They're very weak now."[27]

But while pirate numbers appear to have dropped somewhat since then, the crews' supposed disappearance would come as news to coastal and riparian fishermen. The attacks continue. Off Bhola Island in 2022, I met one man who still bore the scars from a run-in the week beforehand, the *jaladoshyu* taking everything except his clothes in a middle of the night attack. On a ferry from Barisal to Dhaka, I got into conversation with a young man. From the safety of the garishly lit top deck, he eagerly pointed out the inlet in which he and his brother had been waylaid and robbed while fishing recreationally the previous year. According to Mali, some of his amnestied ex-colleagues are accepting pardons and cash, lying low for a little while, and then returning to crime at sea or on land.[28] It may even be that the pirates are reconstituting themselves as more of a poaching force. There are now thirty-two tiger poaching syndicates in Bangladesh, warns Panthera, the big-cat conservation NGO, many using poison to kill animals and supply their body parts to customers in at least fifteen countries.[29]

The key players remain unpunished. For all the coverage lavished on pirate surrenders in the Bangladeshi press, both academics and local community leaders say that they are but foot soldiers in a much bigger racket. Some of the village moneylenders, who charge ruinously high interest rates, are allegedly in cahoots with the pirates. The pirate captains appear to be equally protected, brazenly frequenting fish markets as they sell on their stolen goods. There is simply no way, according to practically everyone I met, that this trade could prosper without the involvement of local bigwigs. "Lots of people who should be in prison—the big guys—are not in prison," Hakim said. Having spent so many hours arranging these surrenders, which he says were only made possible after an internal mutiny in 2015 overthrew an important pirate boss who rejected the idea of yielding, he seems almost cheated by the outcome.

And even in places where the pirate threat appears to have genuinely subsided, few dare to hope that it will remain that way as existing climate and environmental woes worsen, and new ones emerge. In addition to expanded Chinese as well as Indian dam construction, melting glaciers threaten to assail regional river systems like never before, first inundating them with more water—a kind of "false prosperity," as Andri Snær Magnason puts it in *On Time and Water*, his ode to Iceland's disappearing ice—and then potentially starving downstreamers in ways they have never experienced. The Himalayas could lose two-thirds of its glaciers by 2100.[30] How might the "shield" of the Sundarbans weather that? How, indeed, might it manage stronger sea level rise? In a worst-case scenario, in which seas surge by six-plus feet before the century is out, up to half the Sundarbans will be lost, and with it perhaps Bangladesh itself. Even business-as-usual scenarios of 1.5–2 degrees Celsius of warming make for unpleasant reading.[31] If nothing else, there may soon be no locals left there for pirates to menace.

More imminently, how might the mangroves weather the state's own ongoing acts of sabotage? After weaving in and out of a Dhaka neighborhood in a likely unnecessary, not to mention profoundly amateurish, attempt to avoid possible police surveillance, a friend and I paid a visit to Anu Muhammed in 2018. For years, he has helped coordinate a campaign against Rampal, a coal-fired power station that the government is building barely ten miles from the edge of the Sundarbans. He, like so many others, has dipped in and out of jail and house arrest as a consequence. But campaigners have lost. It is seemingly only a matter of time before millions of tons of coal are shipped through the forest to feed the plant—and, ultimately, millions more tons of CO_2 are belched back out over them. This, Mohammed said, is not how climate-vulnerable countries should behave, no matter how much they might need and want the energy to develop. "A project like this will not build, it will only destroy, especially in this location."

But, as bleak as circumstances might appear, there is perhaps no country on Earth that has been more frequently written off than Bangladesh. The state, which was East Pakistan from the end of British rule until it won independence from West Pakistan (now just called Pakistan) in a bloody war in 1971, was born in part out of environmental disaster. The Islamabad-based government's insipid response to Cyclone Bhola, which killed up to half a million people in 1970, exacerbated long-standing Bangladeshi anger with what was essentially a West Pakistani regime. Ever since then, the country has defied predictions of widespread famine to become largely food secure. It has overcome near-universal expectations of absolute poverty to outstrip the GDP per capita of its South Asian neighbors, including vaunted India. Crucially, it has not only maintained but greatly expanded state capacity in the face of worsening extreme weather events. The number of cyclone shelters has leapt from fewer than fifty in the 1970s to more than twelve thousand now. No longer can Bangladesh be called a "basket case," as a senior US diplomat supposedly labeled the new nation at its birth (though that diplomat was not Henry Kissinger, to whom the line is generally attributed).

Climate change poses much its greatest challenge to date, a genuinely existential threat to the state's very being and certainly its viability. Yet, given past successes, one can understand Bangladeshi policymakers' quiet confidence that they can resist the worst outcomes. The big immediate question is whether they will ever include the "small" peripheral peoples in their successes. Those villagers, used to being neglected, are not holding their breath. "Of course, no one cares about us," said Mahmud, a fisherman in the Munshiganj area near the Indian frontier. "We have no voice!"[32]

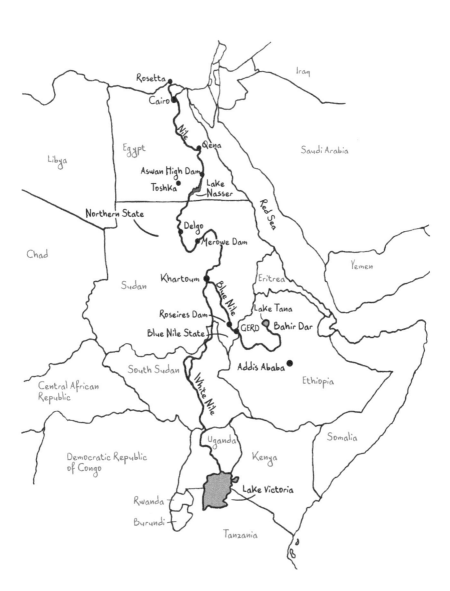

Water Wars?[1]

History tells us that nations do not fight over water.
Egypt and Ethiopia, roiled by a new mega-dam on the Nile,
might break the mold.

To visit the Nile's most contentious site is to run a gauntlet of literal and logistical roadblocks.

Almost as soon as you leave the city of Bahir Dar, the landscape of western Ethiopia morphs into a patchwork of hills and terraced fields that are as exquisitely green as they are ill-suited to travel. Many of the roads are no match for the rains, which pour down from July to September, not stopping until they have sliced the Amhara Plateau into a maze of soggy islets. Streams show little respect for their regular courses. One that we needed to ford had reinvented itself as a small inland sea almost overnight, necessitating a day-long wait for the waters to relent. Certainly, there is no use in turning to the river as an alternative means of transport, as big and tantalizingly smooth as it initially seems.

About thirty miles after it seeps out of Lake Tana near Bahir Dar, the Blue Nile, the slightly shorter but much more voluminous of the Nile's two main constituent rivers, plunges over a majestic waterfall, and then barrels through a roughly four-hundred-mile-long web of deep, cliff-lined gorges. Gathering strength with each arriving tributary, it cascades down five thousand feet from the highlands to the semiarid plains below. It is the most beautiful, most isolated, and, quite fittingly, perhaps the most inhospitable stretch of the entire basin. "Dangerous river, dangerous times," said Eremias, my translator, as we exited our mud-snared vehicle for the umpteenth time that trip and began to push.

But worse, or at least less surmountable, obstacles await the nearer one gets to that hot-button site, the Grand Ethiopian Renaissance Dam (GERD). Ever since Ethiopia broke ground in 2011 on what will be Africa's largest hydroelectric dam, authorities in Addis Ababa have been engaged in a fierce tussle with downstream and mostly arid Egypt, which depends on the Nile for almost all its fresh water and is consequently terribly wary of anything that it construes as a threat to the river.

After Chagni, the road signs suddenly disappear, apparently removed in a textbook ploy to confuse possible foreign (read Egyptian) invaders. The few people we saw in this area with spotty internet connection were not inclined to direct us—or, at that febrile time back in 2015, to even acknowledge our presence. "These are the questions that get you into trouble," said Samuel, a restaurant cook in the crossroads town of Injibera, when I asked about purported land grabs in that area. He was not exaggerating. Days later, security forces raided my hotel room, taking only my reporting pads—and, puzzlingly, some of my Snickers stash. I spent a few panicked hours trying to remember if there were enough identifying details within the notes to trouble my interviewees, before ultimately deciding that the new owners had little hope of deciphering my scrawl, an accidental code.

Crucially, the closer you inch to GERD, the more frequent, more time-consuming, and more brimming with unsmiling armed men the checkpoints become. The first among these are manned by farm militiamen—wiry, hard-looking guys with rusting rifles who are more concerned with stopping cattle rustling than in grilling foreigners. The federal police who follow are tougher. They gave our hard-won travel authorizations a thorough examination, though they, too, have other priorities. With so many guns slipping over from nearby Sudan and big money to be made smuggling alcohol in the other direction to their then-Islamist-governed neighbor where booze can be hard to source, they waved us on after checking every nook and cranny in our car.

However, it was the next layer of security, which I had been warned about—and with good reason, as it turned out. As we pulled into a now-nameless village some forty miles from the dam, an officer from one of Ethiopia's internal security organizations called us over after a tip-off from a previous checkpoint. He grilled Eremias, who suddenly went very pale, no doubt ruing his decision to accompany me on what I had suggested might be a tricky excursion. The officer pored over my passport, raising an eyebrow, I was sure, at my Egyptian residency permit. Then, as I hurriedly and somewhat desperately explained why it was important for me as a Nile-focused environmental journalist to visit the dam, he slowly ripped up our travel permits. We were to go no further, it was clear.

Yet shortly before we were returned to Bahir Dar under escort, the officer treated me to a little lecture, a neat encapsulation of one of the river's tensions. "There are people who want to destroy this dam. There are people who believe that all of the waters of the Nile belong to them," he said with a theatrical dip of his outsized aviator sunglasses. "But this is Ethiopia's time to develop. This is Ethiopia's turn to use the Nile. We are prepared to defend this dam with our lives if that is what it takes." And with that he was off, ready to confront the next real or perceived threat to his country's massive, controversial water project.

Seeds of Violence?

I had come to these parts to try to answer what then looked to be a very time-sensitive question: could the Nile basin ever descend into a "water war"? In Ethiopia, and at almost every step of my months-long journey along the length of the river that followed, the signs were often terrifying. That bellicose Ethiopian rhetoric over GERD has been more than matched by veiled or explicit threats from Egypt. The tough talk has been accompanied by the acquisition of many of the weapons that might figure were the two sides to ever to do battle, including "dam-busting" cruise missiles on Cairo's part, and reportedly an array of Russian air-defense systems to place in the treelined ridges above the dam by the Ethiopians.[2] Indeed, both parties may have already resorted to some forms of covert military action. To put it simply, lots of things are inexplicably going boom and a lot of regional rebel groups appear to enjoy a strength disproportional to their own likely means.

As I traveled north from Ethiopia by bus, boat, and occasionally donkey cart on that 2015 expedition, I encountered no fewer than six different localized conflicts, each one of which had a water angle. And that was just one trip. In many years of reporting across the Nile basin, it has sometimes seemed as if the entire valley is alive with the possibility—and, in many instances, the reality—of water-related violence.

The record suggests that that kind of giddy pessimism is misplaced, reckless even, at least when it comes to water-related clashes between countries. In the fifty years following World War II, instances of "cooperation" between nations along the same rivers were twice as common as instances of conflict, with no recorded cases of countries going to war for explicitly water-related reasons—despite a surge in barrages, babies, and all the other stresses that supposedly pitch places against one another.[3] If, as scholars point out, India and Pakistan can abide by the terms of their Indus River water-sharing treaty through two major wars, then surely so, too, can countries with fewer bones of contention and a good deal less bad blood. Sure enough, as Egypt and Ethiopia have slowly hashed out many of their disagreements over GERD in the years since my river-length journey, a lot of the venom has drained from the dispute.

But—and unsurprisingly there is a big "but," given the nature of this book—it is unclear whether this peace can last in the face of accelerating climate change. First, there is the prospect of a more meager Nile. Because while the Ethiopian highlands on which the river relies for about 85 percent of its flow may actually receive above-average precipitation over the coming years, those rains are also forecast to fall less predictably and so much less usefully for agriculture at both ends of the Nile. And that is key. Even with a well-fed river, officials in riparian capitals fret about their capacity to feed—and employ—swelling populations. For the Egyptian state, in particular, the possibility that climate stresses might stifle Nile-side crop cultivation at a time when the country already imports more wheat than any other in the world is seen as nothing less than an existential threat. Which, indeed, it might be for the regime itself. The Egyptian Revolution of 2011 that brought down the government of Hosni Mubarak may have been partly fueled by a hike in global food prices.[4] Hunger—or the fear of it—forms the mood music to much GERD tension.

Secondly, and very relatedly, there is the impact that these fears might levy on state behavior, which can be especially volatile during trying times among untrusting actors. In the pantheon of risks to the Nile, GERD and other planned basin megaprojects are arguably trifles. However, when added to the specter of looming climate shocks, these highly visible concrete behemoths can take on an outsized significance for politicians, who may be unable or unwilling to address the root causes of water shortages, and so seek out scapegoats, doing so for ordinary people who may not grasp the real reasons for their drying taps and canals. Ultimately, with stakes this high and the sense of powerlessness that climate stresses can engender so profoundly, there is no telling how judicious or honest officials will remain about other countries' water interventions when (and it likely is a *when*) a prolonged drought eventually strikes.

In a potent illustration of the dangers of misinformation, a theme that will crop up throughout this book, I repeatedly met Egyptian farmers who were convinced that the dam was hurting them well before its reservoir even began filling. On one occasion, a little north of Luxor, I got into a very unprofessional argument with a smallholder that quickly descended into a variation of "is not, is so." His insistence that he just "knew" the dam was the problem bothered me more than it had any right to; my use of Google Earth to show the then-unfinished dam only reinforced his resolution.

Thirdly and finally, GERD, climate stresses, and population growth are all bringing long-standing rival Nile narratives into collision in ways that public opinion up and down the valley is not well-equipped to handle. As my farmer friend's reaction suggested, the Nile is an intensely personal beast, a marker of identity for the hundreds of millions who live along or near its banks.* This emotion need not fuel violent outcomes. But getting Egyptian "downstreamers" and Ethiopian "upstreamers" to accommodate one another's narratives when equipped with only partial understandings of the other's needs—and all at a time of that misinformation, disinformation, and spiraling "localized" water violence, which generally sways to a different beat than major water-related conflict but which is contributing to the basin's increasingly ungovernable dynamic—is a big ask. To look back over the past decade's negotiations,

---

* The nature of the Nile may be uniquely dangerous too. Its famed length at some four thousand miles from source to sea; partial unnavigability due to rapids, which are important impediments to historic interaction; and often-hostile basin topography allowed for the emergence of multiple uncompromising state water narratives in ways that few other rivers equal. The large number of riparian states (eleven, second only to Europe's Danube), the mostly authoritarian character of their governments, and the complications that come with having the strongest of those states downstream from the one that is shaking up the status quo make it all the harder to reconcile those competing visions. Together with the fact that the Nile is nowhere near as bountiful as its dimensions might suggest, with a discharge around one-twelfth of the much shorter Congo, the tripwires are many and menacing.

it can almost seem as if states have conspired to tumble over one another's red lines.

Battleground GERD

It was a gathering of many of Egypt's leading political lights, and they were, almost to a man, in a pugnacious mood. Summoned by then-president Mohammed Morsi to discuss potential responses to Ethiopia's fast-developing GERD, they took turns proposing ideas wild, ambitious, and other. Very soon, their suggestions skewed distinctly belligerent. Ayman Nour, a noted liberal politician, proposed "intervening in [Ethiopian] domestic affairs." Saad al-Katatni, a senior figure in Morsi's Muslim Brotherhood movement, insisted the government was prepared to do anything "to protect our water security." By the time the president called time on the session, they had run through a full host of hostile possibilities and a few benign ones.[5]

That meeting, held back in 2013 and televised without the knowledge of its participants, appeared to provide an unvarnished glimpse into the thinking of Cairo's great and good. They looked to be out for blood. But while the Nile basin states have so far successfully avoided fighting the "hot war" that sensationalist media coverage has occasionally hinted is imminent, they have at times done everything else but that.

There have been frequent menacing threats, most of which have followed breakdowns in diplomatic negotiations—and, by extension, domestic pressure for muscular rhetoric by politicians. After being caught unawares by Ethiopia's (very deliberate) decision to start building GERD after a secretive planning phase just as Egypt was reeling from the chaotic aftermath of its revolution, politicians and talking heads in Cairo, from President Abdel Fattah el-Sisi down, have not been shy about ramping up the bellicosity. Two weeks before he lost the 2020 election, Donald Trump suggested that Egypt would "blow up that dam. They have to do something," a comment that some Cairo politicians interpreted as an American green light for military action.[6]

Not to be outdone in their defense of a hydroelectric project that they see as pivotal to developing their water-rich but electricity-poor state, Ethiopian statesmen have responded in kind. "If there is a need to go to war, we could get millions readied" in the event of Egyptian aggression, Prime Minister Abiy Ahmed said in 2019, just eleven days after winning the Nobel Peace Prize for his rapprochement with Eritrea.[7] Were Egypt to bomb GERD, it might find its own mega-dam within a vengeful Ethiopia's sights, an official in Addis Ababa indicated to me. Uncoincidentally or not, the number of military personnel around that structure, the Aswan High Dam, appeared to be a good deal greater on a 2016 trip than it had been when I first visited it in 2013.

There have been military buildups and the acquisition of expensive hardware designed to give those threats teeth. In addition to its bevy of new Rafale jets with their Storm Shadow cruise missiles, the Egyptian military has bought *Mistral*-class amphibious assault ships and a range of high-end German submarines.* "The thing about the Rafale–Storm Shadow combination is that, in theory, it gives Egypt the capacity to strike into Ethiopia in a way that they didn't have before," said retired General F. C. "Pink" Williams, who formerly served as US military attaché in Cairo. "With F16s, you're at the extreme range of their operability. A Rafale has better legs to get there and back." For its part, Ethiopia has reportedly moved many more tanks and heavy artillery pieces to the GERD zone than were there when I made my abortive visit, while simultaneously imposing a no-fly zone over the surrounding airspace.[8, 9] Though impossible to prove culpability or even nefarious intent in every instance, there have been enough snarl-ups during the dam construction

---

* Analysts say that these vessels would be of dubious utility in the event of a strike on the dam, but when added to Egypt's newly expanded southern base at Berenice and its sizeable presence (until 2023) at Sudan's even closer Merowe air force base, they signal serious intent.

process for Western intelligence officials to determine that some kind of concerted sabotage campaign has been playing out behind the scenes, too. Materials destined for GERD at the port of Djibouti have mysteriously exploded or suffered other forms of suspected tampering, one told me. Simegnew Bekele, the dam's chief project manager, was found shot in his car in 2018 in a death that has been ruled suicide but that many Ethiopians deem deeply suspicious (though, in his case, many suspect their own government). He is just one of a number of people associated with the project to have met an untimely end.

From the earliest days of construction, rebel groups in the vicinity of GERD in Benishangul-Gumuz state and elsewhere in Ethiopia have developed capacities—and a willingness to launch assaults—that officials suggest they never previously had. Choosing his words extremely carefully, an American intelligence hand interviewed in 2017 corroborated some of these goings-on. "There are building issues, sure, but that's not the only reason the dam is behind schedule," he said. "There's just a lot of stuff that cannot be explained by natural human error." Whether Egypt is actually responsible (and there is no publicly available evidence to that effect), Addis Ababa certainly believes it to be so. And that is key. Angry, defensive, and embattled by domestic chaos, the Ethiopian state has occasionally retreated into something of a siege mentality in recent years. Officials are less inclined to engage diplomatically—and seemingly more intent on finishing the dam, agreement or not.

That sense of being under siege is taking the landlocked nation in some head-scratching directions. Shortly before I left Ethiopia in 2015, I sat down for a meal with Eremias, the translator, at a shoreline restaurant in Bahir Dar. We soon fell into conversation with a man called Moses. He was all smiles until I asked him about his naval uniform, which struck me as an unusual outfit many hundreds of miles from the sea. There was an awkward silence. "It all looks so peaceful, no?" he said, after a brief pause to gather his thoughts. "But we are all aware that we are on the frontline. This is where the water is, the dam, the best land." Despite losing its coastline when Eritrea broke away in 1991, Ethiopia has maintained a naval facility on Lake Tana. "We might need it in the future," Moses added, cryptically.

An Egyptian soldier stares out over the Aswan High Dam. Security at the facility has increased as tensions between the Nile dispute protagonists have soared. (Photo by Roger Anis)

A Second Front

Three days and a few hundred miles later, I crossed into Sudan, where things quickly got off to a discouraging start. The customs agent at the Gallabat border post was in a take-no-prisoners kind of mood, already annoyed by the number of his countrymen stumbling back from Ethiopia reeking of booze (or so I speculated as I waited throughout the day). The books in my bag—and the nature of my (media) visa—only seemed to add to his prissiness. *Sex and the Citadel*, an exploration of Middle Easterners' private lives, came with an unfortunately vagina-like cover illustration. Alan Moorehead's *The Blue Nile*, a history of the area, was suspicious for reasons I could not begin to understand. As he flicked, uncomprehendingly, through my Egypt guidebook, it occurred to me that its map, which included territory that is claimed by both countries but that looked dangerously Egyptian there, might mean a very premature end to my journey. Eventually, the agent got called away to confront a traveler carrying genuine contraband, leaving me free to scurry, with a ransacked suitcase and no *Sex and the Citadel*, to a nearby guesthouse. However, his heavy-handed attentions were to form a fitting preamble to exploring Sudan's place in the Nile dispute. After all, it might one day emerge as an even testier water battleground.

Much of this tension is connected to the basin-wide geopolitical jockeying that long predates GERD but which has been turbocharged by its inception. As a beneficiary of the existing 1959 Nile treaty, which apportions about 75 percent of the river's waters to Egypt and the rest to Sudan (and, fatefully, nothing to the nine other riparian states), Khartoum was always expected to support its northern neighbor in opposing "unsanctioned" upstream schemes. But, under former dictator Omar al-Bashir, Sudan made a different bet. Enticed by the prospect of securing electricity from GERD to help stanch its own chronic power shortages, and grateful for Ethiopia's refusal to ostracize Bashir after he was charged with war crimes by the International Criminal Court for perpetrating genocide in Darfur, Sudan stunned Egypt in 2013 by backing the dam. Cairo has since expended tremendous diplomatic energy trying to bring the Sudanese back on side.

Drawing off Sudan's strategic location, at least some of these shenanigans may be direct, if slightly tortuous, blowback from the construction of GERD itself. By yoking the Blue Nile, the dam will bring an end to annual summer flooding along that river and thereby free up more land for year-round crop cultivation in Sudan's Blue Nile state. This, Khartoum policymakers consider, is yet another dividend, and they have leased the "new" land in advance to the Saudis and Emiratis, according to Alex de Waal, a Sudan and Horn of Africa specialist. But many residents, who stand to lose their fields and perhaps their entire way of life, see things otherwise. In a part of Sudan that has long been up in arms against the central government, officials allege that Egyptian agents have been disseminating exaggerated reports of GERD's likely impact. "They want to turn people against the dam. They want to stir violence," a senior Blue Nile state representative insisted to me.

American and other Western diplomats in Cairo say that Sudan, with territory that passes to within thirty miles of the dam, has also proven to be a useful hub for Egyptian security services to collect information and sow disinformation among communities in Ethiopia. Further, they say that Egypt has lobbied hard to place its troops among the UN peacekeeping mission in South Sudan, seeing them as extra eyes and ears in strategically useful locations. "The Egyptians are good at using a variety of techniques to make sure that their intelligence gathering is not interpreted as hostile," said Robert Springborg, a longtime analyst of Egypt's military and political economy. "And in this soup of illicit activities, the Ethiopians have not been able to make a convincing case that they're being targeted."

Not, I should add, that it necessarily takes much to penetrate those long, porous borders. On a later Sudan trip, I stopped off in the frontier-hugging Dinder National Park to report on its poaching problem. There, I watched as a group of masked men led mules laden with what looked to be laundry detergent through the undergrowth and past a slightly apologetic-looking coil of barbed wire. Minutes later, they emerged on the other side of the border, the Ethiopian border guards a half mile away seemingly none the wiser. (I soon saw where some of the poached protected species likely ended up too. At Khartoum's downtown arts and crafts market, a shopkeeper tried to interest me in a stuffed Zebra head. "An antique," he said. The thing practically still had blood coursing through it.)

More than anything else, though, it is Sudan's push for expanded irrigated agriculture throughout the Nile valley that is really raising hackles
in Cairo. After being invited around for tea by Asim al-Moghraby, a
leading Sudanese ecologist, I spent several hours talking through the
country's farming prospects. Like most local—and international—
experts, he believes that Khartoum uses nothing like its full share of
the Nile waters. The possibility that policymakers might one day make
good on their pledge to bolster domestic food production within the
valley (or permit more thirsty Gulf Arab mega-farms, whose violent
consequences I will examine in chapter 7) is the stuff of nightmares for
Egypt. This may, Moghraby noted before he sent me on my way with a
wildly generous, if deeply impractical, trove of books, eventually come
to color the two countries' relationship. "We have been too poor and
too badly managed to use our water," he said. "But that surely won't
always be the case." Indeed, in a repeat of that now-common accusa-
tion, farmers in northern Sudan insisted to me that persons unknown
are already tampering with local irrigation and electricity networks.[10]
Watch this space.

The Underlying Fears

Seen from afar, Cairo's reaction to GERD and other upstream development schemes can seem almost hysterically overblown, the bullying
behavior of a longtime hegemon unable to accept its loss of dominance.
But that critique does not necessarily reckon with the wider challenges
that are testing—and panicking—Egypt and practically every other
Nile-side state. GERD, tangible emblem of water struggle though it is,
is not being built in a vacuum.

Officials fear population growth, or more particularly some of its
avoidable consequences. How, these men and women ask, are they
to provide for their surging numbers with resources that are already

faltering due to past and ongoing mismanagement? In Ethiopia (population: about 120 million in 2023, up from around 20 million in 1960), villagers in fast-expanding rural communities have lopped down swathes of woodland to create more space for sorghum, soybean, and teff cultivation. At the same time and for the same reason, farmers are scratching out fields higher up in the hills. Those practices, together with intensifying floods, have fueled one of the highest rates of soil erosion in the world, some 500 tons per hectare (about 200 tons per acre) in places, which is, in turn, slashing crop yields and clogging up smaller dams with sediment. In places such as Tiss Abay, a small town at the foot of the Blue Nile Falls that has more than doubled in size since 2000, the price is clear. "Every year we work harder but get fewer crops," says Addis Gete, an animal herder who supplements his diet with a small vegetable patch. "We fear the future." As if to illustrate his point, a chunk of recently cleared hillside suddenly broke off and tumbled into the swirling brown river waters beneath us.

In Sudan (population: forty-five million, up fourfold over the past half century), swelling cities have saddled the Nile with so much sewage that by the time it reaches the Mediterranean the remaining dribble is nearly unusable. This is a global tale, one in which waterways often bear the brunt of state failures to service booming cities' needs. But it is all the more painful that the sullying of the Nile really starts in Khartoum, where the two main branches of the river, the Blue and the White, meet. It is only here that the river finally takes on its broad, sleepy, familiar form and one can readily identify each branch's distinctive features. The Blue Nile, swollen and colored brown by those soil-heavy Ethiopian rains, roars into the confluence, pushing back for miles its insipid and slightly yellow counterpart from July onward. At other times of the year, during the dry season, the two run alongside one another in what some poetic locals refer to as the "longest kiss in history." Yet nowadays, for all the young couples sneaking quick embraces in quiet riverside nooks, it can be hard to see the romance.

All the while, across Egypt, precious agricultural land is disappearing under houses, highways, and general sprawl. Every year, the country loses around 16,000 acres of Nile-side agricultural land to development, an unsustainable tally in a mostly arid state that has about 8 million acres of farmland total.[11] Almost all of that is jammed into the same wisp-thin valley into which an ever-growing number of Egyptians are also squeezing. On the generally traffic-choked highway between central Cairo and the airport, a population clock on the side of the government statistics body ticks ominously upward, rising a few dozen notches in the time it takes to crawl past the building. It was around 85 million when I moved to Egypt in early 2013. It was a little over 107 million in the summer of 2023.

Then there is climate change, of course, the great unknown. In a snapshot of the basin's countless climate woes, Ethiopia's farmers are suffering from rains that are now coming too strong, at the wrong time, or not falling at all. (Researchers at MIT estimate that by 2050 the Nile's flow could vary by up to 50 percent year-on-year.)[12] Their agrarian peers in Sudan are battling desertification, among many other ills. Those who farm in the narrow shard of greenery between the river and the desert, sometimes only 100 meters wide, wage a daily—and, according to most, losing—battle to keep the sands at bay. "If they brought the map of the area to the minister of the environment, he wouldn't recognize anything," said Osman Abdul Moati, only half joking, as he showed me the dunes that have already smothered his neighbors' fields near Karima and threaten to come for his next.

Throughout the northern reaches of Egypt's Nile Delta, near the river's mouth, it can be a struggle to get anything to grow these days, let alone flourish. Khamees Khalla knows this all too well. He has spent

Rosetta, where one of the Nile's two branches empties into the Mediterranean after a four-thousand-mile-long journey. Dirtied and drained along the way, local fishermen try to get as far away as they can from a river that they once revered. (Photo by Roger Anis)

more than twenty years fishing the country's coastal waters, often reeling in hefty hauls of shrimp for Alexandria's waterfront restaurants. But now, untangling his nets just steps from the fort where Napoleon's troops found the Rosetta Stone, the key to deciphering hieroglyphics, he says he has had enough. Competition is overly fierce, with some farmers trading in their wellies for waders due to the cumulative consequence of sea level rise and soil subsidence. Pollution from the Nile's filthy final stretch is, quite frankly, gross. "We worshipped the river," he said, "but now we want nothing to do with it." In this mutually reinforcing muddle, Khalla feels he has exhausted his options at home. Many hard-up North African fishermen have sold their boats to Europe-bound people traffickers. As coastal jobs wither, he implies that it is only a matter of time before he and plenty of his peers make themselves scarce, too.

Regime Survival

For several years in Cairo, I met on a semi-regular basis with a senior defense official. I initially saw him as an insurance policy, a powerfully placed person who I hoped would feel compelled to at least answer the phone if I, like many journalists in Egypt, somehow irked someone who ought not to be irked. But as time passed and our chats got more convivial, he began to talk more openly about what he saw as the greatest threats to regime stability. Usually, he returned to the same two themes. The first among them, hunger, has long exercised regional authorities, especially Egypt's, where the fortunes of government have often been explicitly tied to affordable food.* In 1977, the mere prospect of an increase in the price of subsidized bread prompted massive protests that forced President Anwar Sadat to change course and keep prices at around 1 cent per loaf, a rate that more or less endures to this day.[13] The 2011 revolution may have been triggered in part by the long lag of the 2007–2008 global food price spike. Gathering in Tahrir and other public squares across the country, protesters chanted for "*bread,* freedom, and social justice."

Even now, as the largest importer of Black Sea wheat, Egypt has been plunged into such a deep economic hole since Putin's 2022 invasion of Ukraine and the subsequent surge in food prices that it may have no choice but to reassess those all-important bread subsidies, to potential messy effect. It is telling that when Cairo officials broach GERD's possible impact, it is most commonly done in terms of its food implications.

---

* Few Nile basin states are democratic and even fewer would relish or know how to handle in a non-repressive manner the societal flux and anti-state sentiment that could quite quickly follow disrupted food supplies. Owing to the inability of these poor, or somewhat poor, states to fall back on sufficient imports as an alternative, it is perhaps only natural that they are extremely on edge about water as domestic harvests yo-yo and prospects for expanding them ebb.

"Did you know that for every 1 billion cubic meters lost due to unilateral #GERD operations, Egypt would see . . . 130,000 hectares of cultivated land lost," the Egyptian embassy in Washington posted in 2021.[14]

The second concern, unemployment, is no less troubling to regional civilian and military officials, like my contact, for whom large numbers of jobless young men have often been a kind of kryptonite. On reporting trips across the basin, I have repeatedly encountered penniless rural migrants on the move. These men and women can no longer cut it as farmers and are seeking their fortunes elsewhere. Insofar as these migrants journey abroad—or die trying—governments appear unconcerned. In 2017, I met a policeman in Delgo in northern Sudan who had learned to gauge the volume of people bound for Egypt by the number of bodies he found rotting along a nearby stretch of disused colonial-era railway. The migrants know that the track extends due north, so they stick to it for fear of getting lost, but then expire from thirst in the desert heat instead.

Yet, as in Iraq, Bangladesh, and most other parts of the world, the vast majority of the basin's rural underemployed remain in-country. It is their responses to worsening water situations that unnerve officials. Many villagers are migrating to already overburdened cities, such as Khartoum and Cairo, adding to urban areas' own infrastructure, service, and employment woes. In parts of Sudan, agrarian areas are emptying out, further reducing domestic food production.[15] Worse yet, from a state perspective, jobless rural portions of the Nile basin are lapsing into varying degrees of lawlessness. On a stinking hot August morning in 2015, photographer Leyland Cecco and I visited an illegal artisanal gold mine not far from Delgo. It was hell. Overseers set truck tires alight to soften the ground. Workers then blasted away at the weakened soil with homemade explosives. Amid fistfuls of drugs popped to manage various pains, and guns to deter rival wildcatters, these men would sooner stand in pools laced with cyanide and mercury for fourteen hours a day than work in the farming world from which most had fled. Why? "At least this way I can maybe earn something," Abdullah Idriss Isaac, a Darfuri miner, told me. "With [agriculture], there is no hope."[16]

Rival Narratives

So is that it? Is the GERD furor just the misdirected fallout from broadly unrelated fears? That argument is compelling enough, and to judge from years of interviews with basin state officials, the growing mismatch between water and food demand, on the one hand, and on the other, the natural landscape's capacity to supply it, is the backing track to much downstream distress over dams. But in a dispute which at least partly predates even the industrial era that is bringing about a warmer world, there is more to it than that. This is, to a considerable extent, a clash of rival historical narratives, all brought into conflict by changing climates and economies.

At the Egyptian end of the river, a lot of the tension hinges on the country's near-total dependence on the Nile. Without the river, this land would never have been able to sustain more than a fraction of its current numbers, its every acre of farmland nourished by Nile waters and with no other source of surface fresh water for hundreds of miles in any direction (and more than two thousand miles all the way to the Senegal and Niger Rivers, if heading west). No river, no Egyptian civilization, either. When I lived in Cairo, I often wandered down to the Nilometer, one of several ancient devices, thousands of years old, through which the pharaohs determined taxes. If the water rose too high and flooded too much, or remained too low and failed to irrigate most crops, that meant diminished agricultural returns and hence a reduced ability to extract any revenue in a then entirely agrarian country. At this isolated spot, from which heralds once circled Cairo to announce the day's water level, it was impossible not to feel that connection.

Without recapitulating every instance of popular Egyptian attachment to a river that features in innumerable songs and soap operas, I always found it most revealing that farm laborers in Upper Egypt (i.e., southern Egypt, upstream from Cairo and Lower Egypt) would sooner earn paltrier wages along what they called *al-bahr*—the sea, than they would working on the generally better remunerated new desert farms. On a visit to Toshka, the biggest and least successful of the agricultural schemes that Mubarak carved out of the Sahara, one of the few farmers to have made the switch blamed its failure on his countryfolk's distaste for leaving the river valley. "We have our maxim: 'Go to the Delta for a year, and don't spend a day in the desert,'" said Suleiman Mohammed Nour, who oversees a team of laborers pruning and picking date palms on the Saudi-owned Kadco farm.[17] By virtue of this intimate relationship, it is only natural, perhaps, that so many Egyptians have come to see the Nile as theirs—and theirs alone.

And the dam? Experience has given Egypt good reason to question the motivations of anyone with upstream designs on that lone water source. As historian Terje Tvedt recounts in *The River Nile in the Age of the British*, Cairo's command of the Nile was repeatedly threatened in the twentieth century. After the assassination of a senior British official by an Egyptian nationalist in 1924, London unilaterally expanded irrigated agriculture in upstream Sudan, an explicit and showy demonstration of its capacity to parch the downstream state.[18] Then, following Egypt's seizure in 1956 of the Suez Canal zone, which was by that point the last bit of the country under (Franco-)British control, the Brits threatened to (though never did) divert the Nile as a punishment.[19] If earlier schemes were potentially hostile, Egyptians think, why would they accept the GERD builders' assurances that this one is not? Certainly, they have not been inclined to stick around and find out. "If I have this room, and it comes to me with fresh air through the door, and then my neighbor next to me says he will close the door because he wants all the air, this will be a big problem," says Ayman Abou Hadid, a professor of agriculture and former minister of agriculture. "If this is the situation, I will force open the door and fight you."[20]

Against this backdrop of possessiveness and suspicion, many Egyptians have been shocked to discover Ethiopia's own sense of entitlement to the Nile. Though the rain-sodden upstreamers have never relied on the river for water, history has imbued it with a spiritual and cultural meaning that Ethiopians see as no less important. The Blue Nile is the Abay—"the greatest of the great" in Amharic, and one of the rivers that flowed from the Garden of Eden, according to Ethiopian Christian tradition. More than two dozen monasteries in or around Lake Tana attest to its religious significance, many of the island ones off-limits to women for fear of "exciting the monks' passions," as the abbot of one of them told me.

Mindful as well of Italy's successive attempts to colonize the country from the 1890s onward, and of several wars with its neighbors since then, Ethiopia is every bit as averse to what it sees as affronts to its sovereignty as are officials in Cairo. Egypt's attempts to stymie the dam, through political pressure and possibly other tactics, have consequently gone down like a lead balloon. "Defiance to foreign rule and coercion is the hallmark of our identity," wrote Addis Ababa University law professor Mesenbet Assefa in 2020 after calls for compromise from the Trump administration.[21] "No pressure and neocolonial mentality can ever stop Ethiopia from using its natural resources and ensure its right to development." "Fill the Dam!" he continued, referring to the time which Ethiopia will take to top off the reservoir behind GERD.*

Still, until relatively recently, Ethiopia did not have the same power to

---

* This was one of the biggest sticking points throughout negotiations, with Ethiopia determined to raise water levels high enough to begin generating electricity as soon as possible, and Egypt desperate to spread the diminished river flow over a more extended period and thereby cushion the dam's impact.

assert its Nile narrative as did its downstream counterpart. The country was too poor, too battered by the horrors of the famines in the 1980s and 1990s, too politically weak to secure international funding in the face of ardent Egyptian opposition. But years of double-digit GDP growth rates changed all that. Over the past decade, Ethiopia has bolstered its economy to the point where it is just about capable of self-funding GERD, albeit while exhorting state employees to contribute their wages toward construction. Ironically, it has since mimicked much of Egypt's own development model. Having built the Aswan High Dam through the 1960s as both a major power generator in a then woefully under-electrified country and as a source of national pride soon after the country had shaken off the last vestiges of colonialism, Cairo inadvertently helped establish a precedent that other basin states have been only too keen to follow. If imitation is the highest form of flattery, then GERD might be considered the greatest of unwanted tributes.

Peas from the Same Political Pod

Anwar Sadat is as close to a repository of political memory as modern Egypt has. A veteran parliamentarian and liberal figurehead in a country where neither role has tended to longevity, he has had a front row seat to the rise and fall of multiple regimes. As the nephew of his namesake President Sadat, who was assassinated in 1981 after a tenure marked by repeated Nile water "scares," the younger Sadat has the pedigree to deliver critiques of the Egyptian leadership's approach to GERD in ways that few others, in this intensely repressive state, might get away with. "Our president has been somehow too soft in these negotiations," he told me.

What I had not necessarily expected when we spoke, though, was for him to have a better grasp of what makes the Ethiopian state tick than many analysts. But perhaps that ought not to have been a surprise.

The parallels between the two countries' rough-and-tumble political scenes run deep, and, in a dispute that has occasionally turned on the pigheadedness of like-minded actors bound to those rival narratives, very pertinently. "GERD is a national project. They are very proud of it. Remember our Aswan High Dam?" he asked, alluding both to the patriotism it engendered and Egypt's extra determination to get the thing built when it also struggled to secure funding (the United States declined to pony up the cash in the 1950s for reasons that included Southern senators' fear that it would bolster Egyptian cotton production at their constituents' expense).[22] "We were very proud of that. They will not retreat."

Inculcated with strong senses of exceptionalism due to their storied pasts, modern Egypt and Ethiopia can both be fiercely jingoistic, which makes compromise awkward or politically unwise, if not completely impossible. Years of messy negotiations tell the tale of that mutual intransigence. Having presented GERD as an existential threat to its citizens, Cairo has been hard-pressed to change tack. Similarly, in Addis Ababa, domestic political pressure has sometimes held its leadership hostage to hard-line dogmas. When Prime Minister Abiy Ahmed agreed to Nile talks in Washington in 2020, a hostile domestic reaction to the American proposals forced him home. And it is little wonder why. Roadside billboards across Ethiopia tout GERD's potential to bring electricity to millions; schoolchildren sing about it. "This is our destiny," some of them chant. Ethiopian history is replete with stories of rulers trading away sovereignty—or being perceived to do so—and suffering the consequences.[23]

Both countries have continually struggled to understand the other. A lot of this is due to their physical distance and historic lack of interaction. Some of it is a byproduct of more-recent events, including former Egyptian president Mubarak's disengagement from sub-Saharan African affairs after an attempt on his life in Addis Ababa in 1995. Plenty amounts to old-fashioned conspiracism. Beholden, it seems, to an out-dated view of Ethiopia as a famine-plagued disaster zone, many Egyptian politicians, including current and former ministers whom I have inter-viewed, have been unable to accept that the upstreamers are now capable of a project of this scale. Someone else, they suppose—China, the United States, or "the Jews," according to Mubarak in a secretly taped recording after he was deposed—must be behind it.[24] For their part, many Ethio-pians think that Egypt just wants to keep them poor and undeveloped and therefore incapable of marshalling the Nile in any capacity. "Our neighbors take our wood, they take our water, they leave us poor and with nothing to improve ourselves," Addisu Melkem, a boatman who plies his trade among Lake Tana's monasteries, insisted to me. "If they continue to repel our progress, we'll simply have to take action."

Altogether, this cascading inflexibility and ignorance has repeatedly pushed the parties into challenging one another's deepest sensitivities—while simultaneously slowing negotiations with talking points that carry little weight outside their respective countries. For example, Egypt has often invoked its historic and legal rights under that 1959 water-sharing treaty, ill-appreciating, it seems, how hollow that claim rings among the nine Upper Nile states, many of whom see it as a colonial-era relic that is scarcely worth the papyrus it was not quite written on. On the flip side, many Ethiopian diplomats have an unhelpful fixation on Egypt's wasteful water practices, which, while undeniable, are neither unusual for a country that has historically been well-endowed with water, nor the sort of thing that is easily resolved. As the great historian Barbara Tuchman noted, "War is the unfolding of miscalculations." And when opposing forces have bombs and bullets but not enough water and little capacity for compromise, bad things can happen, no matter how much they all might want to avoid carnage.

To compound it all, neither Egypt nor Ethiopia permit much space for independent media, academia, and civil society, all of which have sometimes tempered fiery state narratives in other parts of the world. My own experiences have been bad or inconvenient enough. I was detained on a few occasions in Egypt and Sudan, including once in the southern Egyptian city of Assiut. My questions about the city's barrage were suspicious, I was told, and—ironically, given the wariness my Egyptian residency had sparked near GERD—so was the recent Ethiopian visa in my passport. It was seldom easy to speak with water ministry employees. Never more so, in my case, than after one ridiculous episode.

In 2015, I happened to be passing through Qena, also in Egypt's south, shortly after a barge carrying five hundred tons of phosphate had ploughed into a bridge and deposited its load onto the Nile's muddy floor. The ministry, intent on showcasing the river's supposedly clean bill of health, delegated the local police to escort me to the site. But the police captain took to his brief with a bit too much panache. Lapping up some water from the crash location, he declared the Nile "delicious," only to disappear into the boat cabin soon afterward. There he remained for the rest of the return leg, retching into a bucket, and then bounding frantically onto the riverbank when we eventually docked.

Yet, for my local media and researcher peers, the situation has always been much worse. Coverage of Nile issues is tightly controlled throughout the basin, with one Ethiopian journalist jailed for criticizing the way in which GERD was financed, and Egyptian reporters fed talking points by security officials from which they dare not deviate. Many of the experts who truly understand the ins and outs of Nile politics will not speak publicly for fear of losing access (in the case of foreigners) or running into much more dire trouble (in the case of Nile natives). As a result, the airwaves have often been awash with subpar and chest-beating commentary at a time when accuracy and restraint are unprecedently necessary. That has become especially true over time, with many of my go-to Nile interlocutors, including plenty consulted for this chapter, self-censoring themselves into silence. The general climate was perhaps most jarringly captured by an exchange between President Sisi and trailing Egyptian journalists in 2018. As Sisi emerged from a meeting with his Ethiopian and Sudanese counterparts, a journalist asked him, "Was the crisis resolved, sir?" Sisi: "there is no crisis." Journalist and his colleagues: "Congratulations, Sir!"[25]

Many Manassir people displaced by the construction of Sudan's Merowe Dam have tried to stay in the area rather than suffer "internal exile" far from their beloved Nile. Though blocked by authorities, small numbers make an illicit living fishing from the dam reservoir. (Photo by Leyland Cecco)

Water Wars—of a Sort

To end a trip centered on the furor from a Nile-side dam, it felt fitting to finally clamber all over one. Roughly a month after I had been turned away from GERD in 2015, I stood on the parapet of Sudan's Merowe Dam with my reporting partners, and impatiently heard out the director's well-rehearsed spiel. The turbines generated this many megawatts.

The structure was built from that much concrete. From this spot high above what was once the fourth cataract, one of the six sets of rapids that historically obstructed Nile navigation, we could look out over X many billion cubic meters of water. But the one statistic he unsurprisingly neglected to mention was the number of people displaced by the dam's construction. There were some fifty thousand of them, I had read beforehand. And years after its completion, many are still up in arms.

In 2006, security services killed three anti-dam demonstrators. In the period since then, they have shot and imprisoned many more as they protested officials' failure to make good on pledges to provide quality housing. When I passed through Al-Mikabrab, one of the charmless settlements built to replace those that now lie many meters underwater, residents had recently torched a police car. It was a sign of things to come, locals said. "We tried to use every peaceful channel possible to get the government to act, to follow through on their promises," explained Abbas Mohammed Taha, a fisherman turned trucker whom I met as we sheltered from a fierce thunderstorm under the same leaky restaurant portico. "But they didn't, and sometimes there's violence when all peaceful options seem exhausted."

Taha spoke only of his people's troubles. Yet, in his description of the state's ham-fistedness in the water sector, he might have been discussing any one of a dozen or so other hotspots along the river. Because although Egypt and Ethiopia have so far successfully prevented their shared dam quarrel from bleeding into open confrontation, they—and their Sudanese and other basin peers—have still presided over or created an extraordinary amount of *localized* violence. For example, in Sudan's Blue Nile state, where the official alleged that Cairo is stoking anger for its own GERD-related ends, the initial insurgency drew strength from the manner in which the Roseires Dam was built from the 1960s onward. Villagers accuse the state of reneging on its housing promises, as at Merowe, and of shattering their lives in order to serve the interests of other, wealthier parts of the country, again as at Merowe. The reality, a displaced ex-resident insisted to me in Khartoum, is that his community was inundated in order to create electricity which dam-area natives, many still without grid access, will never enjoy.

Then, many days of travel and almost a thousand miles downriver later, I met Nubian activists in Northern State fighting to preserve their ancestral homeland. Sudanese authorities envisage building two more mega-dams at Kajbar and Dal. But even though the bankrupt—and, as of early 2023, civil-war-battered—state stands no chance of realizing these ambitions anytime soon, campaigners are prepared for a long fight. "We have seen what has happened to others before us. Is it any wonder that we all do everything we can to oppose this?" asked one of those activists, Nazar Youssef Saboona, as we traipsed across Sai Island, whose mounds of thousand-year-old textiles and Ottoman-era fortifications would be among the first historic sites to disappear were the new dams to be built. Saboona noted how it just so happens that politically weak ethnic minorities always seem to wind up at the losing end of state development schemes. In the meantime, several more protesters have been killed. Tens of thousands of the community's palm trees have been burned in what they see as an unimaginative attempt at intimidation.

And just over the border from there, Egypt's own Nubians continue to struggle with the violent repercussions of the Aswan High Dam.* As I approached the home stretch of my journey along the Nile, I took a few moments to reflect alongside Lake Nasser, the dam's massive reservoir and one that many locals prefer to call "Lake Nubia" in rejection of the Egyptian president who ordered the inundation of their villages. It had been a dispiriting trip, one full of stories of pain. The Nubian tour

---

* Ethiopia may have displaced as many as 120,000 people for GERD, and some of the intercommunal conflict that has racked western Ethiopia over the past decade has seemingly arisen in part out of the ensuing flux. But with limited reporting from or access to that area, it is something of an information black hole.

guide I had chatted to on the overnight ferry across the lake had just made it even more so. The river, he said, had always had a certain mystique for his people, its irrigating floodwaters always rising at the height of the hot, rainless Egyptian summer, its rich silt stimulating crops in ways that not even modern fertilizers can manage. But now they, like the Manasir people of Merowe, have mostly been resettled far inland. Within this internal exile, it can seem like there is no letup. In 2014, twenty-three people were killed in Aswan after long-simmering tensions between Nubians and the Arab Bani Hillel tribe exploded into fierce street battles that some residents felt were at least partially grounded in the former having been forcibly displaced onto the latter's land.[26]

These mini "water wars" may look like a very different ballgame to their interstate equivalents. And, in some ways of course, they are. There can be more incentive to violence among communities than there is for nation-states, few of which could hope to actually pilfer more water from their neighbors. States, as we have seen, are more likely to tread carefully with their counterparts than they are with their own easily coercible citizens. But only in some ways. The more officials maneuver in order to avoid interstate troubles, the more likely they are to spark violence over water within their own borders. Egypt and Sudan have spent decades pushing for the completion of the Jonglei Canal, which would channel the Nile past the West Virginia–sized Sudd wetlands and thereby free up more water for their use elsewhere in the valley. In doing so, they have fueled periodic hostilities among local Dinka, Nuer, and other now–South Sudanese peoples who fear the loss of their fisheries and pasturelands.

And the more states focus resources and attention on headline-grabbing foreign risks, the less likely they are to note domestic threats to water security. At the same time as Cairo and Addis were coming close to a clash around 2014, villages in Egypt's Beheira governorate were blocking roads in fury at the lack of water in their irrigation canals.

Officials blamed shortages—and even GERD. In fact the canals were just clogged with trash after years of inadequate maintenance. "It is a great shame that government leaves its people in this state," Masood Nosseir, a resident of Kom al-Kaddah, told me. "They have forgotten about us."

Having seen what befell their Egyptian Nubian kin after the construction of the Aswan High Dam, Sudanese Nubians have lobbied furiously against the new dams that would inundate their villages, too. Sai Island, dotted with ancient ruins and populated by aggressive crocodiles, would be among the first places to go under if Khartoum gets its way. (Photo by Leyland Cecco)

The Here and Now

So here we are. By the time of this book's publication, GERD will be mostly or even entirely complete. The 150-mile-long reservoir is filling fast. At least two of its turbines are already turning. That the fighter jets have remained grounded and the tanks parked despite intense saber-rattling, is no small beer for a dispute that has frequently looked ripe for major escalation.

But while that tentative success is to be celebrated, real risks remain. For one, the possibility that some Ethiopians might one day turn to the Nile and its tributaries for river-sapping irrigation, rather than just river-tapping hydropower, horrifies Egyptian policymakers. As well it should. Farmers in the country's west would love to exploit these rivers, their bounty a stark juxtaposition to rural struggle. "Why rely on bad rains when we have all this water in front us?" said Weldemariam, who grows teff just outside Bahir Dar, but by his reckoning not enough of it due to water woes. Abandoning his plow, he strolled across his field and gestured vaguely at the background. "Can you think of any good reason we shouldn't use this?" Privately, Ethiopian agronomists question whether they could ever affordably deploy surface water across their hilly topography, but they are keen to try.

There is another consideration—what happens when intense drought, such as the one that handicapped Ethiopia through most of the 1980s, eventually returns? There is still no agreement as to how GERD would be managed during such circumstances, nor, in an era of climate change, is there necessarily any sense as to how low water levels could go. Would Egypt's minimum water needs be guaranteed? Or would Ethiopia's electricity requirements be prioritized? For the time being at least, with the rains rich and river flow above average, Egyptian politicians are quite literally living on a wing and a prayer. "They think God gave them extra water over the last few years," said one top Egyptian Nile expert. "They hope he will provide again."

More generally, how will the basin, and especially its greatest Nile dependent, handle the water crunch that will likely strike—drought or no drought, dam or no dam? Egypt's National Planning Institute projects that by 2050 the country will require 21 billion cubic meters more water than it currently receives (the equivalent of 8.4 billion Olympic-sized swimming pools' worth), largely due to population growth. Sudan will surely one day use its full water allocation—or allow others to. When meaningful shortages materialize, will officials display the same relatively judicious restraint that they have exhibited in the past? Can they hold their nerve when confronted by an angry, scared, and—by dint of history in the case of Egyptians, water-entitled—citizenry?*

Since about 2018–19, Cairo has largely taken these shocks in its stride. It has proven much the more accommodating Nile negotiator, backing away from many of its red lines even as Ethiopia fills the dam without consulting other basin states. It is also making some moves in a slow transition to a thirstier future. Authorities have cracked down on water-intensive rice cultivation, and are starting to line thousands of miles of irrigation canals with concrete to limit water losses. They have raised water prices to better reflect its value, a vital but inevitably unpopular policy, and they've bolstered desalination. What the tax man cannot do, the cop can. State tolerance for dissent or perceived criticism in the water space has only shrunk. The former editor in chief of *Al-Ahram*, the country's paper of record, was arrested in 2021 after calling for President Sisi to resign due to his GERD "defeat."

---

* On a global level, transboundary water disputes are becoming nittier, nastier, and more common. As in the Nile basin, which gained a new stakeholder with the independence of South Sudan in 2011, there are more states than ever, which means more boundaries for waterways to seep across and more authorities whose needs and wants must be accommodated. Significantly, in an era of climate change, many of these new parties to transboundary water disputes have never previously experienced serious concerns of this sort. That can mean they have limited capacity to safeguard economies and ways of life that were not built with thirst in mind, and no history of negotiating over water with newly minted adversaries in high-stakes scenarios that are practically purpose-built to dispel trust. According to Tad Homer-Dixon, one of the founding fathers of the environmental security field, one of the few instances in which water can contribute to conflict between states is when the nation that feels itself to be losing out has a stronger military. The Nile, unlike the Mekong, the Tigris-Euphrates, or the Indus, has just such a dangerous dynamic.

But there will be a limit to how far policymakers in Cairo are willing or able to go. Parts of the state are still pursuing projects at odds with water conservation. For example, Sisi has talked up the importance of reining in water use, just as he spearheads the construction of a new capital, one replete with a many-miles-long "Green River" and dozens of desert compounds with lagoons and the like. As in so many other countries, officials will struggle to enact sufficient, speedy change at the same time as they reel from expensive climate stresses, global Ukraine War–style "black swan" events, and the limitations of a poor country budget. Importantly, in a military-centric state that derives much of its legitimacy from its defense of the country's borders (and resources), the belligerent rhetoric is unlikely to fully go away, particularly in the face of unpredictable upstream politicians, many of whom appear similarly enamored of bellicose pronouncements. Egypt reserves the right to "take all necessary measures to protect its national security," Foreign Minister Shoukry said in 2022. Barring a basin-wide agreement, Nile experts counsel that the next years could be as unpredictable as past ones.

At the end of my 2015 expedition, I wanted to travel to the point where the Nile meets the Mediterranean, to dunk myself in the water in a silly tribute to a glorious, if terribly besieged, river. Off I went to Rosetta, one of the two places where it empties into the sea. But appropriately, for this securitized and increasingly fragmented basin, that was not possible. There is an Egyptian coast guard and naval installation there, and no amount of pathetic pleading about the length of my trip would grant me entry.

China

Nepal

Melamchi Bazar

Melamchi Project
Headworks

Mount Everest

Kathmandu • Bhaktapur

Lalitpur • Melamchi River Valley

India

CHAPTER 4

Merchants of Thirst[1]

What happens when countries have the bad luck to have
bad rulers during bad conditions? Meet the men feasting
off Nepal's dysfunction.

IT HAD BEEN ELEVEN DAYS SINCE A BROKEN VALVE severed the flow of
water to much of southern Kathmandu, and the phones at Pradeep
Tamang's tanker business would not stop ringing.

A Malaysian embassy residence had run perilously low on water,
and the diplomats wanted to shower. They would pay extra for a swift
delivery. A coffee-processing plant was on the verge of shutting down
production after emptying its storage tank. It, too, would shell out
whatever amount of money it would take. Across the neighborhood
and other parts of the city, the calls were coming in so feverishly that
Sanjay, a tanker driver, jokily wondered if he might get carjacked. "This
is like liquid gold," he said, jabbing a finger at his precious cargo, large
amounts of which seeped from every hatch. "Maybe more than gold."

Dashing from filling stations to houses and factories and back,
Tamang tried to meet demand. His three tanker crews slept in one or
two-hour spurts, often in the cramped, refrigerator-sized truck cabins,
and kept the tankers on the road for up to nineteen hours a day. He
fobbed off business to competitors, an unusual practice in the cutthroat

world of Nepali tanker men, and even sounded out a mechanic about converting a flatbed truck into a new tanker. With fat profits pouring in, the young businessman figured it might soon repay its cost.

But no matter how hard the crews worked or how furiously they pushed their lumbering vehicles over the potholed roads, there was no satisfying the city's needs. The going was too slow. The water shortage too severe. By the time the pipeline was fully restored, some households had subsisted on nothing but small jerrycans for almost an entire month. "You know, it's not even peak season, but this is what happens here," Tamang said. "Just imagine what things would be like if we didn't exist. . . ." He trailed off as his phone rang once more.

Elsewhere in the Nepali capital on that overcast morning in late 2019, Dharaman Lama had spent hours pondering just that question. She had a very different take. The tanker men in her area often bring her half the promised amount and *always* (her emphasis, not mine) provide worse-quality water than advertised. They hike prices for people they take umbrage against, like her. She "complained too much." And sometimes drop customers altogether if they try and summon rival providers. When they sense a genuine, almost desperate need for their services, these men, in her telling, have been known to take corresponding advantage. After once exhausting supplies at the guesthouse for laborers that she operates alongside the Bagmati River, Lama says she had no choice but to pay double the going rate for a timely delivery. The financial pain, she said, forced her to scrimp on food for the rest of that month.

Angry, panicked by the possibility of being left without any water at all, and tired of picking through her purse to settle soaring bills, Lama holds out hope that the state will eventually get its act together enough to supply her with water. But she, like so many others, regards officials with more or less the same disdain as she does the tanker men. For the time being, all she asks is that none of them be deemed heroes. "They're all thieves, rotten thieves, who should be hanged," she says. "It's disgusting what they do to us."

Lost Legitimacy

Nepal might seem like a curious setting for an exploration of violence. Every year, planeloads of hikers, hippies, and architectural afficionados descend on its stretch of the Himalayas, rarely experiencing any danger greater than an overly spicy curry. If, as I have often felt, the accessibility of police stations is as apt a measure of local security, then most of the country is almost monastically tranquil. At one police post in the mountainous Helambu municipality, my colleague Rojita and I had our work cut out just to rouse officers from their midafternoon naps; at another we inadvertently progressed right into the station's squad room, thrown off by its near-total lack of protective measures.

Yet that veneer of calm—"negative peace," a political scientist might call it—is unlikely to last, at least in its current form. For among these stunning peaks are the kernels of climate change's greatest potential security threat, one that threatens to tank many of the world's tottering states—and possibly even some of its more solid-looking ones. As relatively unmenacing as these characters might seem, this probably ought to be the most insomnia-inducing part of the book.

To grossly simplify Nepal's variation of this knotty problem: climate change is blighting agriculture, the main source of employment in all rural Nepali communities. Villages are emptying as jobless people migrate to cities, notably Kathmandu, where inept authorities have struggled to provide for existing residents' needs, let alone those of the many new arrivals. Services deteriorate under pressure from out-of-control urbanization. Citizens sour on officials, and, ultimately, on government at large, whose standing is partly contingent on meeting popular needs. Amid deepening dysfunction and a degree of lawlessness, enter the tanker men: profiteers who fill a space that the state cannot. While their price gouging unquestionably creates hardship, in the long run, it is their very existence—a symbol of government incompetence in a water-rich nation—that inflicts the greatest damage. Think of this as climate change, the destroyer of state legitimacy.*

This sort of displacement of government would be dangerous enough in most countries. States, it is said, are formed by turning from predation to governance. To go back to predation is, in some citizens' eyes, to abrogate the right to govern. However, this loss of face by the state is extra problematic in a country where recent conflict, inaccessible and hence governance-limiting Himalayan topography, and a long record of mismanagement have already whittled away at the perceived legitimacy of Kathmandu officialdom. Citizens need no more reason to disdain their officials.

Moreover, it is doubly infuriating for a city which once knew much superior service. Back when their seventeenth-century urban counterparts in Europe were still stewing in their own muck and drinking beer for want of safe alternatives, Kathmandu and its neighboring sister cities provided regular water distribution through an elaborate system of ponds, subterranean channels, and decorative neighborhood standpipes. The state's apparent decline since then and turnover of a basic utility to widely disliked private operators consequently stands as a painful everyday reminder of official failure.†

---

* In other places, like Lebanon, the lost services are often different, though the behavior of the state stand-ins can be much the same as in Nepal. Despite an eminently resolvable electricity shortfall, that country is unable to provide more than a fraction of its citizens' power needs. Into this void, diesel-generator "mafias" have swooped, sometimes preserving their profits by disrupting attempts to bolster grid output.

† To reiterate, some of the greatest global anger connected to climate change seemingly

After experiencing the full sweep of good and dreadful water delivery in his seventy-eight years of life in the capital, Shyam Dongol, a welder, has come to the conclusion that it is worse to have had services and lost them than to have never had them at all. "In the past we had water. Now we don't. We are supposing to be advancing, but we have less than before," he said in a streetside interview that soon turned into something of a public performance. "How is that progress?"

Warming to the theme as the crowd of mostly appreciative listeners grew, he continued: "Water is life. They do not provide it. Why would I respect the state when it doesn't respect me?" Right on cue, a water tanker drew up at that point, lurching to a screeching halt in a cloud of acrid black smoke.

A Climate of Incompetence

Nepali officials are not wholly to blame for the tanker men's rise, as they are quick to insist to pesky journalists. Those aggressive levels of migration would challenge even the most competent of bureaucracies, with the population of the Kathmandu Valley at times swelling faster than any other urban area in the world. How, officials reason, are they to dissuade subsistence farmers, who make up some two-thirds of the national population, from descending on the capital when climate stresses are making tough mountain growing conditions even tougher? How, they also ask, can they afford to provide good services when already-tight budgets are being ravaged by more-regular and costlier storms, flooding, landslides, wildfires, and possibly even earthquakes?

It is quite the array of climate stresses that they are up against.

---

stems from authorities' failure to meet public service and governance expectations at times of stress. The better their earlier performance, the harder the possible fall.

Mountain ecology is by its very nature vulnerable to even small changes, and the Nepali Himalayas are battling torrential or weak monsoons, more cloudbursts in which dollops of rain suddenly cascade down over small areas, and more glacial melt from the "Third Pole's" disappearing ice sheets, among other woes. To use an ever so slightly arbitrary measure, glacier mass equal to about 570 million elephants has gone "unaccounted for" across the Himalayas.[2] The subsequent reduction in downward pressure may be fueling earthquakes, such as the horror one that shook central Nepal in 2015, killing thousands.[3]

But having exhibited what one political analyst described to me as "management so poor that even enemy saboteurs would admire the damage," the Nepali state has also ensured that climate stresses are almost certainly destined to inflict a greater impact than they otherwise might. Weak monsoons always hurt. They hurt that bit more when most piped water is lost to leaks before it reaches residents—despite decades of warnings and massive injections of foreign donor cash.

Through more than twenty changes in government since the turn of the millennium, Kathmandu and its medley of communist and arch-conservative politicians have often been far too absorbed in politicking to translate carefully crafted climate plans into action.[4] "When it comes to climate policy, Nepal is first in the world," says Dipak Gyawali, a political economist, former water minister, and reliable provider of journalist-pleasing quotes. "But when it comes to implementation, the Nepali state should be put in a dungeon and repeatedly whipped." The net result of all of this, in Kathmandu's case, has been a daily demand of over 400 million liters a day and a government supply of 90 to 150 million liters, all on the doorstep of the world's biggest water tower. The tanker men have been only too glad to help fill the shortfall.

As ever, Nepal's plight is far from exceptional. Globally, countries with the worst rule of law also suffer from the greatest water scarcity, a reflection of the self-reinforcing nature of these forces. Kathmandu's reliance on the private sector for water delivery is also typical of cities across the Global South and especially in South Asia, many of which are swelling just as droughts intensify and the consequences of groundwater overpumping come home to roost. The tanker fleet in Karachi, Pakistan, is estimated to have doubled over the past decade. The number in Lagos, Nigeria, may have quadrupled during that time, though even ballpark guesses are shaky since the tankers operate in the shadows. With about 70 percent of the global population projected to live in cities by 2050—another 2.5 billion people—the opportunities for non-state profiteers will only grow.[5, 6]

In Nepal, the opportunity is here. With its unhappy blend of shambolic governance and challenging geography, the landlocked Himalayan nation is helping to answer a question sometimes posed by historians: "What happens when countries have the bad luck to have bad rulers during bad conditions?" As Nepalis are discovering, the answer, in the form of the rapacious tanker men and other assorted ills, is seldom pretty—and could one day be much uglier.

The Rise of the Tanker Men

Laxmi Magar remembers when she saw her first water tanker on the streets of Kathmandu. It was the late 1990s and Nepal was at war. Tens of thousands of rural migrants were pouring into the relative safety of the capital, fleeing conflict between forces of the royalist government and communist Maoist rebels. The many new mouths aggravated an urban water shortage that had slowly taken hold over the preceding decades.

At first, both longtime residents and recent refugees welcomed these men (and they are all still men) as a solution to interminable water pipeline disruptions. That soon changed as the less affluent began to chafe at their high prices and unsavory practices. Previously run-of-the-mill tasks, like washing, began to require careful financial calculations. "Before, I didn't think about how often I could shower or when I can clean the house," said Magar, a mother of six. "But now that water is so expensive I watch every drop."

Many families have long since been forced to alter what they cook, how they cook, and whom they host. Water-intensive dishes, such as spinach, are off the menu for many. Large open fires in aging apartment blocks are frowned upon because there is often insufficient water to douse flames if they spread. In a country where hospitality is treasured, guests are sometimes unwanted, or almost feared, as extra bodies to be accommodated. At roughly 1,800 Nepali rupees ($15.60) for five thousand liters, tanker water is about forty times more expensive than government-supplied pipeline water at 2020 prices.

The situation is (unsurprisingly) worst for Kathmandu's poorest and most vulnerable, who have less reliable access to water than almost any other urban residents in the world. Because few of the city's slums or distant new migrant-filled neighborhoods are connected to the state water grid, they are completely dependent on outside assistance during the dry season. Some tankers raise their rates accordingly. And because many of these areas have narrow, *tuk-tuk*-wide streets sprawled across steep hills that often turn to mush with the slightest drizzle, the bigger trucks cannot get through, meaning that residents have to buy water in smaller quantities from middlemen at grossly inflated prices. Even ostensibly middle-class families are suffering as a consequence.

Nira Kasaju and her husband work in government factories in Bhaktapur, a city a few miles to Kathmandu's east, and together earn more than their neighbors. But trucks cannot navigate the narrow streets to their crumbling seventeenth-century apartment building, which means they must depend on tractor-drawn tankers that sell water at double the normal rate. They have since had to cut back on everything from toys for their children to holiday decorations. "Whatever it costs, we pay. We have no choice," Kasaju said, as she sprinkled her stairwell with a few drops of water to keep the dust down. "This is unacceptable, of course, but what can we do?" Like most of those in her area, she is wary of displeasing the tanker men for fear that they will cut her off, as they have a number of other critical locals. Unlike other interviewees, two of whom noticeably blanched when asked about the tanker men, she was at least willing to give her name.

Many Kathmanduites say they would be able to manage the expense if only the water came clean. But, amid reports of the tanker men filling from sewage-riddled rivers and, in the case of some of their peers in Bolivia, even heavily chlorinated swimming pools, that is increasingly not the case, either.[7] Residents experience frequent skin problems, intestinal bugs, and diarrhea, which compels those who can afford it to buy jugs of potable water, and forces those who cannot to drink dodgy water, miss school or workdays with sickness, and then fall deeper into poverty. In this "doom loop" of inequality, many poor people struggle to see the escape. Climate-induced drought is only accentuating that divide, with tanker men raising prices and prioritizing their best customers, who are generally the affluent, during periods of scarcity. "Every year, more people come to us, which is great!" said Maheswar Dahal, a tanker man in the Jorpati neighborhood. "But in the winter [dry season] we have to tell them, 'It might take five days,' or sometimes we just have to say no."

Safeguarding Business

And what of tanker "devilry"? Having built booming businesses over the past two-and-a-bit decades, the tanker men are unsurprisingly intent on preserving them at any cost. As a consequence, at least some of them appear to have resorted to extreme measures, striking deals with corrupt officials to limit pipeline flow into "their" areas, and campaigning against public works projects that might break their strangleholds. In Lalitpur, Kathmandu's twin city, residents around the UNESCO World Heritage–listed Patan Durbar Square say that tankers paid officials not to fix many of the free, ornate public standpipes that were knocked out by the 2015 earthquake. In western Kathmandu, local tanker men reported a developer to the police for illicitly connecting his buildings to the water network (and thereby depriving the operators of business), according to a local official.

Throughout the Kathmandu Valley, clashes among the roughly four hundred tanker-owning businessmen have sometimes been so ferocious that they have been known to call in favors from friendly politicians to shut down their rivals—particularly if they feel others are straying onto what they see as their territory. "The competition is just unhealthy," said Dharmanda Shresthra, who owns three tankers and a water-bottling factory. "Everyone is always after each other and after profit, and it affects the quality of the water."

Yet there might be more-damaging developments to come. These businesses appear to have few inhibitions about overexploiting water resources, jeopardizing environmental health and perhaps even their cities' long-term viability. Tankers are tapping groundwater so ferociously that many wells yield up to 20 percent less water every year. Dozens of springs and deep boreholes down to a depth of almost 200 meters have already been exhausted. Unless there is a dramatic change of course, water experts—and many of the tanker men themselves—fear there will soon be few local resources left to tap. It was one thing for Cape Town to almost run dry in 2018, an Indian hydrologist pointed out to me. But for Kathmandu, a city in full view of the Himalayas

The spring at Khahare, on the periphery of Kathmandu, where tanker men some-times wait hours to fill their trucks. (Photo by Poornima Shrestha)

on the rare days when the smog relents, and in a country with about 3 percent of the world's freshwater resources? That would be madness of a different magnitude.

Standing alongside the water-filling station he operates at Khahare, in the hills to the south of Kathmandu, Krishna Hari Thapa was in a wistful mood when we met in October 2019. For the best part of a decade, he has watched —and profited—as the number of tankers at his spring has increased from around thirty to over eighty a day. He has watched too as the once-mighty local spring has slowed to an unimpres-sive trickle. "Twenty years ago, it was like a river here, and now it's not. You can only guess what it will look like in another twenty years," he said. But Thapa will not stop, cannot stop, no matter how low the flow goes, he says. The money is too good. And besides, "where else would people get water?"

The Complicity of the State

Amid mounting public anger and shriveling resources, even big-time tanker operators admit that their industry has often lurched out of control. For all their distasteful ways, though, the tanker men say they are not the biggest villains in this saga. That label, they insist, is best applied to the state, without whose repeated failures they never would have had the opportunity to run rampant. The businessmen have a point. "Let's face it: the private sector came in because the public sector failed," said Dipak Gyawali, the former water minister. "And until you clean up government's act, nothing will change. The tankers are just a symptom."

These failures begin with epic urban mismanagement. Though the influx of climate-battered newcomers from the countryside would tax the capacity of any state, Nepali governments have handled their settlement in the Kathmandu Valley about as poorly as possible. Over the past two decades in particular, officials have stood by as new construction consumed the ponds and subterranean channels that supply much of the historic water network. Where once over two hundred fish or crocodile or serpent-shaped standpipes delivered water to central urban neighborhoods, now fewer than half of them gush anything, even at the height of the rainy season, according to the municipal water body.

The whole time, officials have done little as farms, factories, and real estate developers have dirtied the valley's waterways beyond measure while tarmacking over vital aquifer recharge areas. For much of the monsoon and the months that follow, households use hand pumps to extract from the shallow aquifers under their properties and provide for at least some of their needs. But the more the valley's forested and agricultural land is lost, the less the groundwater is replenished. That is particularly problematic as rains are increasingly weaker than usual, which limits rooftop rainwater collection, or stronger than ever, which fuels floods and can contaminate shallow aquifers. Here, as in so many other places, there is seldom a middle ground these days.

Then, too, in instances where government perhaps should have acted, it seldom has. The pipeline network is so leaky that many recipients average as little as one hour of running water every week, during which they are expected to fill rooftop or underground cisterns. The pressure is so weak that many households capture no more than 250 liters on each occasion. For these people—and the roughly 30 percent of residents who have no pipeline access at all—tankers are their only option. Politicians say that they recognize it is a crisis but blame their predecessors for inaction.

In an interview at her family's tightly guarded compound in 2019, Bina Magar, the then minister of water supply (and, coincidentally or not, the daughter-in-law of the prime minister) insisted that she was well on her way to improving the capital's water woes. "For so long we had unstable governments that have lasted one year, six months, eight months," she said. "Now we have an opportunity to bring stability and fix everything." Her house, as with seemingly all ministerial residences, relies on tankers, insulating them from the consequences of state failure. But predictably, perhaps, her tenure in office passed much the same way as those of her predecessors.

On that trip, I visited the Manohara slum just to the east of Tribhuvan International Airport in Kathmandu. There, I found some 7,500 families scraping by with no pipeline access and relying on tanker men who tried to charge them triple what they charged the middle-class neighborhood down the road. On a return visit in 2023, residents were, if anything, in an even worse position. They still had no pipeline access and now, after repeated squabbles with the tanker men, no truck deliveries, either. In their stead, residents have taken to washing with and sometimes even drinking from the sickly looking stream that flanks some of their houses. The sense of misery was almost as palpable as the water's stench. Rajendra moved here from the distant and very mountainous Mustang district (average altitude: 13,000 feet) in the hope of securing work—and, he admitted, a degree of urban anonymity away from the prying eyes of his relatives, who had no time for his painful, cannot-look-anyone-in-the-eye shyness. But he had concluded that it is better to be poor in the village than poor in the city. There, "at least we won't die of thirst," he said.

Sabotaging the Saboteurs

Compounding this dereliction of governance, the state has also complicated the tanker men's jobs to a point that they likely would not be able to provide a customer-pleasing service even if they were so inclined. For example, most operators source their water in places like the springs at Khahare. But the rural roads are so rough and the potholes so gaping that the drivers crawl along for fear of snapping axles. Businessmen say their trucks could perform double their current daily average of four deliveries and thus sell more cheaply if they could move more quickly. But with no expectation of improved infrastructure, tanker drivers have implemented their own precautions.

Some pad their ceilings with folded newspapers to cushion the blows as they get bounced around their suspension-less vehicles; others deck their cabins out with so much Hindu and Buddhist iconography that they can scarcely see through their windshields. The most impatient, or those who work the most traffic-clogged routes, take things further. Many trucks have equipped themselves with mini-TVs or booming sound systems. After accompanying one crew on their day of deliveries,

I felt discombobulated, stumbling out of the passenger seat like a dazed cat from a tumble dryer.

The corruption can be debilitating. Tanker men field so many demands for bribes that they sometimes keep wads of cash in their jacket pockets for that purpose. If they do not pay sums that vary from 5,000 rupees ($43) to 100,000 rupees ($866) ("political campaign contributions," as they are sometimes called), they can get shut down, a dozen businessmen said. These costs, too, must be passed on to the consumer. Officials are noticeably tentative in their denials. "These claims are not related to our organization, but perhaps the traffic police or someone else," said Sanjeev Bickram Rana, executive director of the Kathmandu Valley Water Supply Management Board (KVWSMB), citing what is widely seen as the greediest branch of Nepali officialdom.

Even attempts at regulation appear to have failed, more due to official failure than because of tanker opposition. The state implemented a color-coded sticker system to gauge tanker water in 2012—green for drinkable water, blue for household use, yellow for construction-quality—but years on it still is not properly enforced. KVWSMB says it lacks the resources to monitor more than three days a week; the tanker men say officials do not care as long as their pockets are lined. As far as Kathmanduites are concerned, there is more than enough rage to go around.

On one overcast Saturday morning, Sunita Suwal waited outside her house in Bhaktapur for the weekly hour-long pipeline delivery to flow. She grew increasingly angry as the scheduled time passed. Then she waited another hour, losing out on a shift at a seamster's workshop that she could ill afford to miss. Finally, as the morning ticked by with no water in sight, Suwal snapped. "The state fails us. The tanker men rob us," she said. "They all just want to make money from us. Really, what's the difference?"

A Solution Gone Wild

Having surrendered control of the capital's water delivery to often-grasping private businessmen, Nepali officials have often come across as remarkably relaxed about its predicament, as if waiting for a hydro Hail Mary play to bail them out. And, in a sense, they have been. That Hail Mary, the Melamchi Water Supply Project, is centered about five hours' drive across death-defying roads from Kathmandu (think trucks laden with propane canisters traveling at speeds they have no business going), and involves redirecting several Himalayan rivers through a sixteen-mile-long mountain tunnel to bolster supply in the thirsty valley. For years, as urban water access deteriorated, officials invoked the project as a panacea that would restore the state's role in the water sector once and for all. "Melamchi," as ex-minister Magar put it with rare ferocity when we met, "is the answer."

However, to the surprise of seemingly no one within Nepal's long-suffering water expert community, that "miracle," too, is failing to pan out. On the contrary, the project threatens to further undermine the capital region's peace and security, while ultimately doing little to loosen the tanker men's grip. No sooner was Melamchi finished on June 15, 2021, than disaster struck. At around 5:00 p.m. that day, about *six* hours after key parts of the tunnel's twenty-three-year-long construction process were completed, a wall of water swept down over ten thousand feet into the project's headworks. It tore through the main site and then through dozens of villages, killing almost thirty people, including at least eight water project employees. By the time the highest of the flood-waters relented more than twenty-four hours later, the river valley had been so brutally reconfigured that returning locals struggled to locate where their houses had once stood.

Investigators are still piecing together precisely how this happened.[8]

This much we know, though. In the days leading up to the disaster, a cloudburst soaked the valley uplands with dangerous amounts of rain. That water then destabilized a nearby glacial lake, one of many formed across the Himalayas by melting glaciers in recent decades and one of about twenty known to have burst their banks of late. Together, this angry tide of mud and mountain roared downstream, taking with it entire hillsides that had been loosened by the 2015 earthquake, which was also centered in this area. Even now, with watchers permanently stationed at several points up in the mountain, project engineers scurry for higher ground when the rains pick up. "We are forever fearful," said Padam Kunwar, gesturing at nearby peaks, many taller than the highest peaks on most continents but essentially nameless in this land of Everest and Annapurna. "That we are even alive at this moment is like a Hollywood movie."

Still, the flood need not have been as devastating were it a matter of climate and environmental disaster alone. This is where the state's unwanted contribution came in. The project was seemingly executed without factoring in those changing climate conditions. For example, there were few precautions to combat the landslides and monster floods that have worsened throughout this area, nor, as the project dragged on for decades after it was first conceived in the 1970s, did planners seemingly factor in the glacial lake outbursts that have become considerably more common since then. There are more than eight thousand of these lakes in the Himalayas, some expanding more than a hundred meters a year, and many liable to burst their wobbly banks at any moment.[9] Most damningly to locals, debris from the tunnel excavation had been left piled along the valley floor. When the torrent arrived, it absorbed these thousands of tons of rock, building itself into even more of a house-eating monstrosity than it might otherwise have been. Years later, entire hotels remain midstream, tossed like outsized Lego bricks into places they have no right being. With almost every "proper" bridge washed away, locals must either chance the wobbly, hand-built tangles of wire mesh and driftwood that a few villages have thrown across the river, or drive hours out of their way.*

From Bad to Worse

To all this might be added the ultimate folly: Not even a fully functioning Melamchi project alters Kathmandu's water calculus in the long run. From the supply side, the tunnel's provision of 170 million liters a day is barely a stopgap for a booming urban area that already consumes double that amount daily. Moreover, the state's failure to dedicate more than a fraction of the resources that it lavished on tunneling to improving the leaky distribution pipeline network ensures that there is a limit to even that water's usefulness. "You could have Lake Baikal on the other end and it still wouldn't be enough," says Dipak Gyawali. So why have so many Nepali administrations gone all in? Here, too, he has an answer. "It's a pocket-filling enterprise for contractors. It's about getting as much money as possible." After all, he added, "what's the kickback on a pond?"

---

* The very fact that people hold Kathmandu mostly culpable for a disaster that it may have worsened but did not cause is illustrative of the difficulties that states with no reservoir of public goodwill face when weathering climate stresses. After experiencing so much governmental corruption and incompetence over the years, disenchanted citizens are forever disposed to accept the least charitable interpretation of the state's role in crises. In Nepal, as in many similarly afflicted countries with equally distrusted political classes, that bodes ill for officials' ability to maintain credibility as climate stresses worsen—or, indeed, for their capacity to withstand intense public anger at all. Pitiful state responses to natural disasters have contributed to frequent government and occasional system collapses, as in pre-independence Bangladesh. Without an uptick in governance, some form of extreme political flux could one day play out at the other end of the Ganges basin.

Worse—or more poignantly—still, the Melamchi disaster and the Nepali state's reaction to it are fueling even more intense migration to the Kathmandu Valley, thereby heightening water demand in and around the capital, and adding to the very challenge that authorities came to the mountains intent on resolving. Bharat Bahadur Karki was once a man of means. Since the flood, he has been left with almost nothing. The waters took his riverside trout farm. A subsequent landslide took his house, a two-story mansion in the village of Gyalthum, about ten miles downstream from the water project headworks. Though his family survived, he is still haunted by how close he came to losing everyone. He is not prepared to chance his luck again. Walking me through the jumble of boulders that stand where his riverside paddies once yielded the "most delicious rice," he explained why he had had enough. "You try and continue but life was hard before this [flood] and now it is impossible. It is time for a change."

Bharat's story is par for the course in Helambu and Melamchi municipalities (and, indeed, across the country at large), where so many broke and desperate farming families are reaching similar conclusions. The loss of up to five-sixths of the upper valley's best agricultural land has kneecapped the area's economy, shedding jobs that locals are mostly unable to replace—and inflicting a financial and psychological blow that they, already reeling from that gamut of climate stresses, are much less capable of bearing.

The diversion of much of their river could render crop cultivation impossible for the relative few whose fields were not washed away. Under the terms of the deal that Melamchi area politicians struck in exchange for dropping their long-standing opposition to water transfers to Kathmandu, the state pledged to leave ample flow for local use. But, in what villagers see as officials' latest act of brazen resource burglary, the river has been reduced to few tame rivulets for much of the year, each struggling to weave its way through the boulder field. By contrast, when I visited the tunnel in the summer of 2023, it was greedily diverting water, back in business after a six-month, post-disaster suspension.

Paralyzed by fear of more floods, more earthquakes, and more government schemes of dubious wisdom, few locals have any intention of sticking around if they can help it. In the years before and particularly since the flood, the youth club near Gyalthum has lost sixty of its seventy members to migration, which has left them with too few players to field a soccer team. Not that there would be anywhere to play now. The flood claimed the only flat land, too. The school in Melamchi Bazar, the main town in the upper valley, is hemorrhaging students, its numbers kept stable only by villagers moving downhill from the earthquake-battered and increasingly parched uplands, which is itself often a first step to onward migration. For those who remain behind, there is an awful lot of alcoholism, an awful lot of suicide, and a deepening disdain for the state that, in light of the Maoist insurgency that took root in somewhat similar circumstances in the 1990s, ought to be sounding alarm bells in Kathmandu.

At around sunset on our final day in the Melamchi Valley, Rojita and I sat down for evening beers, hoping to take the edge off a flurry of depressing interviews. It was not to be. We watched as a group of men, now all landless farmers, put away glass after glass of homemade *raksi*, a vodka-strength liquor. We quietly nursed our drinks as they got that bit more belligerent, some beginning to stumble home to wives who, according to local police, are bearing much of the brunt of that fusion of booze and hopelessness. Finally, one of the remaining men, perhaps sensing our quizzical looks, put his glass down and unburdened himself. "There is no life here. There is nothing for us now," he said. "You ask about tanker men? Sure, they make life difficult. But here everyone makes life impossible."

A Metropolis on the Brink

With its mishmash of tourist attractions and local oddities, Kathmandu can feel like a family fairground, as friendly and charming as it is tired and tumbledown. But away from the storied Buddhist temples, busy riverside crematoria, and stores selling counterfeit adventure wear ("Patagoonia," "The Nort Face") is a city that is coming unstuck in a hurry. The consequences of that largely climate-related rural chaos have a lot to do with it.

Those newcomers to the capital area need jobs, not least because many of them arrive bowed down with debt from their failing farms, but with little education and almost no opportunity to make use of their existing skills here, there is little choice beyond construction work. In this, they are being pitched against Kathmandu's existing troop of day laborers, who understandably do not relish the competition. Workers report more frequent fights on construction sites, often under the influence of *raksi*, and a depression in wages as bosses take advantage of the surplus labor. When I met Sagir Hawari, a whip-thin twenty-one-year-old, he had arrived in the city three weeks beforehand and quickly secured work through his uncle on a building site. But he is being paid about half of what he had anticipated and consequently cannot manage Kathmandu's higher costs, especially, he noted without being prompted, its unexpectedly lofty water tanker bills. He has since chosen to bed down in the site's dank dark basement with about twenty other people, a revolving cast of street dogs, and, by the sounds of their incessant scurrying, a small army of resident small critters.

And Hawari was lucky to find any job at all. In yet another illustration of how climate stresses can trap states in cycles of low development even when they pursue "climate-friendly" solutions, Kathmandu's employment crunch is becoming more marked as hydroelectricity generation wavers due to those erratic rains, which is forcing the state to ration power. For the most part, officials are prioritizing household use, which many businesses say has forced them to slow hiring at a time when they are already burdened with high (again, generally tanker-induced) water costs. When I visited a *kukri*-making workshop in Lalitpur intent on buying a wicked-sharp Gurkha knife, the power was out, the workers mostly made idle for the fifth time that month.

Naturally, that influx from the countryside is also changing the character of the city, to the fury of some long-standing residents. Older Kathmanduites hold these rural Nepalis responsible for everything from diluting their identity and traditions, to spreading disease. This kind of animosity, a globally common one that we will return to in the next chapter and which is only becoming more pronounced as agriculture stutters and rural peoples urbanize faster, appears particularly strong among elderly Newars, the area's historically dominant ethnic group. Perched on the stoop of the Buddhist temple he oversees in Lalitpur, Shyam Bajracharya, a priest in his eighties, waxed nostalgic about how the neighborhood once trilled with Newari celebrations, the Newari language, and Newari food, likely the most delicious Nepali cuisine due to the historic richness of the area and locals' corresponding capacity to afford more varied dishes. No longer, he says. "Our culture is dying. We don't do our festivals. I feel terrible."

But it was on the subject of water that he got particularly excited. People from elsewhere in the country have snaffled their resources, leaving the locals dependent on "these bad people," the tanker men. Those men are "migrants from India" out to make a buck off their backs with the connivance of the state, he suggested. With so much earthshaking construction to house the new arrivals, the last of the standpipes on his street was knocked out a decade ago, the rusting, cobweb-covered device now standing as a vivid reminder of what has been lost. In all this, the

Kathmandu has, at times, expanded faster than almost any other city on Earth. New construction has sprawled over ponds and aquifer recharge areas, and into woodland. (Photo by Poornima Shrestha)

priest was merely voicing gripes that are gathering strength across Kathmandu. Migrants are being scapegoated for worsening traffic, filthier pollution, and more damaging flooding. Little of this finger-pointing is fair, but in the misinformation-heavy climate created by crises, that scarcely matters. Research from Kenya and Vietnam suggests that "environmental migrants" are often less accepted by host communities than those escaping conflict or political persecution.[10]

Then there is the crime. Though the precise relationship between rural-to-urban migration and some forms of exploitation is unclear, the correlation can be startling. These often desperate and unworldly newcomers are both extra vulnerable to abuse when away from their support networks, and disproportionately drawn to petty crime for the same reasons, senior policemen say. Nepal has witnessed an explosion of online scams from fake recruitment agencies directed at migrants, many of whom are keen to join the roughly 2,200 Nepalis who the prime minister's migration advisor told me are leaving for Gulf Arab states and other migrant hotspots every day. Thousands of them have been fleeced through social media, but police say that the likes of Facebook have not been responsive to their pleas for assistance. At the same time, Kathmandu, though still very safe by all big-city metrics, may be experiencing more violence as a consequence. Fueled by a volatile mixture of alcohol-tinged desperation, economic precarity, and perhaps the fallout from climate stresses in the city itself, violence against women is on the rise, NGOs say. At a shelter in a southern neighborhood, administrators struggle to field demand for beds, with near 100 percent occupancy and the director so rushed off her feet that I felt guilty requesting even a few minutes of her time.

A Public Scorned

So where does this all leave the tanker men, the much-maligned emblems of a city spiraling out of control? And where, for that matter, does it leave the state that made them possible? After years of near-unbroken success, during which they have both profited from and in a way helped fuel that increasing urban dysfunction, the tanker men now find themselves in a bit of a bind.

Since Melamchi finally came online, demand for their services has shrunk, and some tanker men, who were convinced that the perma-delayed project would remain perma-delayed, are now desperate. Interviewees told me of frequent attacks on their trucks by competitors, including bullet holes in the tanks and punctured tires. They describe such prolific theft of key bits of kit, like the hoses used to transfer water from trucks to household cisterns, that drivers or other employees must now sleep in the vehicles at all times. With customers at a premium, the cartel-like practices that had governed the trade have gone out of the window, leaving longtime operators finding themselves in a new world in which others are encroaching on *their* turf and paying off *their* favored politicians. From this nadir, the nasty minority among the tanker men are having to learn to play nice for the first time.

But although many of these operators are now suffering, some flogging their old trucks for scrap or converting them back into the haulage vehicles that most originally were, few of them feel they will be in this position for long. The country's climate shocks are intensifying faster than anticipated; according to a 2023 report, glaciers across the Himalayas were melting two-thirds faster in the 2010s than in the previous decade, and up a third of those in Nepal may be gone by 2030.[11] Relatedly, the flow of rural migrants to the capital area is only growing. The likes of Jitendra Das Amartya feel they need only bide their time. Until then, he appears to be keeping a mental ledger of those who have kicked him while he has been down. "If I am even twenty minutes late now, I can lose business," he says. "But the city will need us again. I am confident about this."

Discomfited by bad press and perhaps grateful for the relief from higher tanker bills too, the officials I met are adamant that this success is no flash in the pan. But their new plan—expanding the Melamchi project into three more valleys to compensate for the inadequacy of the first phase—looks a lot like its old one. Few experts rate its chance of delivering anytime soon, not least because of the complications that intensifying landslides and flooding pose for construction. For this reason, too, the tanker men look to be onto a good thing. "In a Nepali context, everyone talks about coordination," says Nava Raj Pyakurel, a senior civil servant in the Ministry of Urban Development. "But everyone wants to coordinate, and no one wants to be coordinated." (This love of big, neat-looking solutions is a global syndrome, or "megapro-jectivitis" as Pakistani social scientist Daanish Mustafa has labeled it, a tendency to favor the grandiose where the small and "unsexy" would likely yield better, cheaper results.)

Meanwhile, public intolerance of the state's poor performance is peaking.* Instead of singling out the tanker men for rough treatment, residents of struggling, waterless neighborhoods have been pursuing the people whom they hold principally responsible for the businesses' unsa-vory success in the first place. I heard three stories of state water employ-ees getting beaten up. I heard of another in which a hapless municipal valve man was yanked aside and berated for tanker "crimes." On occa-sions when residents have taken to the streets to protest poor services, including water, they have sometimes been swept aside by police water cannons. No one in this thirsty city is blind to the irony. No one is getting any less livid. "We get no water from the pipelines, less water from our well, and we can't afford tanker water," said Anjali Tamang, a student and protest participant, giving me the judgiest of looks when I asked one of those infuriating journalist questions ("How does this make you feel?"). "Of course we're angry!"

In other places at other times, this kind of chaos could fuel dangerous degrees of revolutionary sentiment. And in Nepal, with its alarming climate prognosis and distrusted, disliked state, it might yet. There is

---

* The Nepali state's poor performance in the face of climate change has also created rich opportunities for India and China, the landlocked state's two giant neighbors. Though tra-ditionally part of Delhi's sphere of influence—so much so that Kathmandu's Indian embassy is sometimes considered a second center of political power, Nepal has seen significant Chi-nese inroads in recent years. In this, Beijing has been aided by disaster diplomacy, donating excavators and backhoes to landslide-vulnerable municipalities, according to a JCB con-struction equipment showroom in the Nepali capital. For their part, many Nepalis accuse India of building its flood defenses in such a way as to inundate parts of Nepal's low-lying Terai region rather than any of its own territory.

already plenty of antidemocratic feeling, a commonly expressed sense that none of this would have flown under the monarchy, which presided over periodic authoritarian governments in the decades preceding its abolition in 2008. If power is legitimacy, then dysfunctional Kathmandu is in for a rough ride. But for now, many Nepalis are simply heading for the exits. Appropriately, that includes state water employees. At the airport, surrounded by an incongruous mix of Gore-Tex and psychedelic T-shirt-clad tourists, I met "Kumar" as we waited to board the same flight to Istanbul. For years, he had helped manage water supply in some of the outer parts of Kathmandu Valley, and for years, by his account, he had tried to bolster pipeline access. But he had had enough of the poor pay and corruption. In any case, he had little to do. The tanker men did most of the deliveries.

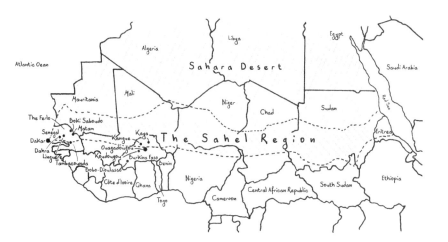

Atlantic Ocean

Algeria

Libya

Egypt

Sahara Desert

Saudi Arabia

Mauritania

Mali

Niger

Chad

Sudan

Red Sea

The Ferlo

Boki Saboudo

Matam

Eritrea

Senegal

Dakar

Kangue

Kaya

The Sahel Region

Dahra

Ouagadougou

Linguère

Koudougou

Burkina Faso

Tambacounda

Bobo-Dioulasso

Benin

Nigeria

South Sudan

Ethiopia

Côte d'Ivoire

Ghana

Central African Republic

Togo

Cameroon

CHAPTER 5

Deadly Pastures[1]

As access to water and land in West Africa fluctuates,
farmers and herders are duking it out over the scraps.

THE TROUBLE STARTED SHORTLY BEFORE NIGHTFALL, when a herd of
migrating cows surged through a low wooden fence just north of the
Burkinabe town of Kaya and went to work on Boubacar Ouedraogo's
crops. They devoured a field of millet, all half acre of it, including the
seeds that he had set aside to donate to charity. Then they inhaled the
cowpeas that, despite their misleading name, were not meant for bovine
consumption. "I lost my family's food. I lost *my* food," he said when we
met in Ouagadougou, Burkina Faso's capital, a few weeks after the incident in the summer of 2021. In their hunger—and haste to sate it after
crossing many miles of inadequate pasture, the cattle may even have
munched their way through a few tools that Ouedraogo had initially
thought stolen. At least he found himself able to laugh at this.

A veteran pastoralist who had spent his entire life (about sixty-five
years, by his best guess) driving livestock back and forth across West
Africa until a gammy leg forced him to slow down, Ouedraogo had
been in the cattle owner's position many times himself. He consequently knew the procedure down to a T. That very evening, Ouedraogo
sat down with the guilty party and soon agreed on compensa-

tion roughly equal to the value of half a cow. That, both men thought, was that.

What neither had reckoned with, though, was the spark this incident would apply to simmering grievances elsewhere in the village. As word spread of this latest "outrage," the most recent of a long line of intrusions by migrating livestock onto local agricultural land, other farmers decided that these outsiders needed to be taught a memorable lesson. After first going door to door to bolster their numbers and amass weaponry ranging from scythes to wicked sharp machetes, about two dozen men descended after dark on herds that were grazing fitfully in the surrounding flatlands—and set about their bloody business by cell phone torchlight. By the time the sleeping owners woke to the pained lowing of their cows, about thirty animals had been butchered and tens of others slashed in ways from which they would never fully recover.

Ouedraogo was one of the first on the scene. At first, he was gratified to find none of the human dead that increasingly accompany these clashes, though he was still taken aback by the sight. "It was a massacre," he remembers, with pools of blood and organ soaking the sands with the first moisture they had seen for many months. Some of the animals were identifiable only by their personalized brands, their patterned hides having been sliced beyond recognition. But Ouedraogo's mild relief soon—and quite presciently—turned to fear as angry pastoralists began to demand retribution. With a hatful of their own long-standing complaints about farmer behavior, these men were in no mood to let the assault pass unpunished. Over the following days, herders shot at least two area farmers, burned a dozen farms, and set the stage for yet another cycle of violence.

Although local tensions have since eased, or at least had eased at the time of writing, an uneasy compact now governs relations between

Sahelian transhumance (seasonal pastoralist migration) is a millennia-old tradition that developed to suit the landscape of a region that is too dry to sustain livestock throughout the year—but which is nevertheless much more abundant than is popularly understood. Typically, herding families leave "home" during the dry season in pursuit of lusher, generally more southerly pasture, and then return six to ten months later when summer rains temporarily transform arid or semiarid areas into something much leafier. (Photo by John Wendle)

peoples who were once happily interdependent.* Social ties have yet to recover, contributing to the kind of toxic mutual mistrust that was eerily reminiscent of some Iraqi and Syrian villages. Herders remain angry at authorities' apparent failure to punish the perpetrators of the initial assault, all part of a generalized privileging of farmer interests, they say—and of the state's steady disappearance. Beset by jihadism, the Burkinabe government cannot administer much of its territory, let

---

* And indeed, who were once, and in some instances remain, one and the same people. As some commentators point out, this conflict can be as much a clash between ways of life as it a clash between individuals.

alone police its citizens' behavior. Above all, both parties fear a replication of the conditions that have time and again brought them to this point. "When the rains are good, everything is fine. But look around you," Ouedraogo said, gesturing at the city's own parched landscape. "Who can live from this?"

A Crisis Foretold?

Ouedraogo's village lies within the Sahel, a strip of drylands that spans the width of the African continent for over four thousand miles and that separate the Sahara Desert from the tropics. (*Sahel* means "coast" in Arabic, as in the shore of the desert, a shifting and possibly advancing sea of sand.) This region is often presented as Exhibit A of climate-fueled conflict, a bitter—and, along with Nile-style "water wars," an eerily generalizable—preview of the sort of violence that warmer conditions are expected to exacerbate across the globe. According to this narrative, drought and desertification are shrinking the region's already meager water and "good" land. In this Mad Max–like world, farmers and herders are being forced to duke it out over scraps.

It is certainly true that, in recent years, the Sahel has experienced an eye-catching surge in violence. Between 2010 and 2021, conflict between herders and farmers claimed at least fifteen thousand lives in West and Central Africa, with half of that tally coming after 2018, and by some suggestions, the casualty counts have picked up significantly since then.[2] Mali and Burkina Faso have recorded tit-for-tat massacres which have left hundreds dead in each country and many thousands uprooted from their homes.[3] In one eight-month span from 2017 to 2018, Nigeria, which has faced more violence between farmers and herders than anywhere else, registered more than 1,500 related deaths, a rate of killing up to six times that of ISIS-affiliated Boko Haram.[4]

But there is more to the story than just scarcity, as farmers and pastoralists (a term I use interchangeably with *herder* throughout this chapter) impressed on me in interviews across Senegal, Sudan, Burkina Faso, Kenya, and Mauritania. Because while drought is unquestionably a problem for these groups, they speak as much, if not more, about the erratic nature of the rainfall than the outright lack of it. How, ask men and women whose very lifestyles prize predictability, are they to know now when to plant their crops or when and where to migrate with their livestock? As in other parts of the world, it is that uncertainty, that erratic deviation from the known, that is principally responsible for bringing farmers and pastoralists into uneasy contact.

And while climate change figures prominently among the region's woes, it is, again, the way climate aggravates long-standing non-climate problems that can push people over the sometimes-fine line between peaceful frustration and out-and-out violence. The region, the world's poorest, has been badly served by the legacy of divisive colonial rule, and then further stifled by conflict and mostly unsatisfactory governance thereafter. The lack of cash, the scale of fighting, and the failure to face up to climate stresses are naturally related.* It is nigh on impossible to establish a functioning government when you cannot afford to hire sufficient administrators. For example, Niger has three civil servants per one thousand people. France, its old colonial master, has about thirty times as many.[5]

Moreover, in a now grimly familiar story, farmers' and particularly pastoralists' capacity to adapt is running into other government

---

* Most poor climate-change-battered countries are trapped in a particularly pernicious climate–finance trap. The same disasters which require adaptation can also hike the cost of borrowing the money that they need to fund those sea walls and other adaptive projects. Countries racked by climate-related conflict are doubly trapped, with donors disinclined to contribute to projects that they fear might soon be damaged or destroyed in fighting.

priorities, in this instance security. Herders have always moved during times of climate stress. Their history of seasonal migration ought to leave them better placed than anyone to adapt to resource scarcity and resource uncertainty. But as fears over terrorism grow, the border gates are now crashing down on many of the roughly twenty million people in the Sahel who depend on livestock for their livelihoods, which means that they can no longer deploy their go-to crisis-management methods just when they require them most. As a result, horrific scenes like the one Ouedraogo encountered near Kaya are increasingly common.

Playing out across villages and swathes of scrubland, these kinds of clashes can seem pretty small potatoes—horrible for those afflicted, but not a threat to broader stability. Yet if that were ever true, it is not now. Conflict between farmers and herders is overlapping with jihadist violence, weakening authorities' grip on rural areas, and likely contributing to the epidemic of military coups that are knocking out both democratically elected and authoritarian civilian governments across the Sahel. There is much more to this chaos than skirmishes over roaming cattle, of course. But, as in other parts of the world, when rural areas sneeze, entire countries can catch a severe cold.

A Climate That Makes No Darn Sense

In his younger years, Idrissa Ba's village-chief father had given him one bit of advice for when he eventually inherited the mantle of authority: look after your people's cattle. Holding court now in his compound's shaded courtyard under the bough of a mighty oak in the now-unrelenting wintertime heat of Boki Saboudo, Ba feels he is failing at precisely that.

Where once most of his people migrated north and east with their livestock during the dry season, now they mostly have no choice but to head southwest from this isolated spot along the Senegal River near Matam into the bushy flatlands of southern Senegal, their traditional pasture being foodless or all but out-of-bounds these days. Where previously they usually waited until March or April to embark on their longer annual migrations, these days they are often on the road by December, or well before, an early start that can require them to travel many hundreds of miles more to find pasture. "If they don't, they starve," he says. Some livestock clearly already are. The decaying carcasses of emaciated animals line the approaches to the village and dot the brush.

In this brave new unfamiliar world, many villagers in Boki Saboudo are ditching cattle, or long-range transhumance, or even livestock-wrangling altogether. When I went looking for the village "brander," the man to whom local pastoralists once turned to mark their animals, I was told there no longer was one. Most people do it themselves to save money, the imam said. There might be insufficient customers to sustain a business even were they to avail themselves of his services, he added. If ever there were a neat little encapsulation of enforced change, I thought, this was it.

Ba, a kindly-looking man with watery eyes and a grandfatherly manner, seems thoroughly bowled over by this transformation. He admits that he struggles to dispense useful advice to the anxious herders who seek out his counsel. "It can be difficult to know what to do," he says. "You start to question if what you know is still useful." Pausing to collect his thoughts—and to still the hubbub from his three wives, nine children, and innumerable grandchildren, many of whom were not-so-quietly listening in, he continued: "You have to change your plans constantly." But, despite minimal familiarity with the science, of the prime culprit he has no doubt. "The climate is not normal. The rains are not normal."

And he is largely correct. In recent years, precipitation patterns in this corner of Senegal and in its Sahelian neighbors have fluctuated wildly—and all in ways that are almost calculated to unsettle the social balance. Sometimes rains are weak, as in 2017, 2019, and 2021, which can mean that pastoralists have all but exhausted their "home" vegetation by February, or even sometimes by early September, if the rainy season has been particularly poor. That is forcing them to travel up to six or more months earlier than usual, which is a recipe for trouble. Farmers have often yet to finish harvesting their crops and so are extra disinclined to welcome outsiders and their livestock onto or around their lands.

Sometimes, as in 2020, rains are too strong, a reflection of the extremes that climate change delivers at both ends of the spectrum. Pastoralists on the Mauritanian side of the Senegal river told me of animals drowned in the mud, tracks rendered impassable by vast expanses of newly created lakes, and of enticingly lush but nevertheless dangerous volumes of vegetation. Thick undergrowth can mean more pasture-expunging wildfires around villages later in the year. Many Senegalese and Malian communities learned this to their peril in 2022. Bewildered by the feast-or-famine nature of annual rains, one old man's plaintive cry to God for clarity brought to mind a passage from Lampedusa's Sicilian epic *The Leopard*: "Water is either lacking or has to be carried from so far that every drop is paid for by a drop of sweat. [Yet] when the rains come, they are always tempestuous and set dry torrents to frenzy, drown beasts and men on the very spot where two weeks before both had been dying of thirst."[6]

Increasingly, conditions are sometimes just plain "weird" too. There are stop-start downpours, and rains falling in one place but not in similar locations nearby. Rains in July, but not August. August, but not September. That extreme uncertainty can force herders to travel into unfamiliar territory where they encounter communities with very different mores.* For instance, villagers in northern Senegal's Ferlo region complain of the arrival, for the first time, of herders from central Senegal, who drink alcohol openly and behave "forwardly" around local women in defiance of the area's more conservative norms. There have been frequent brawls. "These new people do not respect the rules," said Amadou Sow, a community leader in Barkedji. "They are unlike us and just cause trouble."

But that is not all. Like pastoralists, farmers are reeling from their own climate struggles, as weak and erratic rains drastically slice crop yields. For instance, five hundred kilograms of peanut seed can yield as little as one hundred kilograms of crop, as opposed to the usual four or more tons in riverine Senegal. Worried farmers now plant their fields as soon as the first rains fall, rather than waiting a month or so as they once did. It is a practice that shrinks available pasture even more—and at pastoralists' time of greatest need. "We work so hard but get so little," said Ibrahim Djallo in Doundodji, a village to the north of Linguere, which, with its crushing sense of hopelessness and suspicion, was one of the few places I have not felt welcome in the country.

The sheer difficulty of making the crops grow means that some farmers are less interested in maintaining once mutually beneficial arrangements with migratory herders. Historically, landowners welcomed roving cattle onto their fields as natural fertilizers during the dry season while providing free use of the land or agricultural waste for hungry animals in exchange. This no longer holds in some places. Many farmers now have access to artificial fertilizers, thanks in part to state support, which has

---

* This trouble appears particularly common among herders from the few places which once had enough year-round pasture but who are now being pushed by bad rains, land pressure, and increasing herd sizes into periodic migrations. Inexperienced and often ignorant, they are extra likely to fall afoul of their hosts.

Hungry animals often eat whatever they can during times of extreme hardship, which in Senegal, as in other parts of Africa that are reeling from waste-management crises, means they're ingesting ever greater volumes of plastic. Colorful plastic bags festoon the trees and shrubs of the Ferlo. (Photo by John Wendle)

meant they have less need for livestock "services" and, as they struggle to make ends meet, less desire to give away grasses that they could sell.

What is more, those measly crop yields, along with prolific population growth, are pushing farmers to expand their acreage into former pasture in places like Tambacounda and other southern Senegalese provinces. The population of West Africa has tripled since the 1980s and the volume of cropland has doubled. The entire continent's population could be as high as four billion by 2100, a tenfold increase in just over a century. As a result, pastoralists feel like they are running out of room to roam. "Even the areas that we knew we could rely on during emergencies in the past now often have problems as well," said Hadjel Sow, a pastoralist with over thirty years' experience migrating up and down the West African interior (and no relation of Amadou). "Life is just so very, very different."

Bad Governance Galore

Were wobbly rains the only problem, things would be a lot more straightforward. But if climate change is straining relations between herders and farmers, poor governance is generally responsible for translating that tension into conflict. Herders across West Africa insist that states favor farmer interests over their own. After a series of run-ins with farmers outside Bobo-Dioulasso, Burkina Faso's second city, passing pastoralists turned to local police, who, according to the herders, refused to hold their neighbors accountable even though they had reportedly initiated the dispute by expanding their cashew and mango trees into the corridors that herders use to bypass farm areas. Instead, the herders were ordered out and a few of their animals impounded until they paid steep bribes to the cops and two sacks of fertilizers to the farmers. That, shopkeepers in the city center told me when I went to stretch my legs after many long days in the car, is how it should be.

"Herders are not welcome here. They bring problems. They do not know how to behave," said Muhammadu, a pharmacist and the self-described local gossip. Turning for confirmation to one of his customers, who, for a small fee, had left his phone behind the counter to charge while he ran errands, he proceeded to get to the nub of the matter. "They only use the land a bit, so they are not the priority." Farmers, by contrast, are a constant in the community; they tend to have greater prominence in local governments and more political clout to legislate their preferences into law.

Herders say that authorities single them out for poor treatment even when they are not running up against farmers. In this, men like Hadjel

Sow face prejudice from societies that have long been suspicious of their "anti-modern" lifestyle, their identification with multiple countries or none, and, crucially, their border-crossing and hard-to-tax ways. Nomads have been "abandoned by heaven," a first-century CE Chinese observer wrote. "They do not worship God," a later Arab writer put it.[7] In *Rivers of the Sultan*, a history of the Euphrates and Tigris Rivers under the Ottomans, Faisal H. Husain writes of that empire's "dream of a sedentary paradise with its regular, predictable revenues from pacific farmers [that] had no place for pastoral nomads."[8]

Then there are various types of state-sanctioned land grabbing. Already at their wits' ends, herders, and some farmers, accuse domestic elites and foreign corporations of muscling in on their livelihoods. Pastoralism can be lucrative, especially when the rules do not apply, which has incentivized big-city businessmen to amass livestock. These huge herds, protected by heavily armed guards, can overgraze "regular" pastoralists' preferred spots and run roughshod over crops—leaving the victims without recourse to justice.[9] Similarly, countries such as Senegal have long been of interest to international agribusiness. By snapping up fields along the reliably irrigated Senegal River valley and coastal strip and then enclosing them with fences to grow food for export, outsiders from Saudi Arabia to Spain and India have denied herders access to additional tranches of land. According to aggrieved villagers, some of these lands appear to have been acquired in the same contentious manner as in Sudan (chapter 7).

All the while, terrorism has added a desperately unwanted X factor. Over the past decade, jihadists have taken advantage of weak and bad governance to cut a terrible swathe across the Sahel. Some traditional pasture is now prohibitively dangerous, in part because these extremist groups tend to claim cattle in lieu of tax, while other land is completely out-of-bounds because of border restrictions intended to stifle terrorist movements. Fearful of attracting scrutiny from Senegalese security forces, Ferlo herders say that they are careful to remove suspicious-looking messages from their phones as they return from Mali. Jihadists control about 40 percent of Burkina Faso, which as of 2023 is suffering more casualties from terrorism than any other country. Almost half of all global deaths due to terrorism are now in the Sahel.[10]

Worse yet, this conflict has damned all herders and peoples identified with herding by association. While ethnic groups focused on pastoralism are indeed overrepresented within terror groups, they are still a minority and nowhere near as present as is popularly believed. Yet the name *Fulani*, the largest of these West African groups, is all but synonymous with *terrorist* in parts of Nigeria, which risks becoming a self-fulfilling prophecy.[11] Across the continent, jihadi groups are presenting themselves as both champions of these persecuted minorities, and as the only adjudicators capable of forging peace between farmers and herders. For example, Jama'at Nusrat al-Islam wal-Muslimin (JNIM), a jihadi organization aligned with Al-Qaeda, denounced the expulsion of Fulani from Ghana to Burkina Faso in 2023 and called for them to "stand up for their people."*[12]

Some regional states, notably Senegal, have well-earned reputations for superior governance. There is little discrimination against the Fulani

---

* Though commentators might have occasionally overstated climate change's contribution, this terror success may itself be partly rooted in deteriorating growing and herding conditions, as with ISIS in Iraq. A landmark 2023 UN report concluded that Islamist militant group recruits in Africa are primarily motivated by a pursuit of employment, rather than religious beliefs. With fewer "good" rural jobs available, ISIS, Al-Qaeda, and likeminded ideologues are well-placed to hoover up the shortfall. To put the cat among the cattle, so to speak, there is ample research to suggest that climate-induced resource *abundance* may trigger violence of its own. In periods of plenty, there might simply be more to fight over. Equally, over time, absolute resource scarcity might mean less violence if there is nothing left that is worth the trouble.

here, for example, nor as much land pressure. But by herders' reckoning, even the Senegalese government in the capital, Dakar, has compounded their troubles. Starting in the early 1980s, Senegal and its neighbors dammed the Senegal River and began developing large irrigation schemes for year-round, rather than just rainy season, crop cultivation. Those initiatives, though broadly beneficial, deprived herders of pasture and reinforced the perception of inequitable treatment. (The Senegal River, for one, is often seen as an example *par excellence* of transboundary water cooperation in challenging circumstances. However, as along the Nile, officials' success in preventing inter-state water conflict can merely transfer the violence to a more local level). Most policies have winners and losers. Herders just feel that they always seem to be the ones losing out.

Fight Fight Fight

I did not expect to like Usman Diallo, a man so tall and lean that I found myself half-wondering whether he even cast a shadow. He had been introduced to me as someone with the blood of innocents on his hands. He had laughed while killing a child, one contact insisted, though I was unable to verify the story and it smacked of a creative flourish in the telling. Plus, I had a more prosaic grievance with him: he had fed my interpreter such terrible directions that we had bounced from a minibus to a motorized rickshaw, finally trekking through slums of intensifying poverty before we found him in the ramshackle one-room house which his family has shared with distant relatives since the incident. Yet as Diallo recounted his experience over several hours while, curiously, downing an entire party-sized bottle of Coke, I began to sympathize with him, or at least to understand how he had ended up in the middle of a murderous brawl.

It was early 2021, about two months after and roughly a hundred miles from the scene of the cattle killings in the Kaya area, and Diallo and his family had been driven by war and exceptionally weak rains from their usual grazing grounds along the Mali–Burkina Faso border. Moving far to the south, they thought they had finally stumbled on sufficiently rich and jihadi-free terrain for their several hundred cattle. (The Fulani people from which Diallo hails do not count—or admit to counting—their livestock for fear of the evil eye.) They quickly erected their wood-and-tarpaulin shelters just outside the village of Kangue, and settled in for the season. Little did they know, in this area that they had never previously visited and where they struggled to effectively communicate in the absence of a common language, what a storm their presence would ignite among people who had reached the end of their collective rope.

For several years before, locals had suffered repeated setbacks, each adding to earlier hardships. They were poorer than ever after a decade of alternating floods and drought, which had gutted an economy almost wholly dependent on farming. They were reeling from a surge in crime, including the pilfering of many of their own few livestock, as the state slowly retreated under the weight of jihadist violence and its own chronic dysfunction. Deep internal disputes had only worsened as community leaders fled to the cities, but one of the few things that remaining villagers could agree on was their distaste for migratory pastoralists. So, when the Diallos and a number of other herders arrived, accompanied by thick clouds of billowing dust, their very presence was akin to waving a very red flag at a very irate bull.

What happened next depends on whom one asks. The villagers say that the visitors unleashed their almost one-ton zebu cattle on whatever fields had survived the most recent deluge—and then refused to pay compensation when they grasped the local people's powerlessness.

Diallo forcefully denied that account, raising his voice for the first time as he presented his side. By his telling, it was the locals who had failed to adequately fence off fields and then, lacking familiarity with traditional dispute resolution, had demanded extortionate cash, which the herders neither could nor would pay. Regardless, the end result is not up for dispute. Retrieving stashed weaponry, the two parties channeled years' worth of accumulated grievances into attacking one another. At least three villagers were killed and enough cows mangled for Diallo, whose people supposedly also avoid expressions of discomfort in public, to appear close to tears. "We have been left with nothing," he said, clad, I only noticed then, in too-short trousers and sandals that were more patch than shoe. "Our life has been destroyed."

That situation, in all its slow-building escalation, exemplified the sort of circumstances that drive farmers and herders to fight. Years of subpar governance had hollowed out the state's already limited rural presence; Burkina Faso barely has more civil servants per capita than Niger, and the ones whom it does have are often reluctant to follow security services into unstable areas with poor amenities and correspondingly poor living standards. Many months of conflict (at that point) had scared away whatever officials or civil society organizations had been within easy reach of Kangue in the first place, which left few, if any, trusted parties to mediate the dispute while it might have been mediatable. Against a background of continuing climate stress, which had depleted finances and drained psychological reserves, most of these people seemed to be at the end of their proverbial tether. Far from "what doesn't kill you makes you stronger," these cascading crises whittle away resilience, compound trauma, and make it that much more likely that the next trial will trigger an extreme response.

Of course, the state's presence can be as problematic as no state at all. A few years ago, my colleagues and I had a very small taste of its predatory instincts when a policeman pulled us over along Burkina Faso's main east–west highway and, without even bothering to invent a driving infraction, pushed our driver for a payoff. We pushed back, angrily threatening to report him to some of the senior officials we had interviewed. But it was not until darkness approached, the point at which even then it was unwise to be out on the open road, that we escaped his clutches. According to one study, based on Africa-wide data, "Flood disasters are associated with communal violence only for administrative districts that are governed by distrusted local state institutions."[13] According to another, drought reduces cooperative behavior, particularly vis-à-vis other ethno-religious groups.[14]

With Kangue effectively under jihadi control at the time of my last visit, I had to piece together its story from Diallo and the village's displaced residents, now all squeezed into dingy housing on the peripheries of the capital and Koudougou, the country's third-largest city. But the more they spoke, the more this incident felt like an ugly blueprint for future chaos. The very fact that some villagers and many herders now have guns and hence a capacity to inflict heavier forms of revenge is a function of the region's spiraling lawlessness. Equally, the villagers' exceptional mistrust of the herders may have been amplified by "fake news," which thrives when citizens lose faith in their authorities and which in parts of the Sahel is inordinately centered on highlighting alleged herder crimes.[15] At this, Diallo's tech-savvier nephew clicked open Facebook and showed me a video of a Burkinabe politician decrying "Fulani terrorists and murderers." We watched in silence for a few minutes, the older Diallo growing tenser and more withdrawn with every hurled insult.

Even the near-total lack of familiarity between these peoples is largely new. This had been the first time in Diallo's thirty-something years of migrating in which he had had to travel so far in pursuit of pasture that he had no local contacts at all. "None,'" he emphasized. "I knew no one." Tellingly, with the wind seemingly socked out of him by this run-in and with the authorities possibly on his tail (a suggestion which he denied but would explain his frequent furtive looks and the almost willfully bad directions he had given us), it may well have been his last. "When you have to fight, it is time to stop," he said. "This I know."

Business as Usual—of a Sort

Toward the end of a 2022 trip across the Senegalese Ferlo, I stopped in the town of Dahra, where the Association pour le Développement Intégré de Dahra (ADID), a pastoralist NGO, had kindly agreed to assemble a group of migrating herders on my behalf. I wanted to hear how they saw their future. Above all, I wanted to understand how they felt they could stay safe and keep their families and animals satisfactorily fed and watered through worsening conflict. Much to my surprise, these herders at least, their appetites sated with steaming bowls of rice and peanut sauce and many invigorated by recent visits to Dahra's massive livestock market, appeared quietly bullish about their prospects. (Even without being told, I might have guessed that a few of my interlocutors had been to the market; they sported the same mud-streaked clothing as I did after we'd thrown ourselves over fences and up walls to avoid runaway animals.)

Nowadays, they have more tools to navigate trickier conditions, such as motorbikes to scout ahead and cell phones, which enable them to glean information on the best pasture before traveling—and, on occasion, which villages are hostile and best avoided. They have more targeted media, like Radio Ferlo FM, a station run by ADID, which airs animal husbandry tips and weather forecasts, among other programming, and all in Pulaar, the dominant pastoralist language in much of the region and one that is often neglected by state media. Later, in the studio, I watched as an enthusiastic young presenter broadcast advice more than a hundred miles in every direction, all interspersed with music, jokes, and animal impressions of dubious accuracy. His laugh was so infectious and his tone so disarming that I, understanding not a word of what was said, would have bought anything he was selling. Despite living lives that would be familiar to their ancient forebears, these men and women are nothing if not adaptable.

Critically, many pastoralists are also embracing superior herding practices, which should allow them to better exploit pasture that is too marginal to interest farmers and so steer clear of some grazing grounds that appeal to both. Hundreds of NGOs have rolled out training on everything from restoring land with compost and manure, to switching to smaller stock. As well as being hardier, sheep and goats are cheaper to buy—though experts counsel that few "true herders" would ever countenance the change due to the perceived loss of prestige. Sure enough, on this point the men at the NGO fell into a chorus of interruptions, almost competing with one another to talk up cattle's merits. Besides, one of them said, "We know cows better than we know ourselves." And they might. A few days earlier near Loumbel Lana in the geographic center of the Ferlo, I had challenged a teenage herdsman to identify every one of the two hundred or so animals in his care, each one of which looked merely "cowlike" to my untrained city slicker eye. Divvying up the herd by size, hide pattern, and color, he passed my silly test with ease.

More than anything, though, Sahelian pastoralists may have a greater understanding of their predicament than many of their global peers—or think they do. Between the late 1960s and mid 1980s, the region experienced a sequence of deadly droughts that left kids "pulling at the intestines of dead cows for something to eat," as a US Senate hearing heard in 1974, and that cut grain yields in countries such as Mauritania by up to three-quarters.[16] Although struggling mightily now, many draw succor from their success in weathering past horrors. "Things are hard, very hard," said Idrissa Ba, the discombobulated village chief of Boki Saboudo. "But we've seen bad conditions before. People will go to new places, to old places, with some of the family, with none of the family. I might not recognize [future transhumance]. But it will still survive."*

And the farmers? Many of them display the same confidence. Some agricultural communities have been able to at least partially adjust to new growing conditions by reviving indigenous knowledge. For example, I met farmers in Mauritania who had reverted to burrowing their arms elbow-deep into the soil and gauging the amount of humidity between their fingertips and their forearms to determine if fields are ready for sowing. At the same time, they are embracing new technologies to replace the kinds of knowledge that climate change has rendered impotent. Agronomists frequently spoke of the value of quality weather forecasting, much of it now available on printouts distributed to fertilizer sellers or warnings of incoming mega-storms nailed to electricity pylons, and all of it a dramatic improvement on the bird migrations, plant flowerings, and other natural phenomena that farmers once consulted but which often no longer hold up.[17] In theory, the less farmers are hostage to uncertainty, the less edgy they will be about cattle threatening their earnings.

---

* One of the new places to which some Ferlo pastoralists are migrating is the Kedougou area in Senegal's far southeast. According to two local scholars, the area is comparatively unpopulated due to the persistent legacy of slavery, with a disproportionate number of its inhabitants transported to the Americas in the eighteenth and nineteenth centuries. Other parts of West Africa bear different lingering scars. As Peter Frankopan documents in *The Earth Transformed*, rates of polygamy appear to be higher in places where traders filched the most men, the gender imbalance creating a "surplus" of women.

Having ditched traditional mud-brick construction, with its heat-stifling properties, some Sahelian villagers may be suffering the consequences. The royal court
of Tiébélé, near Burkina Faso's border with Ghana, is one of the finest remaining
collections of traditional houses in the region. (Photo by Moises Saman)

Perhaps as importantly in the long run, some Sahelians are returning to traditional house construction. Since time immemorial, villagers
in this toasty-hot region have mostly built in mud, generally the only
material at hand but also one with terrific heat-stifling properties. However, with greater prosperity, many are shifting to concrete, even as temperatures peak. Near the Burkina Faso town of Leo, I met a farmer who
had recently made the change but then lacked the money to artificially
cool his new house. When, soon afterward, he shot a herder following a minor run-in with the man's cattle, his neighbors put it down to
extreme sleeplessness. And that fits a broader global pattern. Many of
those engaged in these disputes appear exhausted by an inability to sleep
well in the heat or a fear of closing their eyes out of concern for what

might befall them if they do, as with some Bangladeshi villagers, who worry that their houses might subside into the rivers overnight. The net result, among other perils, is some mightily poor decision-making.

"The reality is that cement construction is simply sexy," says Francis Kéré, the Burkinabe architect who is spearheading the "return" to mud and who in 2022 became the first African to win the Pritzker Prize, the biggest award in architecture. "But it's bad sex because you don't have the materials you need. It is not producing comfort."[18] At a Kéré-built orphanage in Koudougou, the results appeared to bear out that assessment. Within the mud-brick walls, supervisors report fewer fights, fewer mental health issues, and higher test scores.

Steps into the Unknown

Frightened by change of this magnitude and with nerves frayed by consistent inconsistency, most rural peoples inhabit something of a middle ground, forging ahead without alternatives but barely staying afloat. For every upbeat-ish farmer or herder, there is another who cannot see a way forward. Many feel trapped by a drought that, in parts of the region, is already more intense than anything they have previously experienced. Short on fodder, hungry herds struggle to fight off disease, to give birth, or to suckle whatever young they might have. That change has cut herd sizes and animal sizes and hence pastoralist profits at a time when these fewer, scrawnier beasts, often a sad-looking lot with sagging skin on hulking frames, are producing less milk for market.

Likewise, the political context is only becoming trickier to negotiate. As a measure of that bind, even state attempts to temper herder pain have often created knock-on problems of their own. For example, from the 1950s onward, colonial French and then independent Senegalese authorities dug dozens of wells in previously waterless and farmer-free stretches of the Ferlo. In doing so, however, they inadvertently concentrated livestock in small areas around the wells, which has degraded the land and fueled tensions among pastoralists. The same goes for many state efforts to mediate disputes. Sometimes these initiatives simply undercut existing methods of arbitration, while doing little to endear distant central government to either farmers or herders. Although, as we shall see in the final chapter, NGO-led initiatives have often yielded much better results.*

Against this impossible-sounding backdrop, many people are resorting to short-term coping devices, which prove irresistible but may only fuel fiercer trouble in the future. Farmers are deforesting land as they expand their acreage to make up for weaker yields, larger families, and, in some instances, their avoidance of fields that they see as most vulnerable to intruding cattle. Meanwhile, pastoralists, whose assets are mostly tied up in livestock, feel pressured to marry off their daughters at even younger ages to secure their dowries and offload to others the costs of supporting them. Among both parties, there is more belligerence toward one another and more of what I term climate dislocation—wild, irrational expressions of possibly misdirected rage of the sort that crops up in Iraq, Syria, and other conflict-climate settings. It is said that when Kalashnikov prices rise, "it is time to leave," as veteran war correspondent C. J. Chivers writes in *The Gun*, a history of AK-type weapons.[19] In Burkina Faso, prices are very high indeed, almost doubling on average since 2018, a security official told me in 2021.

Ultimately, it is all creating an environment in which even veteran law enforcement personnel, the kind who take pride in looking implacable,

* It is no surprise, perhaps, that so many regional leaders, including recent past Nigerian and Nigerien presidents Buhari and Bazoum, have been so keen to blame climate change——and climate change alone——for spiraling regional insecurity. They and their peers own some of this mess.

seem very, very concerned. "No problems are becoming small problems. Small problems are becoming bigger problems," says Cheikh Gueye, chief gendarme in Ouro Sogui, a large town on the eastern edge of the Ferlo. "For the moment we can manage. But what if the water situation gets even worse? All work is connected to that water."

Then there is migration, the strategy that crops up in some way, shape, or form in each of these chapters, and one that may feature particularly prominently here in fast-growing West Africa. Pouring out of their villages and into the Dakars and Ouagadougous of the region, rural West Africans are fueling one of the biggest migrations in the world. To descend into the granite quarry pits at Pissy, on the outskirts of the Burkinabe capital, is to encounter laborers from almost every one of the country's provinces and each of its neighboring states, all breaking their backs in hellish heat and air quality akin to car exhaust for wages—of up to $10 a day—that they could only dream of in the villages.*

For most migrants in this region, as in all others, these close-ish cities mark the end of their journeys. Yet, with more urban climate stresses to accompany the rural ones they have sometimes fled, including prolific flooding in neighborhoods such as that of the Diallos, and more cities struggling to provide jobs for all these new arrivals, among many other drivers, an increasing number of them are intent on going a step further. (In Dakar, for instance, I was struck by an environmentalist's admission that he was saving up for laser eye surgery specifically because he

---

* For pastoralists, this kind of migration is generally a little harder than it is for farmers. They are less likely than the others to have migrated seasonally to cities, which is often a stepping stone to permanent migration, and they are less likely to have support networks elsewhere because of that lesser history of relocation. Without access to the remittances that relatives often send and with even fewer resources of their own after spending whatever they have trying to adapt to climate stresses, pastoralists can struggle to generate the funds necessary to make these moves possible. But migrating permanently many of them still are.

was infuriated by his glasses forever fogging up in the oppressive coastal humidity.) By boat from the Atlantic coast or by truck across the Sahara, hundreds of thousands of Sahelians are already trying to reach Europe. As is explored in the penultimate chapter, the impact of a bigger surge could affect far more than just the happiness of the families whose loved ones succumb along the way.

At the Pissy quarry on the outskirts of Ouagadougou, about five thousand laborers from across rural West Africa burn tires to crack the granite, and then use pickaxes and other hand tools to lever and break the rock apart. (Photo by Moises Saman)

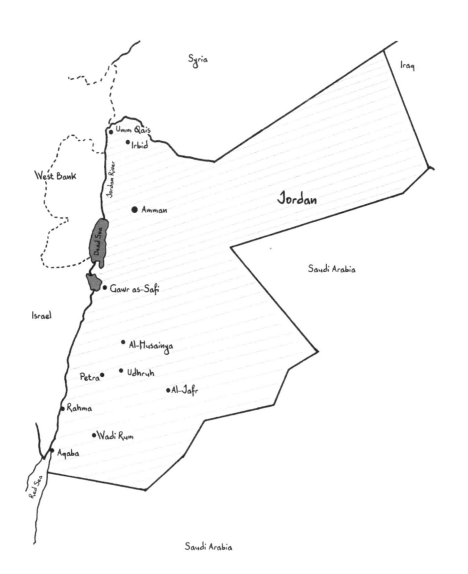

CHAPTER 6

No Jobs, No Peace[1]

For years, the Jordanian government has recruited unemployed rural men into the military. Now drought is torching that strategy, and no one knows what will take its place.

Outwardly, Rahma looks much like one might expect of a village in the semiarid reaches of southern Jordan. It is dusty. It is largely treeless, with nary a waist-high shrub to take the edge off the almost year-round sunshine. Laid out in a loose rectangular pattern a few hundred yards from one of the country's main highways, its one hundred or so box-shaped houses are as spotlessly clean inside their perimeter walls as they are flecked with mounds of litter around them.

Peer a little closer, though, and there are plenty of unpleasant surprises. The fields are fallow—and have been for so long that the soil has become indistinguishable from the surrounding sands. The livestock pens alongside the waterless reservoir are empty, save for a few dejected-looking sheep. And the streets? So quiet that when I visited in 2018 a stray dog sat sentry in a little hole it had burrowed in the middle of the main dirt drag. It would not stir no matter how furiously the driver leaned on the horn.

Pulling to the side of the road, I went searching for people to interview. I knocked on compound gates, levering open one sunbaked metallic door handle with a shirt sleeve after I thought someone inside had welcomed me in. The voice turned out to be that of a very vocal donkey. I visited the mosque, which, even at midafternoon prayer time, was empty but for the imam and a man in mud-spattered overalls whom I took to be a gravedigger. (As far as I could see, the cemetery with its freshly disturbed ground was one of the few hives of recent local activity). Only outside the village's lone functioning café did I find signs of life—of a sort. There, four young men slouched in the shade, identifiable as awake only by their slow, rhythmic phone scrolling.

Over tea and a small ashtray's worth of extra tarry cigarettes, they poured out the story of their village. It was as depressing as its appearance suggested. Not so long ago, much of the population had made a reasonable living herding sheep, goats, and camels back and forth across the rocky plains.* But weakening winter rains had robbed them of the vegetation that they needed to sustain their animals for much of the year. Fast-disappearing groundwater, combined with fiercer heat and other stresses, had hiked the cost of supplementary fodder beyond what many could afford. With little disposable income to go around, most of Rahma's small businesses, including almost all its entertainment options, had folded for good. At least a quarter of the village's residents had departed in their wake.

Had they enough money to set themselves up elsewhere, these men all say they would have joined the exodus in a heartbeat. Instead, with no means of making a living, they whittle away their time sleeping until noon, brewing and then drinking homemade alcohol in rejection of conservative Muslim norms, and seemingly consuming their share of the drugs that are seeping, in ever greater quantities, over the border from Syria. I had thought that a few of my new friends looked preternaturally

---

* Though, according to environmentalists with long records of working in the area, only some local people lost their jobs. They say that Rahma has a reputation as something of a troublemakers' town, with many of its residents disinclined to seek out work in the first place.

perky after returning from the toilet. One of the four, decked out in a black T-shirt with "fcuk you" emblazoned across the front in English, soon confirmed my instinct.

"You cannot understand how bored we are. Nothing to do, no money to spend, so yes, we take Captagon, we smoke hashish when we can afford it," said Hassan, whose last name I have withheld given the illegal nature of his interests. Captagon is a cheap synthetic drug that is mass-produced in regime-held parts of Syria and then smuggled across the country's borders. "And it's not just us. Everyone's lonely because their friends are gone." He went on: "We're scared, too. You hear lots of ringing phones here. Why? Because it might be the bank calling to chase the debts that everyone has. You don't pick up if you don't know who it is."

The Bottom Line

It is an awful thing to see a community fall apart. But, in Jordan, that is the fate of scores, if not hundreds, of villages. Farming and herding livelihoods are shriveling from scorching heat and want of water. Public health, education prospects, and the few nonfarming employment possibilities are declining with them. In these unhappy jobless vacuums, people in places like Rahma are increasingly coming apart at the seams.

In addition to (and perhaps partly as a result of) increased drug and alcohol consumption, many villages are experiencing unprecedented rates of petty crime, like housebreaking, which is snowballing into larger challenges. Communal trust, once shattered, is hard to rebuild. That is extra true as many of rural Jordan's best and brightest, who are generally also the ones responsible for preserving these communities' sense of self, join their global equivalents in migrating. "It sometimes seems like we don't know each other. We look at each other with new eyes," said Mohammed Yehia Dowlat, a farmer who lives just outside Irbid in the country's far northwest. "We are not family anymore."

If any of this sounds familiar, that is because rural Jordan's experience tilts at a global conundrum, one hinted at throughout this book. What do you do when agriculture and pastoralism, the professions that are uniquely vulnerable to climate change and that account for most livelihoods in the countryside, decline, but there are no clearcut alternatives? How, as an almost inevitable corollary, should one manage the often-violent results of government failure to square that seemingly "unsquarable" challenge? As seen in Iraq, where ISIS feasted off state inaction on climate and environmental issues, doing nothing is a recipe for disaster. And as seen in places like Nepal and Bangladesh, where climate stresses are fueling exceptional levels of rural-to-urban migration, even farming families' attempts to address their own struggles can come with knock-on security consequences.

What distinguishes Jordan is that, historically, the state *has* had something of an answer to this rural conundrum, albeit an inadvertent one. Since the earliest days of the kingdom's existence, the ruling Hashemite family has incorporated huge numbers of vulnerable rural tribesmen into the army and other security services—"farms to arms." In doing so, it has not only guaranteed them regular incomes, but assured itself of the support of a demographic that was instrumental in its rise to power and is pivotal to its continued rule.

The numbers tell the story of that century-old arrangement. In some rural areas of southern Jordan, roughly 70 percent of people with full-time jobs work in the army, police, or intelligence apparatus, according to my reporting in about twenty villages, a figure that can rise to around 90 percent in some of the most politically connected communities. About half of all "formally employed" Jordanian men of tribal origin make a "living by soldiering, policing, or spying for the state," writes scholar Sean Yom. As of 2020, that meant more than 200,000 men in these forces, with at least another 250,000 receiving pensions after service of as little as sixteen years.[2] As a result, many districts have practically been emptied of young and middle-aged men, with those in uniform sent elsewhere in the country.

However, having served the state so well for so long, this strategy is beginning to break down. After years of padding the public sector payroll with hundreds of thousands of young Jordanians, government finances are looking uglier than ever, which has forced periodic reductions in hiring—and might, at some point, require cuts to the existing wage bill. Jordan has one of the ten highest military expenditures in the world relative to GDP, according to the Stockholm International Peace Research Institute (SIPRI). Pointedly, its fiscal health is deteriorating for reasons that include the spiraling cost of sourcing and distributing water.

At the same time, drought, worsened by climate change, is making it ever harder to survive as a herder or farmer, killing even more jobs. Jordan's rainfall, fairly meager to begin with, is projected to shrink by up to 30 percent this century, just as higher temperatures require more water for crops and livestock.[3] The kingdom, its people already subsisting on a fraction of what the UN defines as absolute water scarcity, could be among the first countries to truly run dry. What happens then? "We don't really know," said a Jordan-based water engineer with Mercy Corps, an American aid organization. "Because it has never happened before."*

Given these tough realities, one might expect would-be soldiers to temper their job expectations. That is not the view from rural Jordan, though. Having seen so many of their fathers and big brothers find work in the security services and having noted the unsavory "Rahma-like" alternatives (i.e., no jobs at all), the new generation of villagers expect similar treatment. "It's the army or nothing," a tribal sheikh in Al-Jafr in the center-south said of his sons' future career prospects. The state's

---

* With few alternative natural resources and a fast-growing population, the country is having to bore down up to a mile to tap fast-depleting nonrenewable groundwater stores. All told, Jordanians get by on about 1.2–1.4 billion cubic meters a year, which is about a tenth of what Egypt loses to evaporation from Lake Nasser annually alone.

diminishing capacity to meet this need is contributing to passionate public anger. Already, rural Jordan is raging.

During several long road trips across the south, I saw protesting villagers burn or rip up portraits of the king, a previously unthinkable act of *lèse-majesté* from these longtime royal loyalists. In one instance, a shopkeeper on the outskirts of the historic city of Salt yanked an image of the incumbent Abdullah II from the wall—and stomped on it, all while making sure to leave the accompanying portraits of his late father, the beloved King Hussein, and son, Crown Prince Hussein, untouched. (Though in that case, as in so many others, there was a playacting quality to the outrage. When I returned for a follow-up chat the next day, the shopkeeper had sourced a replacement portrait and reconstructed

Though never well resourced to begin with, Jordan's water availability per capita has plunged to about one-sixtieth of the average in the United States. In communities like this one in the country's south, the taps flow about once a fortnight. Some families, fearful of missing those irregularly timed opportunities to fill their rooftop tanks, delegate a son or daughter to stand watch over taps through the night. (Photo by Susan Schulman)

the sequence of past, present, and future monarchs that dot the walls of so many businesses—and those of all government offices.)

These demonstrators have, at frequent intervals over the years, blocked roads; marched on ministries in Amman, the capital; and congregated outside Hashemite palaces to signal their discontent with the lack of jobs. "Twenty years on the throne, nothing green or dry remains," went one chant directed at Abdullah.[4] Unable to address popular grievances but also unwilling to brook this degree of dissent, the state is turning to deeper political repression in response. This is all bringing Jordan, long spoken of as the "oasis of calm" in a troubled region, to a proverbial crossroads. To inelegantly bastardize Gramsci's famous portent: The old rural model is dying and a new one is struggling to be born. In between, monsters and an awful lot of uncertainty lie.

The Pact

The Jordanian military's entanglement with rural woe is as old as the state itself. No sooner had British officials helped carve out Jordan in 1921 from the wreckage of the vanquished Ottoman Empire and turned it over to the Hashemite family, than the fledgling monarchy set about trying to consolidate control over the area, not all of whose inhabitants were inclined to accept the outsiders' authority. Some of this pacification came out of the barrel of a gun. But, as Jordanian historian Tariq Tell argues, the steady collapse of local Bedouin tribes' way of life in the decades preceding the Hashemites' arrival had created conditions that were ripe for the new kingdom's advance.

First, the opening of the Suez Canal in 1869 had eroded one of the Bedouins' principal businesses, guarding or supervising the passage of camel caravans traveling south through the desert to Mecca and Medina. Then, the completion in 1908 of the Hejaz railway, which dramatically eased travel from Damascus to the Muslim holy sites, consumed much of the rest of that custom. Finally and perhaps pivotally, an extended drought and series of locust infestations from 1926 to 1935 savaged the Bedouins' all-important herds and flocks. Having initially struggled to quell the last tribal holdouts, royal forces ditched the "stick" and instead amalgamated many of these struggling herdsmen and their settled farmer peers into their ranks.

Over time, that mutually beneficial royal–rural relationship only strengthened as the state—and the region around it—shapeshifted dramatically. The fragmentation of the Middle East into a collection of often-hostile actors with harder borders stifled access to prime grazing lands, making pastoralism less and less viable—a precursor of sorts to the Sahelian experience. The expansion of crown authority through the incorporation of Bedouin-manned desert patrols eventually put an end to most raiding. With more nation-states strung across regional rivers, farmers experienced the beginnings of the transboundary water disputes that were soon to greatly muddle their lives. The flow of the Jordan river, for one, has shrunk by about 90 percent over the past century, its waters and those of its tributaries relentlessly depleted by Syria, Israel, and to a certain extent Jordan too.[5]

Most significantly, the wars following the creation of Israel in 1948 and the Arab powers' loss to the Jewish state in the 1967 Six-Day War unleashed waves of Palestinian refugees into Jordan. It was after this period that historians say the monarchy's relationship with the tribes hardened into a kind of unwritten contract. Wary of the new arrivals—and particularly of the largest of their representative bodies, the Palestine Liberation Organization (PLO)—the king drew even more villagers into the forces. When the PLO and the army fought one another across Jordan in 1970, he upped military privileges and pay. When a tank brigade briefly mutinied in 1974, he upped them some more.[6] (Nowadays, people of at least partly Palestinian origin account for more than half of the Jordanian population. Very few of them are represented anywhere in the public sector, and especially not in the security services.) "The argument is that we built this country, we protected you, including at the high tide of Arab nationalism, and particularly against the PLO," Tariq Tell told me. "In return we should be given this entitlement."

The more Jordan's immediate neighborhood balkanized into a series of aggressive dictatorships, including Baathist Syria to the north, whose army invaded in 1970, and Saddam Hussein's Iraq to the east, which threatened to breach the border soon after, the more the monarchy prioritized the welfare and loyalty of its armed forces. "Get along, enrich the troops, and care little about everyone else," Roman emperor Septimus Severus is said to have advised his sons. For a dynasty that had seen its royal counterparts in Egypt toppled in 1952, and its Hashemite cousins, the royal family of Iraq, massacred in 1958, that arguably made sense. Yet not even its more farsighted members could have envisaged how wide-ranging a function that force would serve.

An Environmental Safety Valve

This brings us back to the environment. By all rights, the herders of the Husseiniya area, about a hundred miles south of Amman, "ought" to be deeply impoverished. Many of their sheep, enfeebled by weaker rains and the resulting lack of winter pasture, bleat with hunger. The goats display clear signs of starvation—bleeding eyes, bowed heads. With pitiful milk and meat production to match its poor health, the entire flock has become a money sink, one that is sometimes unable to cover even half its costs. But this is where security salaries have ridden to the rescue for men like Awad Ali. With two brothers in the army and a son in the police, each earning between $900 and $1,800 a month, he and his family have enough income to feed themselves and at least some of their animals. He has little doubt as to what would have become of them all in other circumstances. "We would not be surviving," he said. "And certainly not from the land as our fathers did, as our grandfathers did."

Many farmers can relate. Tucked in the rocky lee of the Dead Sea some 1,300 feet below sea level and among the lowest settlements on Earth, Ghwar al-Safi has always been hot. On one of the occasions I visited, it was 99 degrees Fahrenheit in the shade at 9:00 a.m. By that afternoon, it was 124 degrees Fahrenheit, toasty enough to try frying an egg on the car hood and put the classic heat metaphor to the test. It worked, sort of. . . . Yet, crucially for the locals who depend on cash crops, hot conditions are not only getting hotter but also expanding into previously cooler periods of the year. The lucrative tomato-growing season once started in early September. Now it is generally late October before temperatures relent enough for planting, which means two fewer months for residents to earn badly needed cash. Ali al-Ashoush is one of many to have suffered the consequences.

Down to his last few dinars after his entire tomato crop was charred in 2016, he thought he was going to have to join many of his neighbors in migrating elsewhere. "I was exhausted, too. You have to work late at night and in the early morning to avoid the heat," Ashoush said. He remembers thinking that the sting he sustained in his house from a scorpion that had also sought sanctuary from the heat was a fittingly painful denouement to a three-decade-long farming career. But after calling in a few favors, he too took a step that he had previously resisted and enrolled both his sons into the army. Despite the loss of free labor, it has been enough to tide him over.

Government salaries provide for farming and herding families alike in the face of the country's worsening water crunch, a crisis that hurts all Jordanians but that, because of their generally lower means and higher water needs, strikes rural folk hardest. Detached from the piped water networks that feed urban areas, albeit irregularly in their case too, most villages depend on free or heavily subsidized water tankers. However, reminiscent of Nepal, the amounts delivered are seldom sufficient or distributed on time or of tolerable quality. In their stead, many people must fall back on private tanker operations, which, together with bottled drinking water, absorb up to a third of some villagers' total income. According to Abdullah Fahad Abu Tai, a bottled water vendor in Al-Jafr, you can tell who has money and who does not just by looking at them. "The men whose wives clean their *galabeya* [robe] with bad water look kind of beige," he said. "The men whose wives clean their *galabeya* with good water look white because they keep their color."

In addition to providing for many otherwise optionless rural Jordanians, these security jobs have also offered the country a measure of physical protection. As highlighted in previous chapters, terrorist and other non-state armed groups have frequently feasted off rural areas with weak economic prospects and a strong sense of abandonment. This is only becoming truer across the Middle East as climate and other environmental stresses wring more jobs out of "traditional" livelihoods, while intensifying conflict, some of it also climate-fueled in this grim cyclical web, creates an ongoing appetite for fighters.

Had Jordan not reverse engineered that model by providing a safety valve for many of the bored, struggling young men who have often contributed to instability globally, it might have found itself in the same unhappy boat. "No jobs, no peace," explained one pastoralist outside the Crusader castle town of Kerak. Whether deliberately or not, the state has helped stave off some of the troubles that have ailed its neighbors in Syria and Iraq. And that is all very well and very good. The challenge is, what happens then when that model begins to stutter? No one, it seems, has really thought through that eventuality.

Breach of Contract

For a man who had been so reluctant to meet me that he had thrown up all sorts of improbable-sounding excuses ("Are you sure it's not too wet today?"), Mohammed was surprisingly frank when we eventually sat down to talk in Amman. As a senior officer in the General Intelligence Directorate, he is among those responsible for tracking and tackling internal threats to regime stability in Jordan. On the day we met in early 2023, he made almost no effort to conceal his concern.

After years of steady expansion, his branch of the intelligence apparatus had recently received orders from on high (i.e., the royal court) to stop most hiring. Though Mohammed, whom, I agreed, I would refer to just by his first name, did not specifically say it, he seemed to imply that this was asking for trouble. Coming at the same time as the army and other security services had imposed similar or tighter restrictions, he and his colleagues were prepping for a rural backlash. Sure enough, over the following weeks, many towns and villages, including the one in which locals had theatrically burned a portrait of the king in front of me, convulsed with angry protests. "People need work. They have nothing there, and they expect the state to provide," he said. "So when it doesn't, they are angry. It is rational." Patting his paunch, the size of which is, jokingly or not, considered a sign of seniority among security officials in the Middle East, he then leaned back in his chair and called for another round of teas.

None of this is wholly new to security officials, who have kept a wary eye on these communities, generally also their own, for decades. Since the 1980s at least, rural Jordanians have railed—often in fiery form—against deteriorating living standards. Those grievances have only intensified as the state has centralized more services away from the tribally dominated peripheries to the capital with its Palestinian Jordanian majority, where the "newcomers" are theoretically better placed to enjoy them, and as the cost of living has spiraled. Despite higher-than-average private sector wages, army paychecks have not been enough to keep pace with surging electricity bills for those with air-conditioning and eye-catching generator expenses for people who rely on water pumped from ever-deeper water wells. The years since about 2010 in particular have consequently been characterized by frequent blockades of roads with burning tires and the torching of public buildings, among other protest tactics.

Yet in appearing to renege on one of the principal planks in the royal–rural pact just as farming and herding hits new lows, the monarchy may unwittingly unleash a deeper anger that will not be so easily suppressed. My research in rural Jordan certainly seemed to bear out his angst. In village after village, interviewees spoke of the increasing difficulty of securing public sector employment as a betrayal, one which would legitimize the revocation of their acquiescence to Hashemite rule. "We have nothing because of these conditions. Our sheep are dying," said one herder outside Hasa near the country's geographic center. "And now they remove the jobs that we are owed." Several prospective soldiers decried "Vitamin W"—*wasta*, the connections that they say one now needs to procure whatever security sector roles are still available. On a 2019 visit to the village of Um Seyhoun, on the doorstep of the magnificent archaeological ruins at Petra, I was treated to an especially arresting example of rural indignation.

Arriving days after a number of its residents had been evicted from their souvenir-selling spots within the site, my colleague and I were quickly surrounded by a group of young men desperate to tell their story. Calmly at first and then less so as their emotions bubbled over, they rounded on the state for first refusing them security jobs and then depriving them of the livelihood that they had carved out after the collapse of their herding lifestyle decades ago. One of them brandished a gun to help illustrate his point. A few weeks later, someone in the village shot at an empty tour bus. In the years since then tensions have only escalated, with locals frequently doing battle with the gendarmerie. "We have no loyalty to a state that treats us like this," said a man who gave his name as Ahmed al-Bedu, a herder-cum-tour guide, in a rush of what seemed a lot like youthful braggadocio, but which typified many of my interviewees' responses. "They do not deserve our respect." Leading me to his house just off the main road, Bedu pointed out the sewer that ran open to the elements through the middle of the street, a trickle of shit and trash that reminded me of depictions of medieval European cities. One wrong step, he noted, and "not even ten showers will clean you."

Unsurprisingly, this is all very sensitive stuff for the state, and over several of these reporting trips I received regular reminders of both that touchiness—and of the security services' proficiency in keeping tabs on supposed threats. In one instance, while conducting research for an NGO, my Jordanian colleague took calls roughly every hour from an official who would drop in, not so subtly, that he knew which villages we had just passed through and whom we had interviewed. The idea seemingly being to keep us on our toes. On another occasion, in 2015 near Um Qais along the border with Syria, I was followed by two men with bulges along their hips and jackets that did not flap in the wind. They would pause within earshot as I tried to talk to villagers. Fearful of getting anyone into trouble, I soon cut that visit short.

Much of this rural fury is directed against government ministers, the royal courtiers who are often more powerful than ministers, and against the queen, or "Satan" as one tribal leader referred to her in 2018 and was then quickly arrested.[7] As a woman of Palestinian origin, Queen Rania is accused of advancing "her people's" interests and trying to amalgamate more of them into the public sector at the expense of East Bankers, the area's original inhabitants. Commentators have noted a steady increase in anti–Palestinian Jordanian discourse online, much of it coming from East Bankers in the diaspora.[8] Of late, more of this dissatisfaction is being projected onto King Abdullah II himself. He is perceived as having orchestrated some of the betrayal through his economic liberalization policies. In her book *Protesting Jordan*, academic Jillian Schwedler draws from years of protest attendance to highlight demonstrators' increased willingness to call out or insult the king by name. "This is Jordan. Not a Hashemite Farm!" goes one 2020s protest cry.

Deprived of sufficient water, many Jordanian smallholders are ditching their farms in favor of the security services, if they can secure jobs, or Amman, if they cannot. The north of the country is increasingly dotted with crumbling or abandoned farm infrastructure, some, such as this one, partly repurposed as accommodation by homeless Syrian refugees. (Photo by Susan Schulman)

But, more ominously, many young Jordanians appear to be channeling their emotions into a broader anti-state sentiment that might be best described as a massive middle finger to everyone and everything. Researchers suggest that people are particularly likely to turn to political violence when they lose the capacity to imagine a better tomorrow.[9] The very fact, then, that public trust in government almost halved between 2011 and 2020 ought to worry Amman officials and their foreign backers alike.[10] Strikingly, there is so little trust in the state that many of the farmers I have met over the years genuinely seem to believe that the country is well-endowed with water but that it is simply being stolen or frittered away. (This is not wholly incorrect. Though objectively water-poor, Jordan loses much of what it does have to some 3,000–6,000 illegal wells, many operated by protected agro-interests, according to officials and independent water experts). Observing proceedings from the shadows, security men like Mohammed appear braced for trouble. "It is never an easy time," he said. "But now the threats come from everywhere and the challenges are so many."

The Left Behinds

To visit Jordan as a tourist is to have a very different experience from that described above. You fly into a shiny airport, flounce between the manicured districts of Western Amman, and then drive the neatly tarmacked highways to attractions along the Dead Sea, the Red Sea, Wadi Rum, Petra, and more. Throughout this Jordan, the hospitality and sense of safety are without parallel. (Unlike in, say, Egypt, you can travel Jordan without really seeing how the vast majority live.) But, as rural communities drift deeper into a future with less agriculture and perhaps fewer compensatory security jobs, the already yawning gulf between *their* Jordan and the one which visitors—and affluent Ammanis—speed past is only widening. That malaise is giving rise to another danger, one that is less dramatic, and with fewer international implications than anti-royal feeling, but that is no less painful for those concerned.

Most of this starts with migration.* By all accounts, Udhruh has not been a happening kind of place for a while. Spread across a half dozen rocky hillocks with no shade and a bunch of poorly maintained ruins from the Roman era onward, it appears damned by its off-the-beaten-track location and stifled by its poor-quality soils. On the day I visited, the village seemed suspended between lethargy and listlessness, as quiet in the middle of the day as many places of equivalent size are at the

---

* Globally, rural-to-urban migration is generally discussed in terms of its impact on the receiving "host" communities and on the migrants themselves. But that is to skip over the often painful and sometimes violent consequences for the places they leave behind.

dead of night. But it was not always like this, residents say. With worsening rains and insufficient public sector jobs to go around, much of the population has moved to Amman. As in most of the twenty or so other villages I visited during my research, all of which had lost anywhere from 10 to 50 percent of their people over the previous decade, businesses have struggled to survive their departures. "It is only the poor who remain," said Mohammed Saleh al-Odat, who mans what was, as far as I could see, the village's only open store and who said he no longer stocked anything beyond the bare basics and cheapest brands. "And there are not enough of them, either."

The loss of so many people, many of whom are leading citizens and disproportionately affluent and all of whom are friends of at least some of the "left behinds," is pulling the community apart and fueling the kind of loneliness that my chain-smoking interviewees in Rahma so grimly evinced. Another of those four young men, Hassan, spoke of the difficulty of finding a partner as the pool of eligible suitors shrinks and as his family's poverty undermines their attempts to raise a dowry, which, due to the expectation that the husband will provide a home, furnishings, and jewelry, is generally a male responsibility in the Arab world. "I don't know if I'll ever be able to marry," he said. "This makes me feel like less of a man." At that, he lit yet another cigarette and stared off despairingly into space.

In this ostensibly hopeless void, more of these desperately bored youngsters are turning to any number of dodgy distractions. Most of the alcohol they consume is homemade, since commercially brewed beverages are expensive and hard to find in this conservative hinterland. Much of it is dangerous—and disgusting, packing a sort of treacly, chemically punch that had me dashing to a bathroom when I sampled an interviewee's homebrew near Wadi Rum.

None of it, though, is concerning officials or public health experts as much as Captagon. At a military run hospital a few miles from Petra,

Bassem Nawafleh, the chief nurse, has seen much more of this drug over the past years. Though frequently petitioned for advice by the families of users, he appears to have few ideas on how to handle it. The drug's illegality and the perceived stigma of addiction ensures that patients are often overcome by hallucinations, paranoia, and plenty of other ailments before he gets to examine them. The more the economy stumbles and the more that state-linked enterprises in Syria manufacture Captagon (reportedly on behalf of the Assad regime, which then spirits it over the border by drone, catapult, human mules, and other methods), the more of these cases he sees.[11] "This is a crisis like the opioids in America," Nawafleh said. "It's a crisis that's hidden but still in plain sight."*

There is more petty crime, too. While it is always tricky to pin law-breaking directly on poverty and substance abuse, local security officials and villagers themselves insist that there is a link, particularly since crime used to be very rare. In recent years, these villages have experienced an epidemic of burglary, which has forced many residents to lock their doors for the first time, and of livestock rustling, a growing problem from Syria to Senegal. Several herders in the south told me stories that mirrored what I had heard across the Sahel—of young men on motorbikes stealing scores of area animals each month and selling them to dishonest butchers willing to ignore their telltale branding. A cigarette retailer near Aqaba looked thoroughly put out, almost tearful,

---

* If about 5 percent of the drugs that were muled through Jordan were previously kept in-country for domestic consumption, that figure is now 10–15 percent, according to the Anti-Narcotics Department (AND). "We think that the challenges that youth face, such as unemployment, and the absence of targeted outreach, could mean that they are being exploited by criminal groups," Amjad al-Adarbeh, the Jordan representative of the UN Office on Drugs and Crime, told me. The pattern fits the regional experience. By delivering cheap, easy hits, Captagon and other amphetamine-like drugs have attracted a clientele that stretches from exhausted Cairo bus drivers to laborers working construction sites in 120°F Basra heat—through, reportedly, to ISIS and Hamas fighters. AND seized more than forty-five tons of methamphetamines through the first three quarters of 2022, more than twenty times the volume captured during that period the previous year, per *Washington Post* reporting.

as he explained how he now kept his wares under lock and key following a sequence of thefts.

In earlier times, communities could at least fall back on the connective tissue of family, friends, and tribal bonds to better withstand—and perhaps tackle head-on—these cascading difficulties. But amid the crimewave, with the loss of the village figureheads whom they might ordinarily consult during crises, and in circumstances so dire that many can no longer even afford to entertain guests (and certainly not with water-intensive favorites, such as vine leaves and peppers stuffed with spicy minced meats, which are off the menu for some families), rural Jordan is unraveling. Villagers speak of a nascent culture of lying, some of it perhaps an attempt to preserve appearances despite deeper financial trouble. As described at a different time in a very different place by a newly penniless George Orwell in *Down and Out in Paris and London*, poverty "tangles you in a net of lies, and even with the lies you can hardly manage it. You stop sending clothes to the laundry, and the laundress catches you in the street and asks you why; you mumble something, and she, thinking you are sending the clothes elsewhere, is your enemy for life."[12]

Villagers speak of mushrooming enmities, the petty melodramas that have often been part of clichéd and perhaps real rural life but that are escalating in line with the loss of communal trust. Above all, everyone talks of more individualism, more "bowling alone" in societies once characterized by family visits, tribal gatherings, and ad hoc sociability.[13] And that might ultimately be the biggest problem of all. Research shows that communities with strong social cohesion, a sense of belonging, and faith in authorities are much better placed to withstand trauma—and, by extension, more trying water and wider climate woes.[14] Deprived of their long-standing support networks and with declining confidence in the state and in one another, these fragmented villages face uncertain prospects in the more challenging times to come.

More Water, More Recruiting, More Arrests

Prince Hassan took his time answering my question. It was mid-2019, and I had asked how Jordan might manage the rural fallout from more-intense future climate pressures. The prince is a thoughtful man, and as the king's uncle (and a former crown prince himself) he has been at the coalface of state governance for fifty-something years—so much so that he is one of the few people able to name-drop world leaders he has known throughout an interview and not come across as a self-aggrandizing blowhard as a result. But to this query he initially seemed a bit uncertain, almost reticent, as if recognizing the deficiencies of any response. "Well, we need more water, of course. We all do in this country," he said after a long pause and a fit of throat clearing possibly engineered to buy extra thinking time. "But the farmers need it more than anyone. We must manage that."

If Jordan might be said to have a three-pronged strategy for buttressing its climate-battered countryside, then sourcing more water to sustain whatever agricultural jobs are left is the first tine. In pursuit of that goal, the kingdom is displaying questionable judgment. It is exploiting nonrenewable groundwater so relentlessly that ten of its twelve main aquifers are almost depleted. For example, Amman and the populous secondary cities to its north are mostly supplied through a pipeline from the Disi aquifer in the country's southeast. But no one seems entirely clear on where to turn when that store is exhausted over the coming decade or two, or, at a governmental level at least, especially interested in patching the leaky pipes that squander much of the precious water it does extract. In the meantime, security services have had to deploy drones and other monitoring technology to protect that infrastructure from villagers irate that the pipeline bisects their parched lands without providing for their needs. Around Al-Jafr, locals have sabotaged the system on more than a dozen occasions since construction began in 2009.[15]

Jordan is building out more desalination capacity as well, an approach that many officials across the Middle East invoke as a kind of silver bullet, but one that, among many other pitfalls, will do little for farmers. Nowhere in the world is the cost of desalinated water low enough to justify its use in thirsty fields, and certainly not in Jordan, where most farmland is far to the north of, and uphill from, the country's short Red Sea coastline—and where the expense of extracting water from such depths and then distributing it far and wide has already saddled the exchequer with debilitating debts. About 15 percent of all electricity goes to the water sector; the Ministry of Finance has frequently had no choice but to shovel money at the state water body.[16] Still, as in so many other regions, "the state is not interested in small, decentralized solutions [like improved efficiency measures or reining in illegal well boring]," says Samer Talozi, a top Jordanian water expert. "They only want megaprojects."*

Most controversially, among Jordanians, the kingdom is developing deeper water ties with Israel. This is a story of relative success, one centered on mutually beneficial resource swaps—and it holds some promise for farmers, the biggest concentration of whom are in the frontier-spanning Jordan River valley. "We have to look outside Jordan," said Ali Subah, the secretary-general for strategic planning at the Ministry of Water and Irrigation at the time of our last meeting, who has since been accused of corruption and removed from his post. "There are no more water resources here." Yet the arrangement with Israel is deeply unpopular with a population of mostly Palestinian origin. Besides, experts

---

* Jordan's limited natural resources have arguably been as overtaxed by mismanagement as by climate-induced drought or overextraction of river water over the borders. The country's water sector has become so riddled with holes—and corruption—that about 50 percent of piped supply is lost to leakage and theft. Despite massive infusions of targeted donor cash in recent decades, it remains that way, with large additional quantities of groundwater also disappearing into the farms of politically connected elites—and, according to Jordanian analysts, those of the king himself.

say, none of these initiatives will yield enough water for a country that is on track for near-universal critical water insecurity by 2100 without drastic action—and whose water-needy agrarians must, by any metric, lose out most and first.[17] Indeed, villagers continue to ditch their livelihoods apace.

Stubborn but not stupid, the state appears alive to these realities, and it is to this end that Amman may double down on rural military recruitment after all, the second of the three prongs. Despite the weighty existing public sector payroll and corresponding fiscal woe, officials in 2020 mooted the possibility of rolling out mandatory one-year military service for all men between the ages of twenty-five and twenty-nine. They have already taken on small trial groups.[18] At the same time, Jordan is outsourcing troops to Arab Gulf states. These countries generally struggle to attract sufficient domestic recruits, and they all prize Jordanian soldiers for their professionalism and generally Sunni Arab profiles.[19] In this, the current cohort are beating a well-trodden path. From training up the new Saudi army in the 1950s, through to helping suppress uprisings in Oman in the 1970s and in Arab Spring–era Bahrain, well-drilled Jordanians have been deployed by more regimes than just their own.[20]

Ultimately, the end game here is as unclear as official Jordanian water policy. Like "an army with a state attached," as has been said of eighteenth-century Prussia, Jordan risks greater trouble the more its military, or perhaps more accurately, the military elite, swells into private enterprise and claims scarcer public funds at the expense of other needs. Already, retired military and other security personnel enjoy a range of perks, including a monopoly on cabs from Amman airport—and, in the case of palace cronies, access to their share of water-guzzling industrial farming operations.[21] Education and health services are collapsing under the weight of underinvestment and additional climate-induced shocks. But in a region that looks to be getting messier with every bout of warming, bloated militaries appear here to stay. (As some observers have put it, the world is not ignoring climate change. It is just gearing up for the conflicts and harsher political terrain that they envisage arising out of it).

Finally, though generally left (publicly) unsaid within the country, there is the third prong—repression. With a rural economy that continues to deteriorate much faster than the state can source additional water or hike employment to desired levels, Jordan may be running out of runway with the first two approaches. In recent years, as public and particularly rural anger over services and job prospects has mounted, those swollen security services have cracked down on dissent more than any point since the 1980s. Favored protest spots, including the traffic circle outside the Prime Ministry, have been closed off or encased in concrete barriers designed to obstruct large gatherings. When protests do occur—and occur outside the neatly choreographed routines that Jillian Schwedler describes in her book and that police generally accept—state blowback can be profound; thousands have been arrested in villages and towns alone over the past decade. Amid a general hardening of anti-monarchy, and particularly "anti-Abdullah feeling," says historian Tariq Tell, the government tabled a new law in the summer of 2023 that could apply to online discourse the same tight censorship that it does to other forms of expression.

Speaking on the sidelines of a conference in a European capital in 2022, a fruit smoothie in one hand and a double-chocolate brownie in the other, a senior Jordanian talking head insisted to me that rural peoples in his country understand that their troubles are not of the state's making. "The shortage of water is not in the hands of the government," he said. "This is in the hands of God. People recognize this and do not blame anyone." But word—and deed—on the "village street" suggest otherwise. Something has surely got to give.

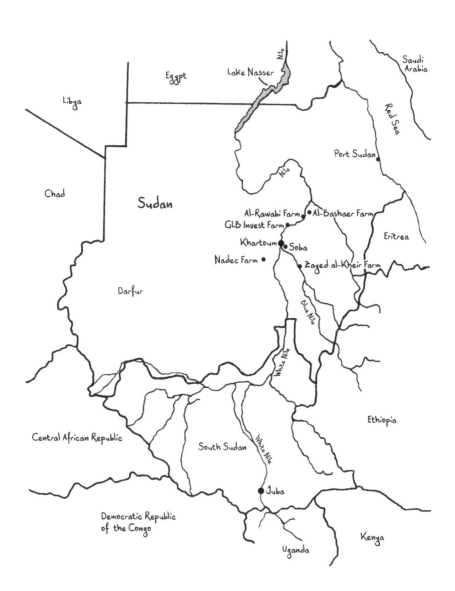

CHAPTER 7

Hunger Games[1]

Having exhausted their own water, rich nations are
seeking food in poor ones, like Sudan. Cue chaos.

WHEN THE JORDANIAN ARMY WENT SHOPPING for land in northern Sudan in late 1999, its scouts came across what appeared to be a
food-growing paradise. The terrain was flat, fat with nutrients, and
abundant. The water it could draw from the nearby Nile was almost
embarrassingly bountiful. And local officials were bending over back-
ward to offer favorable financial terms. It all seemed like a can't-miss
opportunity to supplement Jordan's national food supply while turning
a quick buck. The military pension fund duly snapped up nine thousand acres of backcountry scrub three hours' drive north of Khartoum,
and the farmhands got to work.

Soon afterward, as news of potential riches spread, the surrounding
land began filling up. A Pakistani company leased a large plot to the
south. Syrians began farming to the north. In what seemed like no time,
Emiratis, Qataris, Yemenis, and others had acquired 100,000-plus acres
apiece. The main north–south highway grew so clogged with food destined for those countries' home ports that bored kids in one roadside
village even made a game of it. One point for every truck with animal fodder; two for anything else. "There's good soil, enough water,

sunshine, everything you need to grow a lot of crops," says Abdelazim al-Jak, a Khartoum native who now manages Al-Bashaer, the Jordanian farm. "It shouldn't be a surprise that everyone wants it."

That clamor for Sudanese farmland only accelerated over the following years, reeling in even bigger—and more varied—investors. In 2016, the Saudi government leased one million acres of arable land in the east of the country. Then, Bahrain requested and received 100,000 acres, a plot almost as large as the island kingdom itself. Before villagers across River Nile and Northern states knew it, everyone from Egyptian venture capitalists to the Middle East's biggest paint producer had muscled in on the farming sector. All told, the Sudanese government distributed at least five million acres to foreign investors between 2005 and 2017. By one measure, 9 percent of all land in South Sudan, which is about the size of Texas and was part of Sudan until it seceded in 2011, had been allotted to foreign or domestic agricultural investors in the years leading up to independence.[2]

Initially, people in parts of the country had looked on with wary optimism. Perhaps these firms would provide jobs at a time when their own agricultural efforts were spluttering badly due to climate and ecological stresses? Better yet, perhaps the foreigners' arrival would spur the road and other infrastructural improvements that rural Sudan so badly needs—and from which they too might benefit? But as the farms began to take shape, that vague hope vanished like a fart in the wind. The land that the government distributed to Arab investors was seldom empty. It was often villagers' own private or communally held land! The agribusinesses had little interest in employing locals, and, as many villages found to their dismay, often even less inclination to leave them sufficient water for their own purposes. With allocations as vast as those in some of the most sought-after stretches of the Nile valley, it soon seemed that they were living in someone else's country. "You could walk hundreds of kilometers without stepping on Sudanese-owned land," says Khaled

Khairallah, a herder in Wad al-Habashi, a village to the south and across the river from Al-Bashaer. "What is left for us?"

As the impact of the mega-farms became clearer—and locals pushed back, the state and some of its agribusiness partners got nasty. I learned of at least a dozen deaths, though that might be tip-of-the-iceberg stuff given the isolation and hush-hush nature of many of these operations, and many reports of beatings, severe injuries, and unlawful detentions. I heard claims of livestock killings by mega-farm operators, with one cow's head allegedly placed, "*Godfather*-style," outside a campaigning villager's door. It was a bloody message, said a village imam in North Kordofan state, a warning not to meddle with the business's bottom line. Predictably, perhaps, none of this had the desired effect. Over several trips to Sudan in the run-up to the revolution of 2019, I noticed how anti-agribusiness rage was steadily merging with a rash of other grievances.

As one farmer in Gezira state, a little to the south of Khartoum, told me after the loss of some of his fields to an Emirati agribusiness, "we'll protest until we're dead or we get our way." Events were to bear out his fighting talk.

Vast Resources, Vast Need

This is what a global "land grab" can look like, and though it might resemble an undignified free-for-all, there is a method to (some of) the madness. The Gulf Arab countries from which most of the big agribusinesses operating in Sudan originate have lots of money, but little water or arable land. The Nile basin state theoretically has the inverse. In what has long been presented as an almost glove-like strategic fit, the two parties have repeatedly tried to provide for one another's needs since the 1970s.

Much of this new scramble for Africa is rooted in a mutual pursuit of profit. Crops such as alfalfa and other types of animal fodder command high prices and are too water-intensive to grow in many countries. This has incentivized agribusiness, while authorities in Khartoum have mismanaged their way into penury, leaving them forever in pursuit of external revenue streams. A lot of these deals boil down to hard-nosed geopolitics. After Sudan reduced ties with Iran, the Gulf States' key regional rival, in 2014, authorities in Riyadh rewarded it by pushing Saudi investment, including investment in agriculture. They rewarded Sudan some more when the regime of then-dictator Omar al-Bashir committed up to fifteen thousand troops to fight in the Saudi- and Emirati-led war in Yemen from 2016 onward.

"We have vast resources, and they have vast need," said Mubarak al-Fadil, Sudan's minister of investment and deputy prime minister, when I interviewed him in 2018. His massive office was decked out with armchairs so overstuffed that my feet would have dangled a foot off the ground had I not perched gingerly on the edge. "We just need their finance and expertise."

But in snaffling foreign farmland, the Saudis, Emiratis, Qataris, and others are also displaying something of a *reaction* to climate change at a time when warming temperatures threaten to upend their entire economic and societal modus vivendi. Having long ago lost the capacity to feed themselves as their populations have boomed and their meager water resources dissipated, authorities in Riyadh, Abu Dhabi, and other regional capitals have fallen back on international markets to buy the vast majority of their food. And that should be fine. Dozens of stable states, the United Kingdom and Japan among them, rely on imports for up to half of their food. If nothing else, wealthy petrostates are going to be less put off by higher grain prices than others.

Yet, in the case of the Gulf powers, the scale of their dependence on imported grain, their experience of past barriers to trade, and, crucially, their fear of much greater climate-induced stoppages to come has induced a particular wariness. It is, as an Emirati agribusinessman put it to me, a question of trust, and in a polarized, increasingly unpredictable world they see that as a scarce commodity. "If you're India and you're suffering from a mega drought, you're just not going to export anything," he said in 2020, inadvertently prophesying Delhi's Covidera crop export bans. These countries have consequently sought direct control of their own crop production in geographically accessible and politically pliable countries, like Sudan, as a partial substitute.

Additionally, very slowly and with varying degrees of unhappy foot-dragging, the fossil-fuel-flush Gulf states may be readying themselves for a world that will have less need of their oil and gas—and perhaps none at all. Hence, they are deploying their current riches to snap up farmland or acquire everything from English Premier League soccer clubs to new electric car, green hydrogen, and video games

On the periphery of a Saudi Nadec farm in Sudan's North Kordofan state, locals, this father and young son among them, say that they have been robbed of their pasture. (Photo by Nichole Sobecki)

industries, assets that they think will leave them well placed to build new economies.[3] Again, Sudan—with its largely untapped potential (or, more appropriately, the perception of it) and track record of ostensibly accommodating every investor demand—has often seemed like a strong bet. "We absolutely look at Sudan as the answer to our problems," said a senior Saudi dairy executive in 2018. Like many others interviewed on this subject, he would not agree to be named for fear of imperiling important relationships. "It's 350 kilometers away. It should make economic sense."

A Fixture of the Future?

Were most of these deals to be as mutually advantageous as their proponents suggest, there would not be much of a story. But, as in Sudan, many global transactions have been carried out so clumsily by mostly nondemocratic leaders with little apparent regard for the welfare of those who live on or near allocated land that they have caused more harm than good. Across Africa in particular, state-backed and private investors have exploited resource bounty and poor governance, often to destabilizing effect. In 2009, a deal to turn over several million acres of Madagascar's best farmland to a Korean firm contributed to the violent fall of the government.[4] In the few years after that, Saudi rice-growing projects in western Ethiopia sparked tit-for-tat killings between farm guards and displaced Anuak people, all adding to the climate of intense unease that I found around the Grand Ethiopian Renaissance Dam (GERD).[5]

Even within the United States, itself sometimes accused of corporate agricultural marauding abroad, foreign land investments are making waves. Taking advantage of exceptionally permissive laws in Arizona and other Western states, Saudi and Emirati agribusinesses are sapping nonrenewable groundwater to grow fodder for their big, hungry dairy and beef herds. As drought intensifies and the aquifers empty under pressure from spongelike crops, community fury is deepening.*

The total amount of global farmland under foreign state or corporate ownership is as uncertain as the number of Bangladeshi pirates or Iraqi farmers-cum-jihadists—and what we do know paints a muddled picture. According to the World Bank, there were more than 120 million acres' worth of global land deals in 2008 and 2009 alone, two-thirds of which were in sub-Saharan Africa, yet only a fraction of that land seems to have been cultivated.[6] Not all of the deals were concluded with terms inequitable enough to be described as "land grabbing," a highly charged term. Food security experts frequently push back against some of the more sensationalist coverage of these deals, suggesting that their knock-on effects have been blown wildly out of proportion.

However, while these foreign mega-farms are indeed widely perceived as having failed, even the smallest, least successful ones have often exacted a toll far out of proportion to their size. Why? The extreme lack of transparency on the part of agribusiness can be as problematic as the forced displacements themselves. Through deliberate disinformation and run-of-the-mill misunderstandings, people can come to think that foreign agribusinesses have acquired bigger patches of land and with greater direct consequence for their lives than they actually have. A conversation with a minibus driver in the northern Sudanese Nile-side city of Atbara, a historic railway hub and center of union activity, brought that disconnect home to me. While wolfing down our breakfasts at the same bus depot eatery, Mansour al-Mahdi talked me through his impression of the foreign-owned farms that now ring the city. "All day I drive past fields producing food for other countries and then I go home

---

* The volume of American farm and forest land owned by foreign investors stood at a little over forty million acres in 2022, a 9 percent increase on the previous year, but still only about 3 percent of all privately held farmland. According to National Public Radio reporting, Canadians are by far the biggest investors, owning a total area about the size of West Virginia.

and my wife says she cannot buy any meat because it is so expensive," he said between dunks of bread into piping hot *fuul*, a fava bean stew that is a staple of many Middle Eastern and Sudano-Egyptian breakfasts. "This is our best land. How can it not hurt us?"

Most importantly, land grabbing may yet have another moment in the sun, despite past disappointments. As climate change intensifies, more states are waking to the possibility of disrupted supply chains in the more politically and economically fraught environment that a warming world will likely bring. They are consequently reacting in ways that, through either ignorance or general disinterest in the well-being of others, are almost predestined to spark violence elsewhere. We may see this in the pursuit in poor countries of some of the rare-earth materials needed to decarbonize our economies, as discussed in the next chapter. We see this among some well-meaning initiatives to protect globally vital chunks of woodland through reserves, many of which—from Nepal to central Africa—have been created without the buy-in of the local peoples who depend on those areas.

Sudan's experience shows how one country's climate adaptation can be another's immiseration—and can ultimately prompt as much, if not more, violence as the climate stress itself. With more governments running scared, it seems reasonable to expect more "beggar thy neighbor" approaches, even among those who feel they are doing good. "I think the problem is: Why are these people investing here? Are they coming just to take the land and water? That's not investment, that's rape," said Osama Daoud Abdellatif, Sudan's richest man and himself a bigtime agricultural investor. "We've got to get the formula right."

Oil, Oil Everywhere but Not a Drop to Drink

The seeds of Gulf Arab interest in Sudanese farmland far predate public awareness of climate change—and, like so much in the region's recent history, they are mostly grounded in oil. Before that boom really got going, the Arabian Peninsula's population was small and poor and its food requirements correspondingly limited. Two-thirds of Saudis were still nomadic and mostly self-sufficient as late as 1953; Kuwait had so little freshwater access that it imported boatloads of river water from neighboring Iraq until 1950.[7] When oilmen arrived in Bahrain in the 1920s, sinking exploratory wells into the island sands, its king initially appeared more interested in their capacity to dig for water than any kind of energy resource. On striking water, "the grateful ruler rewarded [them] with an oil concession," writes Daniel Yergin in *The Prize*, a history of the oil industry.[8]

But as the revenues began to flood in, these fledgling and, in some instances, newly independent states transformed at an almost dizzying speed. First, their populations exploded, unshackled as they now finally were from the limitations of the land. The United Arab Emirates (1950 population: 70,000) started its precipitous climb to its current nine million people and change. Qatar, too, swelled faster than perhaps any other country on Earth. It might only have enough "naturally occurring water resources" to sustain about fourteen thousand people, roughly 0.5 percent of its numbers these days.[9] Some of this growth was organic, but much of it was a function of intense in-migration from poor countries to build, service, and operate these exploding economies. Remember those grand Bangladeshi village houses—and, for that matter, those in rural Nepal, Senegal, and Sudan?

Then, as the world around them became thoroughly hooked on their wares over the following decades, the oil producers started to flex their new financial muscles to geopolitical ends. After the United States and other Western countries came to Israel's aid in the 1973 Yom Kippur War, the Arab states implemented an oil boycott in a bid to strangle Washington and its allies into submission. But they had not seemingly reckoned with their own acute resource vulnerability. Flummoxed and desperate to stave off economic disaster, the Nixon administration initially mooted a retaliatory food embargo. "We freeze, they starve," went a popular contemporary slogan.[10] Although that initiative was quickly rejected as unworkable and even immoral, the very possibility that it could have been unleashed just as the Gulf states had become wholly dependent on foreign food sparked deep unease among the monarchies. They resolved to use that immense new oil wealth to do something about it.

At home, the Saudis and, to a lesser extent, their smaller neighbors swiftly carved a globally significant agricultural sector out of proverbial thin air. By persistently tapping groundwater and rolling out vast subsidy programs, Saudi Arabia bolstered its annual wheat output to 148,000 tons by 1981 and then to more than four million tons by 1995, morphing, improbably, into the world's sixth biggest wheat exporter by the early 1990s.[11] The UAE, in turn, increased agricultural land from less than 200 acres in the 1960s to around 170,000 acres in the early 2000s.[12] For years, those flying over the Arabian Peninsula were met with the incongruous sight of traffic-light-green fields arrayed across hundreds of miles of desert. Even now, with significantly less farmland below, I sometimes watch confused passengers triple checking their inflight maps, convinced that their eyes—or the screens—are deceiving them.

At the same time, the Gulf States and some of their Levantine and North African peers looked to maximize production in regional states that had greater food-growing potential but also profiles that, during this period of peak Arab nationalism, were perceived as more politically reliable. Enter Sudan, endowed with a large, and at that point mostly unused, share of the Nile's waters, and which was keen (at a state level, at least) to embrace the Arab part of its complex identity.

As Eckart Woertz expertly narrates in *Oil for Food*, these waves of Gulf Arab interest in the 1970s and early '80s promised much and delivered some. There were mega projects, such as the mostly Kuwaiti-backed

Kenana sugar factory that functions to this day, and an expansion of the 2.2-million-acre Gezira Scheme, a British colonial-era agricultural project between the Blue and White Niles which is Africa's largest irrigation works. There were a whole bunch of symbolic flourishes too. In 1972, the Arab League established an agricultural organization in Khartoum to manage the expected influx of Arab farmers, Arab capital, and Arab businessmen. According to (ex-) Minister Al-Fadil, Sudan's northern neighbor all but sabotaged it, mindful of yet another upstream threat to "its" river. "The management of this fund was Egyptian, and they didn't want it to succeed," he said. The building still stands alongside the airport, its air-conditioning units whirring to keep employees doing who knows what nice and cool.

But as Sudan ran into repeated trouble in the 1980s, including a debilitating drought and two regime changes, that momentum wavered and then stalled. The "dream" seemed as battered as most of its centerpiece projects. (To pass through the Gezira Scheme over the past decade or two has been to marvel at its size—and lost potential. You drive for tens of miles through fields of exceptional richness, all of them arrayed along a gentle slope which draws water through its irrigation canals by gravity from the Blue Nile. However, after years of subpar maintenance the canals and hydraulic gates are jammed with sediment; many of the fields are untilled and devoid of farmers even at the height of planting season.)

Jihadi Intermission

Through the 1990s, the two parties largely lost interest in one another. Sudan became a global pariah under the Islamist administration that seized power in 1989—and then later struck oil in meaningful amounts for the first time, reducing state interest in agricultural investment. Gulf food security concerns diminished as the Saudi wheat sector surged and the promise of an "eternal peace" at the end of the Cold War reduced fears of market turmoil. (Even if, as Woertz notes, UN sanctions against Saddam's Iraq in the 1990s may have reminded the Gulf monarchies of their defenselessness were they to ever to fall afoul of global powers.) However, amid Sudan's international isolation, one man kept the notion of a food-self-sufficient Arab World alive. One man continued to pour millions into the country's farmland. That man was none other than Osama Bin Laden, a then largely unknown jihadi ideologue.

After moving to Sudan in 1992, the well-heeled son of Saudi Arabia's top construction tycoon quickly took up where the state-backed agribusinesses had left off, amassing land holdings of well over a million acres within two years. Some of this he bought, repurposing chunks of it as militant training grounds for the attacks he later helped perpetrate against the US embassies in Kenya and Tanzania. Much of this land he accepted as recompense for the infrastructural projects he built for the cash-strapped government, including the now heavily potholed north–south highway over which truckloads of alfalfa currently roll en route to Port Sudan. All of it, his contemporaries say, Bin Laden oversaw with the nitpicking touch of a micromanaging executive.

At his countryside retreat at Soba, just outside Khartoum and in the shadow of the new US embassy, Bin Laden grew fruits and vegetables for personal consumption, kept chickens, and picnicked with his children alongside the adjacent Blue Nile. As I picked my way through the remains of the estate, I wondered what he might have made of the piles of trash, beer bottles among them, that litter his old orchards. I amused myself speculating as to how he might have reacted to the young couples from the nearby medical school, many of whom snatch kisses in the hedgerows that the jihadi kingpin had planted to keep the surrounding sands at bay.*

---

* Bin Laden's main home in Khartoum's Riyadh neighborhood is in altogether much better shape. Flanked by high walls and with curiously well-tended fruit trees visible through the

But though Bin Laden appears to have derived such pleasure from farming that he reportedly bragged to Sudanese ministers that his massive sunflowers were worthy of inclusion in the *Guinness Book of World Records*, his calculus was not radically different from that of the Saudi state he had rejected.[13] With its bountiful water and arable land (or, again, the appearance of such), Sudan was perfectly placed to feed the wider Muslim world, he felt. As late as 2010, Bin Laden chastised Sudan in video messages from his Pakistani hideout for leaving so much land "idle."[14] In *The Looming Tower*, Lawrence Wright describes how Sudan-era Al-Qaeda "had become largely an agricultural organization."[15] If only it had remained that way. . . .

System Failure

By the early 2000s, the Gulf States appeared to have largely fulfilled their food security ambitions. Saudi Arabia was still producing almost all of its own wheat. Across the wider Middle East, trade in foodstuffs was ticking along so nicely that the region was every year importing another Nile River's worth of "virtual water," that is, the amount of water needed to grow the crops and other products from abroad that people consume.[16]

But although some of the signs of impending trouble had been obvious for a while, Gulf authorities seemed to have been caught unawares as that carefully constructed food-security edifice collapsed like a deflated soufflé over the first decade of this millennium. Hydrologists had warned that the aquifers on which almost the entirety of the Arabian Peninsula's agricultural sector was based were vanishing fast. Having exhausted roughly the equivalent of Lake Erie's contents since the 1970s, over 80 percent of their groundwater, the Saudis—and their neighbors—had to

---

iron gate, it appears just about big enough to have housed the three wives and roughly one dozen children he then had.

hastily rein in most domestic crop production.[17] By 2016, up to a third of Abu Dhabi's 24,000 farms had been abandoned.[18] To visit places like the UAE's Liwa oasis now is to see abandoned farm machinery and sand-blown crop pivots, some now five miles out into the desert.

Severe climate woes also began to bite, bringing into sharper focus the difficulties and costs of growing almost anything, water or no water, in these parts. In one of those twists that repeatedly crop up in climate discourse, these countries at the very heart of global fossil fuel production are also reeling from some of the most inhospitable conditions (even if widespread access to air-conditioning tempers the horror). Kuwait has experienced what might be the highest-ever recorded temperature, about 143 degrees Fahrenheit. Emirati authorities counsel against leaving aerosols in cars during summer for fear of explosions.[19] The cattle herds that form the core of the region's enormous dairy sector require millions of dollars in cooling costs simply to survive.

In this, the Gulf states are suffering from early attempts to diversify their economies. Having established the dairy industry back in the febrile 1970s, they must now sustain the fantastically hungry beasts— and the jobs that depend on the export of hundreds of millions of liters of milk every year, more than Germany—in an environment that is ever-less-conducive to their well-being. It means millions of tons of alfalfa, that water-guzzling crop but one that businesses appreciate for its high "bang for the buck" nutrition and that farmers love because of the speed at which it grows and the prices it commands. Simply put, "agriculture is not sustainable here, and that's why we're looking in other countries," said Najieb Khoory, the head of Mirak Group, when we spoke in 2016. The company grows strawberries, mushrooms, and cherries in warehouse-like greenhouses on Dubai's desert periphery. "The water is nothing. It just trickles."[20]

Exacerbating that rising sense of panic, international markets wobbled badly at more or less the exact time as domestic food production cratered, sparking a devastating and essentially ongoing loss of faith in the system's reliability. In 2007–2008, the world was struck by a perfect storm of drought-induced harvest failures, rising oil prices, and the increased use of some grains for biofuel production, among a bevy of other challenges. Major food producers, such as Russia, responded by enforcing restrictions on the export of key foodstuffs. This was the stuff of nightmares for Gulf rulers, who wondered if there might come a point when food was not available for love or any amount of money. That concern only intensified as the food crisis spiraled into global unrest, from Haiti, where the prime minister was overthrown, to at least a dozen African states, reigniting royal fears over their own longevity in a part of the world where the fortunes of governing classes have often risen and fallen with food accessibility.

"Agriculture is like high blood pressure," said an advisor to former Egyptian president Hosni Mubarak, who must himself have been acutely aware of the peril of food prices in light of their likely part in his 2011 demise. "If untreated, it becomes a silent killer for the ruling classes."[21] Glancing desperately around, Gulf powers once more hit upon the prospect of growing food in friendly, better-resourced neighboring states. Sudan was back in vogue.

Back to Sudan

Since the previous waves of foreign farming, Sudan had stumbled from one crisis to another, its president wanted by the International Criminal Court, and the country under sanctions for harboring Bin Laden until the mid-1990s, among other reasons. Brand-hungry Khartoumites had to make do with the likes of Starbox coffee and Kafory Fried Chicken. But from a Gulf perspective, this deprivation was not an entirely bad thing. Bashir's regime was so eager for any kind of funding following the loss of South Sudanese oil revenues from 2011—and the sharp decline

in domestic agriculture due to its neglect throughout the petro-boom—
that the land allocations and water shares were more generous than ever.
The country soon experienced its biggest and most controversial slew of
foreign land acquisitions to date.

Over various trips to the country between 2015 and 2019, I visited
six foreign-owned mega-farms— as many as cagey executives and jumpy
guards would allow. The appeal to agribusiness was always obvious. At
the Lebanese-owned GLB Invest farm, about a hundred miles north of
Khartoum, lush alfalfa fields rise from the desert like great green mirages,
their gleaming new irrigation systems extending for miles along the west
bank of the Nile. The farm's monster pumps inhale enough Nile every
half hour to fill an Olympic-size swimming pool, propelling it inland
through a subterranean pipe network. When, roughly every thirty days,
crops are ready for harvest, they are packed into neat rectangular bales,
stacked with shiny John Deere equipment, and loaded onto trucks for
the seven-hour drive to Port Sudan, midway along the country's roughly
five-hundred-mile-long Red Sea coast between Egypt and Eritrea.
Within days, the alfalfa is feeding cows in Dubai. "It's really quite an
operation," said Khalid Kahin, GLB's general manager, when we met
following a trip to his farm. "You see why we're all excited, right?"

After scrambling up a towering stack of bales to get a better view, I
certainly understood his delight. The fields extend for so many miles
into the desert that one farmhand told me he waited for darkness and
fired off a flare to indicate his whereabouts when his car died in a cell-
phone-signal-less corner of the estate.

Kahin, a jovial businessman who spoke in carefully considered Brit-
ish-accented clips, typified the enthusiasm that many agribusiness executives expressed back then. But much of that buzz could only really
be captured in raw statistics. GLB's water allocation was enormous
and free: 900 million cubic meters of river water a year, roughly half
the amount Lebanon and its more than five million inhabitants use

annually. Land leases were cheap (often less than 50¢ per acre), long (generally 99 years), and, again, enormous (GLB had 226,000 acres). Importantly, given the chaos to come, GLB and most of its peer enterprises were also able to take advantage of state protection.

On one occasion, soldiers seconded from Sudan's security forces took umbrage with my colleagues and me as we interviewed villagers about the impact of the farm that they were guarding, Saudi's Nadec holding in North Kordofan. We soon found ourselves scrambling through the desert to get away, the car's tires struggling mightily in the soft sand, and then took a circuitous route to bypass police checkpoints on the lone paved road back to the outskirts of Khartoum.

Sudan's generosity toward deep-pocketed investors was all thoroughly par for the course. A former manager of a now-defunct Egyptian operation says his company was granted about 750 million cubic meters of the Nile around the time of the global food price spike, a volume of water that he estimated would have set the company back about $1 billion a year elsewhere. An operations manager for Rajhi, an enormous Saudi business with grants of land in Northern State that extended 120 kilometers by 50 kilometers, bragged to me that the entire project would pay back its costs in just two years. "If you do it right, agriculture here is a piece of cake," Mohammed Azhari said. "The margins are just incredible." Some of the prices need to be heard to be believed. In South Sudan, a Texas-based company secured 1.5 million acres for 49 years for $25,000, before a public outcry forced officials to reconsider.[22]

Welcoming me into his office at the Investment Ministry for a second interview, Deputy Prime Minister Mubarak al-Fadil was at pains to justify the generosity of government terms. "Sudan is a unique economy. It defies all norms," he said. "They are taking a high risk, so we give them a high reward." And he was not wholly wrong about that. Rules and regulations are subject to such sudden change that local officials sometimes double or even triple tolls on their section of the highway to the sea

Arrayed across thousands of acres of Sudanese desert just inland from the Nile, the Lebanese-owned GLB Invest farm produces a wealth of water-intensive alfalfa for the Gulf market. (Photo by Nichole Sobecki)

overnight. US sanctions complicated the import of some farm machinery and the export of earnings—until they were lifted in 2017, though banks continue to shy away from Sudan-related transactions. Then there is the corruption. Sudan has routinely ranked near the bottom of Transparency International's Corruption Perceptions Index—170th out of 176 countries in 2016, and bribes are still often the only way to obtain timely approval of paperwork, according to several agribusiness executives.

"Put it this way: Gulf investors don't take out political-risk insurance with us, because they're already protected at the highest level," an official at a regional development bank said. But in doling out so much land on such favorable terms, there was one obstacle that neither the regime nor its Gulf partners had seemingly fully reckoned with. As it turned out, it was that people-shaped problem on which these efforts would ultimately founder.

The Gathering Storm

From the moment the Emirati company Anhar broke ground on its new farm, the elders of Mahas village had a feeling they were going to get screwed. For months in early 2005, they had watched nervously as the forty-thousand-acre Zayed al-Kheir project took shape along the northern fringe of their village in Gezira state. And for months, as infrastructure started going up, they had sought and received assurances they would not lose access to any of their land. But one mild spring morning, when they escorted their camels to the usual grazing ground and found the way blocked by hastily erected coils of razor wire, they knew their worst fears had been realized. "Everything that we own was taken from us," says Osman Abbas Mohammed, chairman of the local agricultural association, as his neighbors nodded sadly in assent. "Our fathers and our fathers' fathers used this land. Now we have been left with empty hands." (Anhar did not respond to multiple requests for comment.)

Bashir's government consistently claimed that foreign agricultural investment would be a boon for all Sudanese after their years in the economic wilderness. The view from the countryside is that it is anything but. The land that the state distributed was not empty, contrary to government declarations. (Under a 1970 law, most undocumented land belongs to the state, a convenient provision for the government, since communities often do not have paperwork to establish traditional, centuries-old claims.) Promised compensation seldom, if ever, arrived. With the regime having freed agribusinesses from a long-standing requirement that they employ Sudanese workers, many preferred to fly in more "politically reliable" Egyptians or Pakistanis instead. There were not even jobs for locals to partially offset the loss of land.

In the case of Mahas and thousands of other villages, the impact of these mega-farms on their own food security was often immediately tangible. Residents lost swathes of the land they had used to grow vegetables for themselves and fodder for their livestock during the rainy season. That forced them to purchase animal feed that they could barely afford—and strip their own diets of all but the most basic foodstuffs. Others told me that they had stopped planting up their fields for fear of spending what little they had on seeds and fertilizers and then receiving nothing in return if their property was filched. Still others lost the capacity to grow anything even if they retained control of their land.

AlRawabi for Development, a Saudi-Yemeni company with more than 200,000 acres in River Nile state, pumped water from the aquifer under its property so aggressively that it ran every well in the area dry, including those servicing neighboring villages. Instead of being punished, the business entered into talks with the government to dig a canal and extract water directly from the Nile. (AlRawabi, too, did not respond to requests for comment.) Sudanese scholars saw all of this as the natural, if bitter, upshot of regime policy. "It's rational. The Saudis ran out of water, so they're now basically offshoring their polluting industries to countries that don't care about the costs," said Omer Egemi, a professor at the University of Khartoum, referring to businesses' clamor for alfalfa in Sudan around the time that their own countries had outlawed its cultivation at home.

His words brought to mind an encounter with an amusingly foul-mouthed farmer near the pyramids of Meroe in 2016. Having planted mesquite trees around his fields to stifle encroaching sands but later regretted it when they and their notoriously dense thickets then spread into his crops, he had branded the trees the "National Congress," the name of Bashir's political party, "because they are deep rooted, suck up everything in sight, and try and fuck you when you really can't afford it."

Through 2017 and 2018, as news of the size and nature of the foreign mega-farms spread, public fury began to build well beyond the afflicted areas. Urban Sudanese took up rural protest slogans, chanting that "Freedom, peace, and justice! Revolution is the choice of the people!" (It rhymes in Arabic.) At one of the many street markets in Omdurman, Khartoum's twin city just over the river from the capital, vendors alternatively advertised their wares and condemned "foreign food thieves" through their bullhorns. As food prices spiraled across the country, turning even salads into rare-ish luxuries for poor families and leaving millions with insufficient food in general, land grabbing was beginning to emerge as a grievance of national significance. "It's just what the government does. They take people's possessions, they steal money, and they ruin everything," said an accountant in Khartoum who declined to be identified for fear of police reprisal. "Now they've made us hungry. It can't last."

Rebellion

Ironically, at least some of this nationwide anger at agribusiness was misplaced. Coming at a time when the cost of crop staples, such as sorghum, had doubled, and that of produce, such as tomatoes, had quadrupled over 2018, many residents of the capital understandably assumed that their hunger and the seizure of food-producing land were linked. The sheer opacity of mega-farm operations allowed this impression to flourish, although, in reality, price increases were much more related to fuel shortages, poorly orchestrated subsidy reforms, and the collapsing currency and its impact on imported agricultural inputs.

Doubly ironically, the state's rationale for forking over parcels of land may have been partly premised on misinformation, too. Officials had wholeheartedly bought into the frequently cited notion that Sudan has up to two hundred million acres of farmable land, only a tenth or so of which is cultivated. They also seemingly believed that that "wasted" potential was due to their own farmers' laziness. But that statistic assumes water supplies and temperate growing conditions that did not necessarily ever exist and almost certainly do not in an era of climate change. It also fails to reckon with the extreme lack of support that small Sudanese landholders receive, a situation which leaves them trapped in a vicious circle of meager yields and hence minimal investment in their fields. There are very good reasons indeed why farmers are decamping en masse to gold mines of the kind described in chapter 3. God-awful working conditions in the mines are bad. The near certainty of destitution on their own lands is worse.

Yet, more than anything, popular fury was rooted in shock at the government's seizure of land—and the accompanying violence—in a country where even most city dwellers are no more than a generation or two removed from rural living. At Zayed al-Kheir, dozens of locals burned down the farm's Nile pump station in 2016, retribution for the loss of fields and for the shooting of a local who had strayed over the barbed wire. At the Nadec farm where we were chased through the desert, a guard shot a young woman twice in the leg in early 2018 after she pursued her runaway camels into the company's fields. Among many other incidents, security forces killed at least five men who were demonstrating against land appropriations in East Jerif, just over the Blue Nile from Khartoum, in 2016 and 2017. "We have martyrs now," said Abdelmajid Mohammed Ahmed, a farmer and protest organizer there, shortly before the protests really took off. "This has become about more than just the land they're trying to take."

Were these land grabs to have snaffled just any land and at another time, the protests may well have petered out—or simply morphed into the sort of localized unrest that Nile dams have frequently ignited. But the largest of these mega-farms are in the central Nile valley area from which an inordinate share of the Sudanese elite originate and where people are less accustomed to being treated as poorly as those in the country's peripheries. At a time of deep economic woe, fury at the state's removal of wheat and fuel subsidies, and open cleavages within the regime, among many other grievances, the stage was set for revolution.

When on April 11, 2019, Omar al-Bashir was toppled after thirty years in power and months of massed street protests, many of the mega-farms that had aggravated his unpopularity went with him.

Divergent Fortunes

Since the end of that wave of land grabbing in Sudan, the Gulf states have adopted savvier strategies. They have prioritized the acquisition of global food businesses, rather than food-producing land itself, actions that they feel will leave them well placed to claim first dibs on grain if the markets wobble. The Saudi government, for one, now has stakes in everything from big Indian rice suppliers to major Brazilian meat processors. In 2021, the UAE bought 45 percent of Louis Dreyfus, one of the four "ABCD" companies that dominate global food-commodity trading. They and their Kuwaiti and Qatari counterparts have been fairly open about the economic imperative here too. After all, we might shake our demand for their oil and gas, but never our need for beans, barley, and bread. "The amount of capital that is being funneled into food security is incredible. But it makes sense for them," said one UAE-based businesswoman who works in this space. "It's about diversifying, it's about staying economically relevant in this new time."

Moreover, the countries and companies that are still seeking out land investments have shifted their focus to more politically stable places, though recent experience has shown that that approach is not without its difficulties, either. Some Saudi agricultural acquisitions are in Senegal, where they, along with Western, Indian, and East Asian investors, may have played a small part in aggravating farmer–herder conflict, as mentioned in chapter 5—and some are in Ukraine. Enticed by that country's famously fertile black earth, a state-owned Saudi company bought several of its largest agribusinesses prewar, with well over half a million acres of leased land between them, only for those interests to stutter following the Russian invasion.[23] Most contentiously, a chunk of that land is in Arizona and neighboring states.

There, in the driest, most drought-ridden corner of the United States, Saudi and Emirati businesses are growing thousands of acres of, what else, alfalfa. But even though these companies have done nothing illegal, simply harnessing dangerously loose state laws, their massive consumption has become a lightning rod for discontent. Already, officials in the Phoenix area are starting to curb suburban development because of insufficient groundwater.[24] Many smaller farmers are going without sufficient irrigation in conditions so hot that planes sometimes cannot generate enough lift to take off from state airports. The very fact, then, that Gulf dairy giants have been permitted to pump unlimited amounts of water for free and then ship the crop home—having allegedly secured the land at discounted rates—has taken on a new resonance.[25] In 2023, Arizona's governor announced that she would terminate or not renew the companies' leases in the state. The "Saudi water grab," Kris Mayes, the state attorney general, said, is over.[26]

But for Sudan, the years following this most recent flirtation with foreign farming have only brought greater hunger. First, companies connected to the Sudanese security services, many of which long ago developed agricultural ambitions of their own, expanded operations, allegedly taking over some abandoned Gulf investor farms. Just to the north of Khartoum, villagers complained to me in 2018 of land grabbing by Zadna, an army-owned company which they said had drained local wells dry. Likewise, the Rapid Support Forces (RSF), a militia descended from the Janjaweed forces that perpetrated much of the killing in Darfur in the early 2000s, and which joined the army in toppling the partly civilian-led post-Bashir government in 2021, reportedly acquired 200,000 acres of farmland in River Nile state soon after the revolution.[27] According to Sudanese sources, the RSF and its erstwhile Russian Wagner Group allies (of Ukraine invasion notoriety) have used some of those agricultural interests as fronts to extract gold. Many Sudanese villagers have since experienced the dubious honor of being displaced by their own people rather than just foreigners.

Then, since April 2023, when the army and RSF fell out, sparking a brutal ongoing civil war, there has often been no food at all. Bolstered by some of the same Gulf states that wreaked mega-farm havoc, these forces—especially the UAE-backed RSF—have actively targeted food supplies. Both parties have dislodged so many people that enormous tracts of farmland are going uncultivated, which has helped pitch about half the population into "acute hunger," according to the UN in late 2023, about double the number in the previous year.[28] Given the damage that rural Sudan's already-limited infrastructure has sustained during the fighting and the climate stresses that are going unmitigated throughout the collapse in governance, it seems unlikely that the country will be able to feed its people again anytime soon, let alone the foreign countries that had previously placed their hopes in the Nile state's agricultural potential.

In the summer of 2023, I contacted a number of Sudan's top food-security experts to ask what had become of these mega-farms. But few of them knew much. Like eight million other Sudanese, as of early 2024, they have all been displaced far from their homes.

Now What?

In these hopeless-sounding circumstances, with bad press and worse returns for the land grabbers, this phenomenon might seem to have had its day. But future trends suggest otherwise. Demand for meat is only growing among swelling urban middle classes, placing more of a premium on fodder. So far, most of that has been supplied by clearing millions of acres of Brazilian and other rainforest, but as blowback to deforestation builds, clearing people from places like Mahas may sound simple by comparison. At the same time, the risk of failing harvests in multiple major food-exporting countries is surging amid climate-induced drought. By 2045, almost three-quarters of the world's food will come from countries susceptible to extreme heat; many breadbaskets are mining groundwater resources about as unsustainably as Arizona.[29] Together with the probability of more export bans from big-time producer states, who fear increases in food prices among their own populations, the stage is set for more panicky, reactive global governance.

It is for these reasons, among others, a royal courtier in Jordan suggested to me, that his country has not yet reduced the amount of land that it has under cultivation and that its dire water situation demands. The psychological ramifications of having no domestic food production in a messy region are too fearsome to fathom, he said. It is for these reasons too, that countries such as China are redoubling efforts to bolster food production while also acquiring swathes of land abroad—some sixteen million acres, according to Land Matrix, an independent land monitoring initiative.[30] "The rice bowls of the Chinese people must always be held firmly in our own hand and filled mainly with Chinese grain," President Xi Jinping said in 2020.[31] For states with insufficient water to make good on this ambition at home but no confidence in the reliability of the markets, land grabbing can seem like the least bad option.

Finally, Sudan and many of its African peers are likely to continue to form the centerpieces of future interest, however poorly past ventures have panned out. That is the way it should be, many of their political and business leaders (contentiously) say. The continent has 65 percent of the world's uncultivated arable land, according to the African Development Bank. Building out that agricultural capacity could relieve more than its own people's hunger. "We can and would be happy to feed the world," Raajeev Bopiah, general manager of Tanzania's East Usambara Tea company, told me at a Cairo trade show in 2016. "We just need the knowledge and the funding."[32] But many African states' rocky governance can make them extra attractive to a certain kind of investor, too. Sure enough, after the investigation on which this chapter is based went to print in *Bloomberg Businessweek* in 2019, I received no fewer than five emails from excited agribusiness directors. One of them, from a Karachi-based company, read: "We're trying to secure our country's needs. As you might know, Pakistani agriculture is suffering badly from climate change. Sudan sounds fascinating. We must speak."

CHAPTER 8

The West and the Rest

We think Western democracies are immune from climate violence. They're not.

T HE BEGINNING OF THIS CHAPTER ended up writing itself. After more than two weeks of the longest heat wave Greece has yet recorded, Athens in July 2023 felt as if it were coming apart at the seams. The streets stank, with garbage collectors instructed not to work during daylight hours for fear of heatstroke. Ordinarily delightful Athenians were snappy and on edge. I saw three fights in a day, having never witnessed one in five previous years of residence. With the shadeless Acropolis closed by government order and some restaurants shuttered after their uncooled kitchens reached dangerous temperatures, many tourists looked thoroughly miserable, mutinous even, as their much-anticipated holidays soured.

Sweating over a blank Word document in my apartment, I understood how grimly apt this all seemed. Here I was trying to write about climate-induced dysfunction in the West. Now I had rich, highly relevant material on my doorstep. Perhaps it would finally grease the keyboard? But as my long-suffering air-conditioning unit started to protest, I felt another desperately unneeded pretext to procrastinate coming on. My partner, Katrin, and I made a break for the relative cool of the mountains.

Little did we anticipate, as we exited the city, what a tour of Greece's wider climate woes we would receive along the way. Driving north, we came across our first wildfire near ancient Thebes, a now largely non-descript town that, like almost everywhere in the country, is neverthe-less littered with world-class ruins. Shortly afterward, we encountered another wildfire inside the village of Kato Tithorea. Groups of mostly South Asian farm laborers tried to douse it in the absence of uniformed firefighters, who were badly overstretched combatting many of the ninety or so other blazes that had broken out that day. But with the wind kicking up and the browning vegetation almost asking to burn after a rainless winter, the flames leapt like grasshoppers from olive grove to greenhouses and across the train tracks as we watched. In one of those painful ironies, it was the arrival of the summer *meltemi* wind that finally snuffed out that heat wave but that in so doing simultaneously fanned the fires into even less containable beasts. By the time we neared Mount Pelion in central Greece, we had not seen a speck of smoke-free sky for several hours.

Even three thousand feet up on the mountain, a stunning and densely forested massif which curls for almost a hundred miles into the Aegean, the fires loomed large. A huge pall of inky black plumes from the biggest inferno to strike the country that month shadowed the surrounding sea, forming an incongruous backdrop to an international youth sail-ing championship—many of whose participants were soon to join an emergency flotilla evacuating locals trapped with their backs against the water. We watched as the flames enveloped a valley, ultimately killing a disabled woman whose elderly husband had been unable to carry her to safety, and a shepherd who died trying to save his flock. Up to 80 percent of all livestock in parts of the province died. We looked on as the fire ate through industrial areas on the periphery of the city of Volos, releasing chemical-tinged fumes so noxious that we tasted them high up on Pelion. Locals looked increasingly scared and bewildered. They were also getting angrier. "What about us?" a shopkeeper asked. Most media attention had turned to an even more photogenic mega-fire that had flared up concurrently on the heavily touristed island of Rhodes. "Where are the cameras?"

Then came the booms. The first, a faint one, originated in a wine and liquor warehouse, the fire having made a beeline for its barrels of locally brewed brandy. The next few, from a military munitions depot, were of a different magnitude. The noise of exploding bombs and bullets took out windows several miles away and almost knocked me off my feet as I balanced awkwardly on a log trying to tie my laces. Those detonations were followed, over the next hour, by the roar of low-flying F-16s, which I half-suspected of trying to blast the fire into submission. In actual fact, the Hellenic air force was evacuating billions of dollars of hardware before the flames got to them. So culminated Cerberus, the most menacing of a crop of newly named heat waves.

But if people in this area and elsewhere in Greece thought that was to be the end of their horror summer, they were to be sadly mistaken. Over the next two months, the country was rattled by additional climate-related disasters, each as or more destructive than the last. Another massive round of fires culminated in modern Greece's largest ever, a forest-munching monster along the Turkish border. That blaze killed at least twenty-six undocumented migrants, many of whom were themselves fleeing climate-related disorder elsewhere and who had been trekking through the area en route to northern Europe. Though there was no evidence that migrants were responsible for any of the fires, some locals held them culpable and launched "hunting parties" amid online calls for extrajudicial executions.

Having been scorched, Greeks were then drenched to within an inch of their lives in a storm that climate scientists say was made ten times more likely and 40 percent more powerful by climate change.[1] In one twenty-four-hour period in early September, central Greece received more rain than London does in a year, with almost a meter's worth falling on parts of Pelion. Many of the livestock that survived the fires did not survive the floods, which were aggravated by the prior loss of vegetation, all contributing to surging prices nationwide for feta cheese and other dairy products from this area, the country's agricultural mainstay. More than that, there was the dread. With at least one village voting to displace itself for fear of future floods, and the country's main north–south roads and rail lines severed, it slowly began to dawn on people that this was how things are going to be, perhaps from here on out. As my friend Eleni Myrivili, then the chief heat officer of the city of Athens, put it, "We used to look forward to summer. Now it terrifies us."

A Rich World Problem, Too

Most of this book dwells on the experience of poorer countries, the places where we are unhappily used to hearing of chaos and distress of varying kinds. And there is good reason for that. Those are the parts of the world suffering the worst climate impacts and those are the ones with much of its shoddiest governance. They are also, owing to the interplay between those two ills, subject to most climate-related violence. But not just them. The more the West's weather conditions come to resemble that of its less affluent, generally less climatically temperate peers, the more its degree of peacefulness might too. In this chapter, I will try to illustrate how and why "our" own political stability and security may be compromised by climate much more than many readers might have imagined. In fact, I argue that they already have been.

A lot of the risk in richer countries depends on climate crises elsewhere, or, more particularly, how authorities in places like Greece respond to them. For one, migration from war-worn Syria transformed Europe's politics in a more hard-line, exclusionary direction for at least a decade. Climate-related challenges may spur many times more people to try to journey over the Mediterranean. To what end for the continent's declared liberal values? Similarly, the supply-chain shocks unleashed by the pandemic and the Russian invasion of Ukraine have fueled severe inflation across our unprecedentedly interconnected world. Those, too, may pale in comparison with the consequences of failing harvests in major food exporters, the destruction of industry and infrastructure, and disrupted transit through globally significant choke points, such as the intensely climate vulnerable Panama Canal. As a sign displayed by the Pakistani Pavilion at the COP27 climate conference in Egypt in 2022 stated in bold letters following the floods that inundated up to a third of the country months earlier, "What goes on in Pakistan won't stay in Pakistan."

And what of the impact of the green transition on major fossil fuel producers, the largest of which flank or are near Europe's peripheries (or, in the case of Venezuela, near-ish to the US's southern border)? If you are Iraq or Algeria, dependent on oil and gas for almost all state revenues, it is a mammoth ask to rework much of your economy while simultaneously navigating severe climate woes and all without collapsing into an unmanageable mess with consequences likely to be felt near and far. It is tricky to imagine that all parties will be able to pull off this balancing act. To that might be added the rich world's potential contribution to instability in the poorer world as it pursues the minerals required to decarbonize our economies—and the deals it strikes to keep migrants at bay.

But from within the West as well, we can see the makings of significant climate-related chaos. Europe and the United States already experience more crime during periods of the kind of extreme weather that climate change makes much more likely. Plenty of our own economic sectors, including Mediterranean tourism and coastal American real estate, could take major, possibly existential hits—to uncertain societal effect. And though the green transition may be an economic boon over-all, not to mention an absolute necessity, it will not be possible without generating losers at home. The fact that those losses are unevenly distrib-uted is already providing rich pickings for demagogic politicians, some of whom are making hay from the loss of identity that can accompany the process—and climate change in general. Omar El Akkad's *American War*, a "cli-fi" novel, is premised on the idea that the United States will refuse to ditch fossil fuels, leaving it broken and at the mercy of pre-viously poorer parts of the world that had successfully adapted. That seems highly improbable, but disinformation and foot-dragging from vested interests are at least slowing the transition and creating openings for extremists of various stripes.

In this chaotic, potentially more violent world one might imagine that we will have greater need of militaries. Early evidence certainly seems to bear that out, with troops from scores of nations now called upon to help during natural disasters, and security officials girding themselves for extra climate-related challenges. "I think it's pretty clear that even modest sea level rise will trouble North America and Europe no end," said James Woolsey, who directed the CIA during the Clinton admin-istration—and whose agency played an important and largely unsung role in identifying how swiftly polar ice caps were melting through the 1990s.[2] "It can radically affect the operations of ships, of ports, of air bases. People who don't get this should read more." But for all that demand and perhaps necessity, militaries' ability to operate in this more complicated environment may be affected too—as seen in Greece with its evacuated air bases and exploding arsenals. About half of all global US military installations have been in some way damaged or affected by extreme weather, the Pentagon said in 2018.[3] Some, such as the world's largest naval base, at Norfolk, are now almost routinely partly submerged, at a cost of many billions of dollars.[4]

Most dangerously, if most nebulously of all, it is unclear what unfamiliar conditions will do to "us"—and by extension our decision-making, our behavior, our hopes, dreams, and fears. Conventional wisdom suggests that wealthier states will withstand these pressures better than the kinds of countries described in previous chapters. It sounds logical enough. We have more money, more state capacity, and, for the time being at least, generally less exposure to the most debilitating climate stresses. But some scholars question that premise. As seen in previous chapters, popular frustration with government frequently peaks when officials fail to deliver services to which citizens have grown accustomed. If that is the case in the West, we, with our generally strong senses of entitlement, might be in for an awful lot of bother.

Already, people in parts of Europe and North America have experienced the following in recent years: water shortages and bans on hosepipe use in places usually overendowed with drizzle (Belgium and the UK), mainstream churches resurrecting traditional prayers for rain at times of extreme drought (South of France), hospital burn units at capacity with people who have fallen on sun-baked sidewalks (Arizona), wildfires so hot that water from plane dumps evaporates before it strikes the flames (Canada), large numbers of Amazon drivers vomiting from heatstroke while doing their rounds (California), and the much-vaunted reemergence of the "hunger stones."[5, 6, 7, 8, 9] "If you see me, cry," reads one seventeenth-century message placed in Germany's Elbe River to warn of imminent famine.

As these sorts of shocks become more severe, more common, and afflict more people who, because they have never experienced anything like them, are especially psychologically ill-prepared, there is no telling how we will respond. Saleemul Huq, the late great British Bangladeshi champion of climate justice, suggested that it might galvanize us. "Perhaps this will prompt action?" he said, almost to himself over a London coffee. "That's always been the hope."

In 2021, much of Evia, Greece's second-biggest island, was consumed by wildfires. Without their beehives, forests, and farms, many villagers are struggling to make ends meet. (Photo by Ayman Oghanna)

Perhaps. But others have less rosy projections. "It is the people who live in the greatest comfort on record, more cosseted and pampered than any other people in history, who feel more threatened, insecure, and frightened, more inclined to panic, and more passionate about everything related to security and safety than people in most other societies, past and present," philosopher Zygmunt Bauman wrote in 2006.[10] Ultimately, even the uncertainty is problematic. From farmers to financial markets, humans are not much keen on that.

I have partly centered this chapter in Greece for reasons both strategic and slothful. The country boasts the sort of climate impacts that befit the world's fastest-warming continent, Europe, one that is averaging temperature hikes about twice the global mean. At around 3 degrees Celsius (5.4°F) since the preindustrial age, some neighborhoods in cities like Madrid and Milan are warming even more quickly.[11] Greece also still displays the scars of the financial crisis of 2007–8, which sliced its GDP by a quarter, and which, along with its "frontline" geography and complicated modern history, has left it with more cleavages than most for climate chaos to exploit. Not irrelevantly, I live here, using it as a lovely base from which to write, report, and ingest industrial quantities of olive oil. Moreover, there is a weighty symbolism to all of this as well. In the land in which democracy was born we can see how one of the greatest threats the system has yet met could horribly corrode it.

Hotter Heads and Higher Crime Rates

The group smiled nervously at one another. It was late 2023, and two anthropologist colleagues and I had gathered a dozen Greek and refugee women in the snug surroundings of an Athens NGO. The idea was to determine whether there were any climatic conditions that they saw as being particularly physically risky. Things had gotten off to an uncertain start. A few of these women, hailing from countries that were routinely plagued by extreme weather, appeared perplexed by our line of questioning. Translation sometimes slowed things down. Between lengthy digressions on "inappropriate dress" and appropriate sugar-to-coffee ratios, I wondered if we were destined to learn anything at all. But bit by bit, and through a few intensely emotional moments, a clear narrative began to spill out over the next few sessions.

Hot weather was more dangerous because men were liable to lash out when sweaty and uncomfortable, said a Gabonese woman who had been attacked three times in Greece and in her country of origin, all at the toastiest periods of the year. In those conditions, women either wore less clothing, which could be seen as a "come-on," according to a Greek therapist, or were sometimes violently prevented from doing so by conservative heads of household. Welling up a little, a Moroccan translator spoke of more aggression against the refugee women she assisted in the summer months. It was often a function of sleeplessness among poor families unable to snatch sufficient rest in their sweltering rooms, of increased alcohol consumption in the heat, of sudden bursts of anger that came "out of nowhere" (and in this she was backed up by the room). By the end of our fourth workshop, during which we heard from a Ukrainian woman who liked to wear nice jewelry but feared robbery when it was exposed, almost all of our participants had reached similar-ish conclusions. "The more I think," the Moroccan woman said, "the more I realize that everything bad that happens, happens more in the summer."*

That higher temperatures can mean more hostility is not a new finding. In a classic 1980s experiment, two Arizona State University researchers idled their car at a traffic light over a period of months, refusing to move even when the lights turned green. They found that the number of honks increased with the outside air temperature.[12] City planners have long known, though have often seemed to forget, that trees and their calming, heat-sapping properties can temper violence.

---

* As many of our workshop attendees noted, there are many other reasons why summer is extra dangerous that have little to do with the heat itself. Kids are out of school, which can be an extra stressor, and financial pressure may be greater. Holiday activities can be beyond many families' reach, while certain forms of agricultural or construction work can be harder to come by during those periods. In southern Europe, NGO and government support programs are often closed in August. With windows more likely to be open, some abuse may just be more audible or visible, rather than more common, when it is hot.

A 10 percent increase in trees corresponds to around a 12 percent drop in crime, as per a study of Baltimore.[13] According to the Gun Violence Archive, 278 out of the 324 mass shootings (86 percent) in the US in 2022 were between June and September.[14] Less tragically, researchers have recorded more sporting violence in these circumstances (i.e., more baseball pitchers beaning batters on hot days).[15] Not that one necessarily needs data to grasp the heat/rage nexus. To ride the New York subway or London Underground in August is to see—and smell—these cities at their most belligerent.

But (that big *but*) what many Western states are beginning to see, even with built landscapes designed to better shield their residents from nature's unpleasantries, is a violence seemingly more correlated with climatic hardship than at any time in their recent pasts. As suggested by the experiences of my NGO interlocutors, a lot of this is directed at women. In 2021–22, Greece recorded the biggest increase in femicides in Europe, the majority of them, by my analysis, perpetrated between June and September.[16] The number of days over 99 degrees Fahrenheit in Athens has surged more than fivefold over the past century, according to its National Observatory.[17] And, as seen in almost every part of the world, it is those on the margins—those with less access to that "protective shield"—who are most vulnerable to climate change's severest impacts. Violence in generally uncooled US prisons increases around 18 percent on hot days, per a 2021 government report.[18] NGOs and officials working in Greek island refugee camps tell consistent stories of more hot-tempered, fight-filled summers. Though it's not "of the West," I found the experience of one recently released Iraqi inmate telling. The prison turned a blind eye to "fight clubs" through the summer months, he told me, all part of a hope that the jailed would take out elevated aggression on one another rather than on the jailers.

Harbingers of Disorder

However, as conditions become more uncertain, richer states appear to be experiencing variations in miniature of the climate-related disorders that are battering poorer ones, rather than just more extreme versions of past ills. Take the plight of olive farmers across southern Europe. Incentivized by the crop's higher prices after years of drought in Spain, the world's largest olive oil producer, criminal gangs and opportunistic individuals are filching many tons of the fruit.[19] I saw a few pilfered trees near Athens Airport, the tree branches closest to the road sawn off during what the owner says was a middle-of-the-night swoop. Many of their farming counterparts elsewhere are similarly exercised about water, the ultimate resource tussle and one that is by no means the exclusive preserve of the poorer countries described elsewhere in this book. Since 2022, thousands of French police have been deployed to face down environmentalists angry at the construction of new reservoirs in fragile biodiverse wetlands.[20] The reservoirs are meant to provide irrigation for farms through ever-drier summer and spring months. Similarly, in 2020 near the border with the United States, Mexican farmers seized a dam, angry that the water behind it was going to their neighbor, as per a 1940s treaty, despite their own, drought-induced shortages.[21]

Western security officials worry about the potential that climate stresses might present for extremist group and gang recruitment, as seen from Bangladesh and Iraq to the Sahel. The economic and psychological dislocation of the pandemic created significant opportunities for the Mafia, which dispensed aid to struggling Italians—and for white supremacists in the United States, who fostered a sense of community through lockdown isolation.[22, 23] The comparable atmosphere of constant crisis that climate change may unleash is potential manna from heaven for those and like-minded actors who provide a veneer of clarity and familiarity in a world with less of either.

Security officials also warn of various forms of ecoterrorism, which they fear could worsen as climate change becomes more pronounced. In its hard-right incarnation, this extremism is perhaps best exemplified by the self-described eco-fascist who killed fifty-one people in two New Zealand mosques in 2019. He and other similarly minded mass murderers invoked variations of the "blood and soil" rhetoric of early-twentieth-century fascist groups, the idea basically being that resources are scarce and that they should consequently go to "*Über Menschen*." It seems deeply unfair to lump ecoterrorism's largely bloodless left-wing equivalent under the same rubric. Yet many Western governments are doing just that, using anti-terror legislation to tackle the road blockages and other disruptions of groups such as Just Stop Oil. But there is the potential for escalation. The best-selling book by Swedish philosopher Andreas Malm, *How to Blow Up a Pipeline*, calls for, well, what it sounds like it calls for. "Damage and destroy new CO_2-emitting devices. Put them out of commission, pick them apart, demolish them, burn them, blow them up," he writes.[24]

Disillusioned by government failure to check climate change, many citizens may even turn on authorities, feeling, as in Nepal and other places, that these authorities have morally recused themselves through their neglect of an existential crisis. This is an amorphous point, but to look back through history is to see the carcasses of civilizations that faltered or collapsed under the weight of phenomena beyond their control. In failing to manage plagues, as in late-stage ancient Rome and in Sumer, sovereigns were perceived as repudiating their right to rule, or "inviting punishment from heaven," as the last Ming dynasty emperor supposedly wrote shortly before he committed suicide in 1644 after a reign tarred by unfavorable climatic conditions.[25] An interesting, if contested, study of seven hundred years of Nile River flows suggests that state power falls off during "deviant" weather.[26] The author measured flood data against sultans' ability or willingness to dismiss religious leaders, who were essentially rival power centers, during periods of dangerously high or low water.

Although there is a limit to the applicability of some of these parallels, we may already be seeing more political disorder during hotter months. Protest numbers and certainly protest intensity appear to increase in line with temperatures.[27] Above all, in our comparatively cushioned societies with more to lose, often-limited recent experience of major turmoil, and high expectations of states that may struggle more than ever to live up to their own ideals, commentators fear blind panic. Researchers have found that search queries related to "climate anxiety" in English were almost thirty times higher in 2023 than they were in 2017.[28] There is a growing cottage industry in books of the "We're all going to die" variety.* Ultimately, ancient Greece, the wellspring of democracy, may one day provide a template of a different, less desirable kind.

During the Great Plague of Athens, which may have killed as much as a third of the city-state's population in 430 BCE, society descended into anarchy, with many people contemptuous of the law when they thought themselves as good as dead. Then, in a possible hint of how our own political systems might one day fracture when confronted by extreme stress, Athens turned to strife and demagoguery, its system torn apart by factionalism and despair.

---

* Even without climate change, extreme weather conditions can exacerbate mental health woes. A majority of suicides in Greece, as in so many other countries, occur in July and August. Experts from organizations such as Klimaka, a Greek charity, attribute this uptick to heat-related disturbed sleep, the reduced effectiveness of anti-depressants in hot weather, and the trauma triggered by worse natural disasters, among other reasons.

A Harder, More Violent Politics

It was not until I watched the small, heavily laden boat bobbing across the narrows between Turkey and the Greek island of Lesvos, that I fully appreciated how terrifying an obstacle the Mediterranean can be, even on relatively calm days. Rising and then occasionally dipping from view in the waves, the Zodiac boat sat low in the water, its ribs steadily deflating under the weight of its passengers, most of whom likely could not swim. In the half-light of early evening, the man at the tiller, himself also a refugee, kept his eyes fixed on the bright red lights atop the wind turbines that crown the hills of the island. It was only because of these lights, a local told me, that these men, women, and children sometimes avoided dashing themselves on the rocks.

That boat, unlike so many others, made it to dry land, to a stretch of coastline that, until recently, was coated with life vests from thousands of other migrants who have previously made landfall. Yet, if these passengers were hoping for a warm welcome, they will have been in for a shock. Almost from the moment that large-scale trans-Mediterranean migration began in 2014, European politics has been captivated by popular blowback to it. The fallout from these new arrivals, a growing share of whom appear to be coming for reasons related to climate, has frequently been very ugly.

There was—and remains—considerable violence at the borders, much of it perpetrated by law enforcement with tacit or explicit central government approval. On Poland's frontier with Belarus, police have beaten migrants and reportedly them left to die in the no-man's-land between the two countries' border fences.[29] In Greece, authorities have allegedly harnessed the sea itself to "push back" boats. According to Forensic Architecture, a research group which uses technology to investigate human rights abuses, coast guard cutters tow arriving migrants to positions from where they know the currents will float them back to the Turkish shores from which they departed. When, after being invited on board a coast guard cutter in Lesvos's main harbor, I got up the nerve to ruin a friendly conversation by asking about these allegations, my new acquaintances quickly clammed up and brought our chat to an abrupt halt. The United States has a long, parallel history of its own, one that has often hinged on both the political climate in Washington and the size of the influx from Latin America. These days, there are dozens of armed vigilante groups with presences around the Mexican border, some boasting hundreds of militiamen apiece, and many accused of perpetrating serious abuses.[30]

Within countries too, attacks on migrants and refugees have surged with the empowerment of hard-line populist groups, many of which have ridden anti-immigration fervor to electoral success. In Greece, refugees, migrants, and those who advocate for them have been repeatedly targeted and, in a number of instances, murdered by hard-right assailants. The climate of fear was so pervasive when Golden Dawn, a nakedly neo-Nazi party, was at its mid-financial-crisis peak around 2015, that Mohammed, a Pakistani man who operates a bodega near my apartment, would not stray outside the neighborhood after dark. Even now he appears unable to shake some of the habits from that time. I walked with him on one occasion, watching as he tensed into a kind of fight-or-flight mode whenever we passed groups of young men. Targeting minorities or vulnerable groups at times of turmoil is a long-standing global tradition, and one that has often turned on climatic phenomena. For instance, data drawn from more than a thousand European cities between 1100 and 1800 shows that persecutions of Jews were closely correlated with drops in average growing-season temperatures.[31]

Most recently, since about 2016, the EU has tried to strangle migration at its source by striking deals with many of the countries through which migrants transit. This can be an effective strategy, but policymakers ought to have noted the possible pitfalls. By underscoring Europe's fear of migrants, these deals have enabled the likes of Turkey's Recep Tayyip Erdoğan and Viktor Lukashenko in Belarus to effectively hold the continent hostage, sometimes hurling people over its borders when they feel their demands are not being met—and arguably such deals have reinforced those regimes and others whose interests are in many ways antithetical to our own. For example, the EU's ability to help stifle Tunisia's return to dictatorship has been much reduced by its reliance on said dictator for assistance in stymieing departures from his country.

In truth, none of the consequent takeaways are especially encouraging. If Europe is struggling to accept roughly 2.5 million undocumented migrants arriving over the course of a decade, then what of the impact of the many more who are projected to follow over the coming years? The farmers and herders of the Sahel generally know the risks of illicit migration, but, mired in poverty and at one another's throats, many are intent on chancing it all the same. And if states resort to even tougher tactics in defense of "Fortress Europe," how might that blatant rejection of liberal values affect European self-image, soft power, and ultimately its domestic politics? "Welcome to the biggest cemetery in Europe" reads a massive new mural painted three-stories-high near my Athens apartment building, drawn up following the drowning of an estimated 650 migrants off Greece in June 2023. The anti-migration activists are angry. So too are the advocates.

On a steamy September day in 2023, I stood outside the refugee camp on Lesvos talking to Zahra, an Afghan woman. She was visibly furious. The facility, a stand-in erected after its notoriously overcrowded predecessor burned down in 2020, was inhospitable enough, she said, with a high wire fence on one side and, on the other three, the sea (which she, like so many others in the camp avoided, with even its sound sometimes enough to traumatize them anew after frequently hairy crossings). The boredom was paralyzing. But more than that there was the bitterness. She had fled Kabul after the Taliban takeover and had then made her way mostly on foot through Iran and Turkey. She said that she had always aspired to build her country in the image of the West. Now, trapped in limbo and with no clear prospect of securing asylum, she said she was not so sure. "This is not how you treat people," she said. "This is not how democracy is supposed to be."

It's the Economy, Stupid

Into this toxic political environment has come tremendous climate-induced economic trouble, itself so often a recipe for wider popular discontent. More-frequent shocks are already toying with global supply chains, bolstering inflation and wreaking havoc with the just-in-time logistics that many major companies favor. The Mississippi River and the Panama Canal, two of the world's greatest transit arteries, are reducing the number and size of vessels that they convey due to drought.[32, 33] The canal passes through a few now-depleted lakes, a design flaw that its builders could not have envisaged a century ago in one of the world's wettest countries. Many of Germany's biggest businesses rely on its rivers for cheap transport. That, too, has emerged as a loss-making weakness as the Rhine, Ruhr, and other previously reliable waterways fall to depths as low as eleven inches, as happened in 2022.[34]

And foodstuffs? As with farmers, the most climate-vulnerable of people, agricultural production is uniquely vulnerable to shocks. That, needless to say, is a big problem. With almost half of all wheat and rice coming from areas susceptible to drought, scholars expect yo-yoing harvests, intermittent surges in food prices, and perhaps more and more land grabbing of the sort described in the previous chapter.[35] In a survey in the UK, about 40 percent of food-security experts believe that food could be a source of civil unrest there within the next decade.[36]

Then there is the impact on electricity generation, on insurance companies, on worker productivity, to name but a few looming mega-challenges. The first faces myriad risks, including grid overload at times of temperature extremes, and nuclear plants shutting down for want of water to cool them, as has happened in nuclear-power-happy France.[37] Reeling from more extreme weather events, insurers are hiking premiums beyond many people's means—or backing out altogether. In 2023, State Farm, the largest home insurer in California, announced that it would no longer sell that kind of coverage in the state.[38] And worker productivity, a long-standing problem in poorer countries, could cost a hotter United States $500 billion a year by 2050.[39] Economists warn of the possibility of a "Minsky moment," a sudden collapse in asset values if markets determine that investors have not adequately priced in the potential impact of, for example, sea level rise on trillions of dollars of coastal real estate.[40]

In the long run, some tourism hubs might find themselves in the stickiest situations. Like most countries along the Mediterranean, Greece relies on holidaying foreigners for thousands of hard-to-replace jobs—and at least a quarter of the country's GDP. But if recent summers are any guide, then fiercer heat, more prolific wildfires, and almost biblical deluges bode ill for its financial future. There is nothing quite like scenes of families fleeing fiery beachheads on Rhodes, or stories of people stumbling, stricken by heatstroke, through antiquities sites to give tourists pause. On the island of Lesvos, tourism numbers fell about 70 percent between 2015 and 2016 as the migration crisis unraveled.[41] With cooler regions, such as northern Spain, beginning to successfully advertise themselves as less risky alternatives, the Greek islands, as stunning and replete with delicious octopus as they are, might not always exert the same pull. "WE ARE NOT IN THE LINE OF THE FIRE," one Airbnb listing near Athens screeched as a third of Mount Parnitha, one of my favorite hiking spots, burned to a crisp over the summer of 2023. That might not always be sufficient.

The Trouble with the Transition at Home

It was the early hours of January 30, 2020, when the saboteur struck. Stealing out to the spot where contractors had temporarily moored the pipeline in a cove of the Saronic Gulf, this person or persons unknown punctured it in thirty-one different places with a hand drill before disappearing back into the night. By the time the damage was discovered the following morning, the project to transfer freshwater from the Athens area to the nearby island of Aegina had been knocked many months off track. Residents—and environmentalists—were furious. Here, at last, was an opportunity to rework the island's unsustainable water ways. Locals relished the prospect of relief from above-average water bills. But surprised? They were not.[42]

For years now, desalination plants and other forms of water infrastructure across archipelagic parts of Greece have faced frequent fires, spurious-sounding legal challenges, and a range of "inexplicable" breakdowns. (Though impossible to prove malicious intent in most cases, desalination technicians say that not even poor maintenance could explain away so many problems.) This Aegina attack, and the undersea bombing of the island's by-then-operational pipeline that followed in the summer of 2022, were but the latest in a long line of island water improvement projects that had gone awry shortly before or after completion.[43] "You see a whole lot of monkey business everywhere you look," said Panagiotis Hatziperos, a veteran Greek politician and one of more than a dozen former and current officials across a half dozen islands whom a colleague and I consulted as we tried to piece together what was going on.

Islanders have been quick to pin this devilry on the so-called *nerouládes*, the businessmen who ship water in large, smoke-belching tankers from the comparatively well-resourced mainland to many of the parched Cycladic and Dodecanese islands. And despite having only limited concrete proof, the accusers are likely at least partly right. Since the 1980s, these operators and their peers in the bottled water distribution business, who have cultivated a captive customer base because the shipped water is seldom as potable as promised, have made a killing as tourism boomed, the islands' own groundwater and rainfall levels dissipated, and panicked officials in Athens resorted to costly piecemeal solutions. As with so many others at the losing end of sustainability initiatives, some of these businessmen appear unwilling to forgo those profits without a fight.

The green transition is often presented as an unambiguous economic good, and insofar as it is many times cheaper than allowing climate change to run its course, that is true. But processes this enormous are often riddled with complications—as climate champions on either side of the Atlantic are discovering to their dismay. Efforts to develop domestic sources of the critical raw minerals needed to electrify our economies are stumbling, hamstrung by many communities' objections to major new mining and industry on their doorsteps. A proposed $2.4 billion lithium mine in Serbia has been at least temporarily stifled by fierce protests, while other attempts to extract key minerals from Sweden to the United States are proceeding slowly. Although understandable, the geopolitical implications are unsavory from the West's perspective. China dominates the rare-earth minerals market. In reducing Russia and Saudi Arabia's sway, Western countries might simply be switching from one strategic weakness to another. "This is the dark cloud of the clean energy story," says Sharon Burke, who previously served as US assistant secretary of defense for operational energy. "You've got to decide: do you want to despoil small parts of your country, or do you want to be dependent on another part of the world?"

The race to build out enough renewable energy to supplant fossil fuels, though advancing briskly in many countries, can also be messy, despite tumbling costs. Industry insiders in Greece told me of frequent mischief-making between companies competing for the same wind turbine locations, and from locals who reject these projects altogether. They allege that communities have tampered with infrastructure for fear that the projects will ail surrounding nature, a not wholly misplaced concern in parts of the country. According to Greek investigative media, wind turbines have often been sited wherever is cheapest, irrespective of the damage caused by their construction in biodiversity-rich areas, rather than where is best.[44] On other occasions, oil- and tourism-related businesses have allegedly spread rumors about these projects, suggesting, for example, that their developers are responsible for the wildfires in order to free up forested land for construction, or that tourists will steer clear of Greece if their views are tarnished with wind turbines.

Above all, the green transition has losers, or those who feel themselves to be such, and many of them are pushing back. Farmers and ranchers are up in arms about emissions targets, which might require cuts in herd sizes, among other changes. In the geographically small but agriculturally mighty Netherlands, the blowback from a government plan to halve nitrogen emissions, much of it from its millions of farting, burping cows, has been particularly fierce. Under the direction of groups such as the Farmer's Defense Force, thousands of protesting Dutch have blockaded government offices with tractors, torched haybales, and flown the national tricolor upside down across the country.[45] On a 2019 trip to Amsterdam, I encountered the most pungent of their tactics as I tiptoed through piles of steaming manure on my way to the train station. The reality, one of the farmers there explained to me, is that they, like their counterparts the world over, are being hit hardest by climate impacts. That their communities, with their generally thin profit margins and worse access to public services, must then shoulder what they see as a disproportionate share of the "climate cleanup bill" has been a bridge too far. "This is a question of fairness," one of them, Johannes, told me. "People in cities don't even know what it takes to produce their food."

The same goes for those working in fossil fuel industries, where livelihoods are frequently every bit as wrapped up with identity as those in agriculture. Their jobs are concentrated in areas with few alternatives and where generations of environmentally destructive extraction have often swallowed farmland and tarred the landscape with tourism-unfriendly pollution. That means when the hammer comes down on coal mines, oil rigs, and power plants, the pain is laser-focused on communities that lack the resources and, given the close identification with their work, perhaps the wherewithal to adapt. In the isolated Greek region of Western Macedonia, one in ten jobs (and much more than one in ten "good" jobs) are in some way connected to lignite, the most polluting kind of coal.[46] The country's turn away from the fuel has subsequently ripped through the local social fabric, contributing to one of the highest regional unemployment rates in Europe and increasingly prolific out-migration. This, Greece's main left-wing party insists, is "violent decarbonization."

(On paper at least, the green transition looks very doable across the West, not to mention desirable for those at the literal coalface of polluting industries. "Green" jobs pay more on average than "brown" jobs, and through the $369-billion Inflation Reduction Act (IRA) in the United States and similar-ish EU schemes, funding is being made available to cushion the blow in fossil-fuel-producing heartlands. Crucially, the scale of the reallocation of employment in richer countries is much less aggressive than that which accompanied the shift from manufacturing to services in past decades.[47] However, while the IRA may ultimately direct twice as much funding to poorer red states as it does blue ones, a lot of the new job creation is still going to different, generally more affluent areas than the ones where the majority of the old-job losses are occurring—and Americans, in particular, are much less willing to move these days.[48, 49])

More Misinformation, More Problems

Thrown by ill-conceived policies, even people with no economic stake in the energy or agricultural status quo can feel assailed by the transition. This was perhaps best exemplified by the green fuel tariffs that sparked the "*Gilet Jaune*" ("Yellow Vest") protest movement, and roiled France in 2018–19. By hiking prices at the pump, the government inadvertently hurt rural and small-town car owners, many of whom have no choice but to drive because of the paucity of local public transport options, much more than generally wealthier Parisians. "They talk about the end of the world. We are talking about the end of the week," went one possibly too-good-to-be-true protester quote. The cost-of-living crisis that followed Covid and the Russian invasion of Ukraine has inspired similar blowback across Europe against policies for reaching the goal of Net Zero greenhouse-gas emissions by 2050. With prices up and disposable income down, many families have soured on the idea of anything that could require financial sacrifice now, however much these electric cars and heat pumps might save them in the long run.

Amid widespread unease with the pace of change, it is unsurprising that swathes of the public have come to question the green transition, especially when its costs are so conspicuous and those of climate change are often not. Yet, a lot of the time, the committed naysayers among them have received ample assistance in reaching their conclusions. Poor countries are not the only ones susceptible to climate mis- and disinformation. Some of this comes via the extensive ecosystem of think tanks with big budgets and deceptive names that the oil and gas sector has created to sow confusion. Despite acknowledging the connection between their wares and warming as far back as the 1980s, these companies have since changed their tune, pouring a large fortune into campaigns to obfuscate the causes of, solutions to, and severity of climate change.[50] Between 2008 and 2018, the oil and gas sector spent at least $1.3 billion on political causes, more than twenty times the outlay of renewable-energy companies.[51]

Plenty more has come from largely online conspiracy theorists, who have been able to spread their own and perhaps others' fabrications more easily as social media moderation, never strong, drops off even more. Among many instances, this was brought jarringly into focus by the experience of Chris Gloninger. As a meteorologist for a CBS affiliate in Iowa, he frequently explained to viewers how climate change was contributing to the state's ever weirder and wilder conditions. But one local man was enraged at Gloninger for pushing his "liberal conspiracy theory on the weather," and, in an echo of the harassment meteorologists routinely endure, inundated him with death threats. "A lot of the time when I said something on TV, someone would come back and say, 'It was cold today in Iowa. What are you talking about? Why are you lying?'" Gloninger said. "Some people cannot broaden their viewpoint. They're just seeing so much stuff that confirms their beliefs." He has since quit TV meteorology altogether.

As some governments have outpaced voters' enthusiasm for change, populist politicians have been extra quick to identify the transition as fertile electoral turf—and spread even more fake news accordingly. In some instances, they have inflated the possible impact of climate action on farming, fishing, and other richly symbolic activities, presenting mitigation as an attack on traditional ways of life—and themselves as the defenders (never mind the effect that unadulterated climate change might inflict). Given how powerfully rural areas resonate with our various senses of national self, or at least romanticized notions of them, this can be a compelling electoral narrative.

In other instances, populists have cast these policies as the unthinking playthings of "bed-wetting" urban elites—while simultaneously twisting them in such a way as to mesh with other favored talking points. In doing so, they have transformed the green transition into a tribal political issue that is almost totally divorced from discussion of its own merits and pitfalls. "Wind is woke," etc. A case in point: appearing on Fox's *Tucker Carlson Tonight* show in 2022, a Dutch hard-right activist insisted that officials are scuttling agriculture in order to turn the land over to housing for migrants, a variation of a long-standing racist conspiracy theory. "The farmers are standing in the way of the 'Great Reset' plans that the [government] has for us. They are hardworking, God-fearing people standing in the way of the globalist agenda."[52] None of this has to make sense. With a wink and a nod at one another, neither Carlson nor his interviewee really seemed to believe it either. But it was a good story, and good stories win elections.

The Trouble with the Transition Abroad

The room was in agreement. Rich countries were mostly responsible for historic emissions. Rich countries must pay. That conference, held in Beirut before a group of largely Middle Eastern environmentalists, reaffirmed the necessity of a "just transition." Without funding, much of the Global South will go without effective adaptation. No adaptation, no hope of withstanding the worst climate impacts. The city around us, its traffic lights down for want of electricity and its streets patrolled by well-dressed panhandlers, inadvertently spoke to the salience of the activists' calls. After years of financial and political crisis, the Lebanese capital—and places like it—are liable to lurch even deeper into distress if extreme stresses strike undiluted and with the country's brittle coping mechanisms unreinforced.

But what the participants did not do, quite understandably given the event's focus, was touch on the turmoil that might unfold if the world continues on a two-track green transition (or, given the "damned if you do, damned if you don't" nature of so many climate issues, the chaos that might emerge even if it does not). It took a drink later in the day for that head-scratcher to surface. As I described our discussions to a European diplomat, he keenly if slightly agitatedly heard me out, before eventually cutting in with a point that he clearly been itching to make all along. "I get that this is essential, climate-wise. Oil bad and all," he said, his voice rising a little. "But can a region like this one handle the shock?"

Much of this concern is centered on major fossil fuel exporters' ability—and willingness—to transform their economies as the rich world's transition takes off. Look at Iraq, for example. Like Algeria, Nigeria, and about a dozen other countries, Baghdad depends on oil and gas for well over half its revenues (about 90 percent in its case, and almost 100 percent of foreign export earnings). The very idea then that it might one day go without that bounty is something that not even its smartest, best-informed officials can envisage. "Oil is hardwired into the state," Hussain al-Shahristani, a former minister of oil, told me in an interview in 2017. "It is all salaries, all pensions, all spending." He was not exaggerating. When the global oil price tanked in 2014, Iraqi government expenditure went with it, the ministry of water resources' investment allowance falling to $30 million from $1.7 billion the year before, according to the then minister. If you journey through the glistening oil fields in places like Rumaila in the country's south, you truly are seeing, smelling, and, given the volume of gas flaring, almost tasting the life-blood of the state exchequer.* Local tribespeople, many of whom suffer severe health consequences from that flaring, are aware of the leverage their guns and proximity to these facilities gives them.[53] In 2018, I was in the area during one of their periodic oil-field blockades, watching as they closed off roads with burning tires and threatened to breach the fences unless their demands for more jobs were met.

And even if some of the more able statesmen in Baghdad and its similarly fossil-fuel-rich, state-capacity-poor peers embraced a green transition, there is no guarantee that they could pull it off, at least in a timely manner. In Iraq's case, the political class appears more committed to divvying up that oil largesse than to confronting the climate chaos that is partly emanating from it. It seems unrealistic to expect them to suddenly display superior statecraft and, in many instances, less personal greed, just as the complexity of the challenge swells. In the case of coal-dependent South Africa, crime is an obstacle. Gangs have stolen many hundreds of miles of the overhead copper cable laid to facilitate hybrid electric trains, which risks a reversal of one the country's clearest "green" successes.[54] Most of these petrostates face some kind of conflict

---

* It is no coincidence, of course, that so many fossil fuel producers are governed by ham-fisted authoritarians. As economist Chris Blattman outlines in *Why We Fight*, oil is a resource that lends itself to one-man rule. It "doesn't care if you oppress your people or if you attack your neighbors. It's concentrated in an easily controlled space," he writes. For that reason, if for no other, many rulers may resist transitions to less easily controlled renewable-energy networks. For that reason, among many others, one ought to welcome a post-fossil-fuel era—and the uptick in representative government that it may ultimately help foster. Norway, its oil-sodden sovereign wealth fund devised, ironically, by an Iraqi immigrant, is perhaps the only state to have wholly avoided the fossil fuel governance curse.

too. Though not itself a major fossil fuel exporter, Ukraine, where most solar and wind capacity has been destroyed or rendered unusable by Russian missile strikes, is bitterly reflective of the impossibility of transitioning while fighting.[55] Its climate action plans are now in tatters; its coal use as a percentage of its total energy mix higher than any point in years.

At the same time, all parties will eventually have no choice but to confront the consequences of shrinking global demand for their resources. The EU forecasts a 79 percent drop in oil imports by 2050, a scenario that is extra-problematic for countries such as Libya and Algeria, which export most of what they extract to Europe, but that, in time, will rip gaping holes in all petrostate balance sheets as well. Put simply, by the time the most recalcitrant leaders wake to the unavoidability of economic diversification, they may well lack the resources to do so, let alone gird themselves for climate stresses that, by dint of their geographical locations, they will likely feel more than many others. "The world needs to move in this direction. This is obvious," says Ali al-Saffar, director of the energy transition program at the Rockefeller Foundation and formerly the International Energy Agency's point man in the Middle East. "But, if we move in that direction overnight, we're going to see a crater where the oil producers are now." It was this fear, I was sure, that underpinned my diplomat friend's outburst. For here, through the specter of violent state collapse, lies the potential for even greater migrant flows to come.

A Rich World Not Paying Its Bills

At the time of writing (and almost certainly your time of reading), emissions continue to climb. No manner of apocalyptic warnings appears sufficient to shake us from our fossil fuel dependency, no form of weather freaky enough to generate adequate action. This brings us to a second security concern. Because although it is far too premature to capitulate on "conventional" climate action, our apparent failure to phase out fossil fuels on schedule might mean that carbon capture and other largely unproven technologies will be required if we are to prevent truly catastrophic warming, or so some leading climate scientists say.[56] That is potentially exciting, given how many of our climate successes have been technological—the rapid development of renewables, dramatic breakthroughs in battery life, and so on. But insofar as these tools will require our collective agreement if they are to be deployed safely and equitably, it is also worrying. After all, securing cooperation among competing states has been our Achilles' heel throughout.

Solar geoengineering seems particularly prone to abuse. In late 2022, a small American tech startup, Make Sunsets, released weather balloons full of sulfur dioxide into the Mexican sky.[57] The idea was to trial one of many ways in which sunlight might theoretically be reflected back out into space. But, amid widespread outrage from worried locals, the stunt also signaled how much of an anarchic free-for-all the field could become. As climate change bites, the fear is that the hardest-hit countries, most of them poor, will unilaterally turn to this tech in desperation, and all without necessarily grasping the possible knock-on consequences of their use at scale. That is a formula for future international strife, as attested to by the violent outcomes of the war-gaming exercise I mentioned in the introduction. It may already be one. Mindful of the UAE's years-long cloud seeding program, an Iranian general insinuated without evidence in 2017 that the neighboring state's activities had fueled his country's drought—like "atmospheric pirates."[58] Ultimately, not even "success" may be wholly desirable. Were we to geoengineer our way to a cooler planet, "we would be moving under the sword of Damocles," as one scientist put it, forever in danger of imminent destruction if we stopped.[59]

Finally, though no less significantly, there are the tensions that could accompany rich countries' continued failure to help climate-proof poorer ones, the just transition that my Beirut colleagues invoked. The longer the world pursues varying quantities and qualities of climate action, the more vulnerable the West and other major emitters will be to Global South fury. Some of this might be unfair. The Kremlin in particular has sown disinformation about how much Western countries have fueled climate change, while itself doing little to rein in its massive gas flaring. Warming might even be good for Russia, Vladimir Putin once suggested—"We will spend less on fur coats!" China officially denied that the world was warming until about 2011; the country continues to extract and burn record amounts of coal.[60] Although starting from a high mark, most Western states are at least cutting emissions, while the likes of Saudi Arabia, intent on hiking oil production, and India, desperate to develop at any cost, are merely adding to them.

Regardless of how much blame is warranted, the optics can still be unfortunate. For example, Morocco's Noor solar power plant, one of the largest facilities of its kind in the world, dispatches some of its production over the sea to the EU, which partly funded it. The field requires millions of liters of water a day from the Draa River for cleaning and cooling, and in order to supply that volume in a drought-ridden state, many downstream farmers must go without. Their withered date palms, many now abandoned and neck-deep in Saharan sand, tell the tale of lost livelihoods. The mostly depopulated *ksars*, centuries-old fortified villages, speak to the difficulty of making a living in the area without the trees. For those who remain, Noor is an avatar for the costs that wealthier parts of their country and the world place on poor people in order to meet their own climate obligations. "Europe is stealing our water and killing our farms. Why? To power its houses," said Faez Baood, a teacher in M'hamid El Ghizlane. "Where is the fairness?"

More symbolic still are the lengths that Western nations, struggling to develop critical raw-material sources of their own and wary of China's stranglehold, may go to in pursuit of them abroad. Africa, in particular, is rich in elements like cobalt, which is vital for manufacturing electric cars. Leaders of some of the most mineral-rich states, such as the Democratic Republic of the Congo (DRC), clamor for investment. The DRC is a "solution country" for climate change, its president, Félix Tshisekedi, says. But even if Western firms are more sensitive to human rights and environmental concerns than their much-criticized Chinese equivalents, it is unclear whether they can secure these resources without repeating the abuses of the past. A new "green colonialism," some observers have labeled this, the extraction of adaptation-critical materials without granting the countries in which they are found the funding to launch their own transitions.

Yet, as the many kinds of fallout from climate change come into sharper focus, it could get trickier to quibble with the Global South's fundamental grievance: that they are suffering most from a problem that is largely of our making and which we in the Global North appear insufficiently willing to help stanch. There is a reason why the intelligence community in Washington rates fiercer blowback from angry developing countries among the most immediate climate risks to climate security and US interests.[61] "Those who produce the garbage refuse to pay their bills," said Kenyan president William Ruto in discussion with the UK's King Charles in 2023, an impression that was likely only furthered by many Western countries' momentary backtracking on their own fossil fuel phaseouts following the Russian invasion of Ukraine.

When climate shocks intensify and their impacts worsen, Western leaders might imagine that afflicted peoples will turn their ire on the underlying source of their troubles—fossil fuels and those responsible for producing and deploying them. Not so fast, says Indian novelist and climate commentator Amitav Ghosh. "That's a complete fantasy," he told the *New York Times*. "In the Global South, everybody understands that energy access is the difference between poverty and not poverty. Nobody sees fossil fuels as the basic problem. They see the West's profligate use of fossil fuels as the basic problem."[62] If key Western countries were to renege on whatever progress they have so far made toward Net Zero, there is no telling what effect that might have on North–South relations. Multilateral climate action, already deeply troubled, might breathe its last.

Fast Times at Military High

Hot, bothered, and possibly ready to fight, the world of tomorrow looks distinctly thorny, a metaphorical and, in many places, literal minefield of geopolitical tripwires. But even if, as most climate security theorists believe (and all ardently hope), we avoid large-scale conflict related to climate change, our future is still likely to make greater demands of militaries than perhaps any other state institutions. For a start, they will be called upon to help tackle climate change fallout. In many countries, they already are. According to the Center for Climate and Security's Military Responses to Climate Hazards Tracker, dozens of militaries respond to fires, floods, and more every month. In the United States, members of the National Guard devoted 172,000 days to fighting fires in 2021, about ten times more than they did in 2019.[63] In Switzerland, soldiers have airlifted water to cows high up in the Alps over several recent summers, their ordinarily plentiful watering holes scorched into nothingness.[64] For all my sarcastic bluster on Greece's Mount Pelion, it turns out that the Swedish air force actually has bombed forest fires into quiescence. (Like blowing out candles on a cake, the shock waves can douse flames.)[65, 66]

In conversation with strategic planners from a dozen different militaries, many have come across as deeply ambivalent about these new responsibilities—as well, perhaps, they should. There is a strong suggestion that Russia's capacity to combat mega-fires in Siberia, hundreds of which scorch areas the size of Ireland on an almost annual basis, has been badly compromised by the redeployment of resources to prosecute its war in Ukraine.[67] In 2022, Slovenia delivered a timely reminder of the difficulty that smaller states might experience in marrying new duties to their core missions. With the country riven by wildfires and much of the military deployed to fight them, the government canceled a $300-million-plus deal to retool its forces with armored personnel carriers, a deal that policymakers had deemed necessary in light of its newly threatened near-neighborhood.[68] But, as the challenge mounts, militaries are unlikely to have much choice. "The reality is that this is just a big part of national security," said James Woolsey, the former CIA director. "People would say to me at certain environment or water conferences, 'You're CIA. Why are you here?' But if you care about national security, you've got to care about this stuff, probably even more in the future."

Similarly, militaries will be required to respond to new crises in new places and possibly all in ways that they cannot yet anticipate. The Arctic is probably the best-known "climate arena"—and the one that, back in the 1990s, helped interest the likes of the Pentagon and the Dutch army in climate's national security implications in the first place. Melting ice floes may free up the strategic Northwest Passage while thawing open geographically sensitive and materially valuable waters on Europe and North America's frigid doorstep, which their navies must patrol. In its assessment of challenges to US national security through 2040, the National Intelligence Council expects increased military activity "as Arctic and non-Arctic states seek to protect their investments, exploit new maritime routes, and gain strategic advantages."[69] Russia, it notes, has many more icebreakers than all Western states combined. However, almost every military is wrestling with a changing strategic landscape, or soon will be.

For example, in Greece, military planners worry that changing fish migration patterns, which are partly a function of warming waters, are bringing naval and coast guard units into riskier, more regular contact with their Turkish counterparts in the Aegean. Competing for high-value tuna, fishermen—and their respective authorities when they have interceded on their nationals' behalf—have clashed around the contested islets that have previously brought the two countries to the brink of war, and that were seldom previously prime trawling grounds. "The fishing patterns are all messed up," Vasili Lydas, a fisherman from the nearby Greek island of Kalymnos, told me in 2020. "Sometimes they come later. Sometimes they come earlier."[70] For overstretched high commands, these kinds of new considerations are planning quagmires they would very happily live without.

All the while, militaries may find it increasingly difficult to perform even their day-to-day duties. More bases are being struck by floods, rendering them useless for months or more at a time, as at Nebraska's Offutt Air Force Base, which is home to the US Strategic Command and which was inundated in 2019.[71] Others must contend with fiercer fires, more regular sandstorms, and stronger hurricanes, all of which have ground operations to a halt for extended periods. After the fires and mega-floods in September 2023, US and Greek officers determined that the jointly used helicopter base at Stefanovikeio, in the shadow of Mount Pelion and its devastating floodwaters, was too vulnerable for future use. Others still are increasingly unfit for purpose due to extreme heat stress.

In recent years, militaries have experienced an epidemic of munitions depots exploding in the heat, and, in some instances, of planes struggling to take off in inhospitable conditions. Many of Greece's most strategically placed airfields are on small, isolated islands and cannot be easily extended. But, amid high heat, planes require greater distances to generate sufficient lift, which has rendered some of these runways off-limits to transport aircraft for the hottest periods of the year.[72] Critically, many militaries are struggling to keep their troops alive in these conditions, with three thousand reported cases of heatstroke and heat exhaustion in US forces in 2018 alone, and to keep their vehicles serviceable in temperatures for which they were not designed.[73] There is nothing quite like watching a bunch of American special forces soldiers pour out of a Humvee in Mosul and greet the 110-degree-Fahrenheit exterior as if it were an atmospheric cool bag for you to grasp the sauna-like properties of their equipment.

Officers suggest that Western militaries, which are generally more adaptable, may be able to adjust their practices, equipment, and infrastructure accordingly. But they—and plenty of their "poor country" peers—question the abilities of some less affluent, more regimented forces to do likewise. And that, at a time when those militaries may be called upon to manage the many kinds of security fallout described throughout this book, should keep their own governments' officials awake at night, officers suggest. "The militaries of the Third World or the Global South are very ill-prepared to respond," wrote Munir Muniruzzaman, a retired Bangladeshi major general and chairman of the Global Military Advisory Council on Climate Change, via email in early 2024. "Since there is not much understanding of the [climate] threat itself, so the policies have not been geared to the procurement policies of the militaries to prepare them or to tool them for this kind of task."[74]

Finally, to compound this complex mess, militaries will come under stronger pressure to decarbonize themselves, a requirement from which they are exempt under existing global climate legislation. That is likely necessary, given how emissions-heavy many of them are. The US Department of Defense is frequently cited as the biggest institutional polluter in the world, its carbon footprint—and that of its peers—standing as jarring additional reminders to some of the inequitable nature of climate action pain. Decarbonizing the military need not be strategically bad, either. From Afghanistan to Iraq, oil convoys were frequently the very exposed, very explosive logistical underbellies of American operations. NATO forces sustained at least one casualty for every twenty-four fuel convoys in those countries, according to an official at the organization, a statistic that, given the force's thirst for gasoline, may have added up to hundreds of deaths.

Yet even some generals who favor greener approaches caution against pushing militaries to move too far, too fast, particularly at a time when they have so much of the above to consider. "Regions or states or countries that are in conflict are not going to be thinking about this, because it's more important to win the fight," said Richard Nugee, a recently retired British lieutenant general who was until 2021 the UK military's lead on all things climate. "Don't think I'm going to sacrifice operational advantage to be greener. We're paid to win a war. We're not paid to come second." Predictably perhaps, these initiatives also risk turning into yet another pawn in the never-ending culture wars. "They wanna make the army tanks all electric, so that as we go in to obliterate a country, we do it in a hospitable way," Trump (incorrectly) told a New Hampshire campaign rally in December 2023. "We do it in a way so that we're not hurting their atmosphere. . . . These people are crazy."[75]

Out of Chaos, Hope?[1]

In the right circumstances, environment and climate can bring warring communities back together.

THE VILLAGES OF NEPAL'S INDRAWATI MUNICIPALITY are as stunningly picturesque as their inhabitants are miserable. Perched high enough up in the Himalayas to make you feel you are among the monster peaks, but low enough to remain verdant year-round, these communities *should* be idyllic. If nothing else, with forest so dense that leopards can—and sometimes do—creep to within meters of houses before pouncing, they surely ought to be richly resourced. But try telling that to the locals. I speak from firsthand experience when I say that they will fix you with glares potent enough to melt lead.

The freshwater springs on which the villages rely are increasingly lifeless, leaving them, quite literally, high and dry and unable to irrigate crops for much of the year. The landscape is too capricious, too riven with landslides, earthquakes, and lightning strikes for the villagers to ever fully admire, they say. Even moving down some four thousand feet to the well-watered valley floors, as so many highlanders have done, offers no guarantee of a better life. Quite the opposite sometimes. Far below runs the Melamchi River of chapter 4 notoriety, its relative lowlands reached via a road of such outrageous steepness that you pass from upland conifers to tropical valley vegetation (and sometimes back) at an almost indecent speed. Having descended from the parched mountaintops, scores of Indrawatians then lost land or their new houses in the 2021 mega-flood. "We can feel we're cursed," said Dhana Kumari, a villager who took it upon herself to show my colleague and me around after overhearing us interviewing her neighbor. "We suffer no matter what we do."

Walking us through her village, she explained where those crises had led. Many of the men drink like fish, with the bars conspicuously busy at 8:00 a.m. and two evidently much-worse-for-wear punters propped up along the verge not long after. One sported a nice, fresh-looking shiner; the other appeared wary of releasing his grip on a road sign for fear of where he might end up next. Attacks on women are on the rise, too, some perpetrated while the women make their daily, sometimes ninety-minute round trips along lightly trafficked paths to collect water. This, Kumari clarified, was awful in itself. But it was made worse by what she said was by many local husbands' and fathers' ignorance of why they, with their adherence to traditional gender roles, must expose themselves to such danger. "They do not understand how little water there is because they do not cook, they do not clean, they do not see the springs," she said.

Most damagingly, Kumari and other locals maintained, many of the municipality's nine villages—or wards, as they are called locally—are at one another's throats. Comparatively water-rich in the case of Ward 1, and with barely trickling springs in most others, these communities have engaged in frequent tussles over resources. In one instance, residents of Ward 1 blocked the road to their village and then hurled boulders from the heights when villagers from elsewhere tried to force it open. Judging from the gouges in the hillside and the gash in the forest through which the massive stones bounced, it was more by good luck than good management that no one was killed.

In other contexts, and at other times, that is just how things would have remained. Yet, in a measure of how even much-maligned authorities can temper environment and climate-related conflict with savvy management, successive mayors may have found a partial solution. Starting in 2018, former mayor Banshalal Tamang struck a deal with Ward 1's chief whereby he would sanction a pipeline from his community's spring in exchange for an improved road, a new school, and a suspension bridge. His successor as mayor, Jhamka Nepal, has carried on the project. It is too much to say that peace now reigns, with many Ward 1 residents convinced that their ward chief sold them out and many of them muttering darkly about the "foolishness" of trading away water. But for the time being, no one is throwing rocks at one another. Attacks on women appear way down. In this pea soup of environmental and climate crises, that counts as success.

The Concept

This has not been, I will venture, the kind of book that has filled you with hope. Climate security can be a dispiriting topic, and it is flat-out gloomy when centered on places that lack the tools, bandwidth, or political wherewithal to prevent stresses from bleeding into all-out violence. But, well, here is a little optimism. For just as climate change is helping to pitch people against one another, with the right leadership and under the right circumstances, it can also bring hostile, tense, and warring communities back together. In fact, instances of environmental peacebuilding, or EP, as this practice is generally known, can be found in every country described in this book—and sometimes in spades. The nexus between conflict and climate need not mean only blood, guts, and society-splitting fights.[2]

The basic idea behind EP is that shared climate and environmental concerns can form mutually attractive entry points for conflict resolution, conflict reduction, conflict prevention, and conflict recovery. As supposedly soft topics that span boundaries and often self-evidently demand engagement with foes, they are subject to cooperation between communities and governments in ways few other issues are. In time, that interaction could or should generate trust and momentum for action in other areas, all while delivering superior environmental outcomes—a win-win-win. Or so the theory more or less goes.

None of this is entirely revolutionary, and most of it has been deployed in some form in the past. Though rarely cast in explicitly environmental terms, the European Union originated as a variation of this concept, its forebear—the European Coal and Steel Community— starting life as a bid to bind France and Germany together through mutual economic interdependencies after the horrors of the two world wars, and simultaneously maximize the efficient use of one another's resources. Throughout the Cold War, the United States and the Soviet Union cooperated on scientific projects even during the darkest days of near–nuclear Armageddon. More recently, US-Iranian exchanges over water and renewable energy in the years running up to 2015 went some way toward making the nuclear deal happen, according to those involved in the dialogue. "My old boss argued that you have science diplomacy once you have a relationship," says Alex Dehgan, a former chief scientist at the US Agency for International Development (USAID). "History has shown us that it's the other way around. That's what leads to breakthroughs."

But with worsening climate change and environmental degradation— as well as the conflicts that can emerge out of both forces—peacebuilders suggest that the moment cries out for something a bit more ambitious. To that end, they and their development and aid agency peers have started incorporating climate considerations into as many conflict-zone interventions as possible, a recognition in part of how often war and warming dine off one another and how tricky, if not impossible, it is to disentangle the two.* They are rolling out environment-focused programming in places where other forms of peacebuilding have yielded few or insufficient results. Animated by the half-expectation, half-hope that contemporary statesmen will exhibit the same attitude as their predecessors—and talk climate change even when they will exchange on little else—climate advocates are trying to leverage these issues to douse tensions the world over.

All of this, scholars of EP agree, is tremendously exciting, an opportunity to deliver wide-ranging benefits to communities on the frontlines of climate and conflict chaos and help revise the climate-change-must-mean-misery narrative. "This is partly about optics," as Erika Weinthal, a leading scholar of environmental peacebuilding, puts it. "A rewriting of the script about environmental and climate troubles." The most immediate questions are: Can practitioners implement projects without generating additional problems? And, on a planet in which climate stresses and political mismanagement are spiraling, can they keep pace with the rot?

Cooperation across Unhappy Borders

From the inexplicably popular *Mona Lisa* to the unexpected smallness of Stonehenge, the world is full of touristic letdowns. Never, however, have I seen or heard more immediate sighs of disappointment than among those viewing the Jordan River for the first time. Its waters are manure-brown, sometimes producing a whiff to match. Its flow is meager—so much so that I once watched an American mother grip her teenage son by the shirt collar as they stood on one of its banks, seemingly wary that he might attempt to make good on his boast that he could jump

---

* To understand that reasoning, compare the world's most conflict-ridden countries to lists of the most climate-vulnerable. These states—Afghanistan, Mali, Yemen, and so on—are mostly one and the same.

it. Between the iffy water quality and unimpressive quantity, administrators at the reputed site of Jesus' baptism on the Jordanian side of the
Jordan have a job just to maintain a semi-sacred aura. They do not, as
I found in one testy interview in 2014, take kindly to suggestions that
pilgrims are immersing themselves in filth. "It might be muddy, but it
remains the holy river," said Rustom Mkhijian, a senior manager at the
site, his face straining to maintain a smile, after I broached a local water
expert's conviction that the Jordan was more feces than fish. "Be careful
whose data you believe."[3]

Yet, as improbable as it might sound, this piddling stream is a success
story in more ways than one. Ever since Jordan and Israel struck a peace
deal in 1994, environmentalists from those countries, along with their
Palestinian counterparts, have worked wonders to slow and in small
ways reverse the waterway's decline. Were it not for their efforts, there
is no telling quite how rotten the biblical river—and, for that matter,
much of the area's natural landscape—would have gotten.

This kind of cooperation is tricky no matter the context, bogged
down, as it frequently is, by the greater costs and bureaucratic complications that come with navigating multiple jurisdictions.[4] It is doubly difficult across these particular borders. For the most part, Israelis and their
neighbors remain mutually hostile after decades of hot war, cold war,
and something in between. Government-to-government relations are
poor—so much so that they sometimes barely extend beyond military-
to-military contacts. Amid a half-century-long Israeli occupation of the
West Bank and repeated cycles of violence there and in Gaza, most parties to the conflict have merely added to the environmental destruction
rather than tempered it.

But cooperate they have—and for very good reasons. For a start, the
Holy Land is tiny, a patch of land barely bigger than Vermont, and one
in which those walls and fences subdivide states with no regard to natural boundaries. Almost every water resource is shared. What happens

in a frontier-side Palestinian community invariably affects nearby Israelis—and vice versa. There is, simply put, no avoiding cooperation with the other, however much many people might want to disengage. "You've got mayors and teachers who are talking to each and cooperating on a regular basis, and not because they love each other, but because they're in the same boat," said Gidon Bromberg, the Israeli co-director of EcoPeace Middle East, an Israeli-Palestinian-Jordanian NGO that has worked for the three countries' environmental betterment since the 1990s. "We sink or swim together."

In the West Bank, for example, environmentalists have collaborated across borders to stifle wastewater flow from poorer Palestinian communities, which, given the fragmented political landscape, cannot help but sully shared aquifers. In Gaza, Israeli environmentalists have been instrumental in getting as many solar panels and mini desalination stations as possible into the blockaded strip. They have done this above all else to help residents who receive insufficient electricity and water and whose meager supplies of both have been repeatedly knocked out during Israel–Hamas wars. But there is a degree of rational self-interest, too. The less diesel Gazans burn, the less the pollution that wafts, in this very interconnected land, into the Israeli towns next door. Conservationists from all three nations have most energetically banded together to protect wildlife, which, as the saying goes, truly knows no borders.*

For another (related) reason, the Jordan basin states all have things that their neighbors need. Israelis lack space for solar plants to meet their climate action commitments, their own desert almost fully allocated

---

* I had originally intended—and written up—this chapter as a deep exploration of Israeli–Palestinian environmental peacebuilding, a genuine "good news" story in a land increasingly bereft of them. Given the risk of imperiling projects and perhaps participants' safety, I was always going to have to go easy on details. But since 2023 the situation has become so sensitive that anything more than vague descriptions is now inadvisable.

to nature reserves and military facilities. Palestinians need more water, with Israel granting them an unequal portion of their shared aquifers, and better-managed water after years of infrastructural neglect by their own authorities. For them and, especially for thirsty Jordanians, Israel's vaunted environmental know-how and much-prized desalination technology, which now provides about three-quarters of its citizens' drinking water, is only becoming more attractive.

As Mansour Abu Rashid, a former head of Jordanian military intelligence and a longtime advocate of transboundary EP, explained to me after a visit to some of his country's struggling farmers: "They tell me their palm trees are dying. They are being eaten from the inside by some insect. I told them: 'Give me photos and I will send them to Israelis. They have agricultural expertise and their farms are so close. What is there to lose?'" This is all supposed to culminate with EcoPeace's Project Prosperity, a partly implemented plan through which Israel will supply desalinated water to Jordan and later to Palestine in exchange for solar energy from Jordan's bigger, emptier desert.[5]

Crucially, in peacebuilding terms, the longer this cooperation has persisted, the more its participants have come to view their exchange as an end in itself rather than just a means of improving their collective environmental prospects. As the peace process has faltered, most contact between Israeli and Palestinian politicians has evaporated, leaving environmentalists—and sometimes *just* environmentalists—to maintain dialogue. That is no small thing in a land where water concerns have contributed to major hostilities in the past, as with the Six-Day War in 1967, and where climate change threatens to drip-feed new tensions that states stand no chance of addressing unless they work together—or, at the very least, avoid conflict. "Jaw, jaw is better than war, war," explained one Palestinian conservationist, repeating a line generally (if incorrectly) attributed to Churchill, when I asked what motivated him. Meeting within the desert confines of the Arava Institute for Environmental

Studies, a center which trains up cohorts of young Israeli, Palestinian, and Jordanian environmentalists, he then launched into an impassioned discussion with a visiting Israeli parliamentarian, not relenting until the bell sounded for dinner.

Peacebuilding on a Local Level

Enamored with this sort of work, donor and afflicted governments are trying to replicate variations of it elsewhere. Despite countless efforts, including those by Iran, which is trying to assemble a coalition to combat sandstorms with its neighbors, they have little to show for their efforts so far.[6] (It may just be that the issues that help make the Israeli–Palestinian conflict so horribly intractable, such as the small, exceptionally entwined nature of the land and an inopportune person-to-resource ratio, may also make it especially well-suited to EP action.) But, on a local level, environmental peacebuilders have much more to brag about.

Take the experience of Demboi Sow. When we met near the northern Senegalese village of Younoufèré in 2022 I had spent weeks documenting farmer–herder fights across West Africa. The very fact, then, that he and his neighbors were at ease with one another came as a happy change of pace. His cattle were appropriately fat. His house, a sturdy mixture of mud and concrete, looked a good deal better-kept than most others I had seen. With the aroma of roasting beef coming from his yard, a rare delicacy even for families who live and breathe livestock but one they were about to enjoy in celebration of a son returning from a year away in the capital, life seemed very tolerable indeed. But none of this, he conceded, had looked likely in the previous years. Until 2020, this chunk of the Sahel had been as riven with tensions as many of those described in chapter 5. It was not until a herder killed another herder in a tussle for scarce pasture —and tit-for-tat animal killings picked up—that relations started to improve.

As Sow and his neighbors tell it, they had tried to establish mediation mechanisms themselves, but had stumbled for lack of trust. Things changed very quickly with the involvement of Agronomes & Vétérinaires Sans Frontières (AVSF), an international agricultural NGO with a big local presence. First the organization recruited representatives from villages across the Ferlo, each chosen by local elders to ensure community buy-in, and all of them divided among twenty-five "pastoral units," including one in Younouféré. Then they provided a forum for these representatives to meet and hash out herd placements, maximum herd numbers, and compensation in the event that herders wronged one another or area farmers.

While still struggling with the impact of erratic rains, herders across several pastoral units say that they are experiencing less violence than at any point in the past decade, even as clashes mushroom in other parts of the Sahel. For that, interviewees told me, they have the pastoral units to thank. "Life is still hard, but we've found that we can provide for most people and protect the land with better coordination," said Demboi Sow. "I'm not sure what we would have done without this mediation."

The Sahel in particular is dotted with such initiatives, impressive peacemaking counterpoints to destabilizing pressures, and their success stands as a handy illustration of where, why, and how EP is most likely to yield results.[7] Largely small in scale, these schemes can be put into place on a relative shoestring, which, in an era of deepening humanitarian funding crunches, is key.* For the most part, the efforts are led by locals and so are more in tune with the needs and desires of the intended recipients than are many interventions from

---

* According to an official at the UN Peacebuilding Fund (UNPBF), one of the largest organizations of its kind, the fund dispersed about $130 million to EP projects in the years leading up to 2023, with about half of these projects in Africa's Sahel. But, the official added, they cannot meet demand for assistance as more humanitarian crises absorb donor cash.

on high. For example, within the same areas that AVSF has enjoyed success, the Senegalese government has introduced a significantly less welcome mechanism to mediate farmer–herder clashes. It is not working, one farmer about fifty miles from Younouféré told me. Worse, by supplanting some of the informal arbitration bodies that communities had developed themselves, government-imposed mediation could ignite more violence.

Importantly, in regions as riddled with overlapping conflicts as the Sahel, localized EP can be at least partly divorced from wider geopolitics. This has certainly been true of Wadi El Ku in Sudan's Darfur, where the UN Environment Programme (UNEP) built a series of weirs to conserve rainwater and thereby spread its use through the dry season.[8] That program, which reduced farmer–herder fights, has continued to prosper even as Sudan has collapsed into an almost countrywide civil war since 2023. "The evidence for environmental peacebuilding at a local level is compelling," says Silje Halle, an EP expert at UNEP. "The challenge for us is scaling it up without losing that nuanced understanding. A cookie-cutter approach simply won't work."

Do No Harm

But what if EP programming does go wrong, or is poorly conceived in the first place? As snapshots of severe environmental degradation go, Jebel Abdelaziz, in northeastern Syria, is hard to beat. The mountain's long, low, rocky flanks offer little for livestock. The surrounding plain, now riddled with artillery proving grounds and landfill sites, is no more hospitable for man or beast. Extending about thirty miles from Hasakah city into the lightly populated desert scrub, the *jebel*, or mountain—and the villages that border it—are a study in scarcity, a highly visual depiction of hopelessness and grinding poverty. Life, according to locals, is wretched.

"We are the poorest of the poor," said Abdelaziz Abdelrahman, who had recently lost half his sheep to starvation and whose five remaining animals looked like they might soon join the others. "We have nothing," echoed Om Mohammed, a mother of seven and resident of Jouran Abyad village, when we met on a trip to the area in September 2021. Her clothes threadbare and lone field uncultivable, she was barely exaggerating.[9]

But while these communities' struggles owe much to the same killer blend of drought and mismanagement that ails nearby Iraqi villages, they also have a more specific man-made gripe. Starting in the 1980s, officials in distant Damascus began planting the mountain with trees, a bid to re-green the area after decades of degradation. Soon after, in 1994, they demarcated it as a protected area, closing off villagers' pasture without consultation or compensation and upon pain of imprisonment were they to breach the new restrictions. To twist the knife, they did not grant many of them jobs as forest rangers either, instead choosing Syrians from elsewhere in the country.[10] It is no wonder, I thought, that so many people, from South America to southern Africa, have come to see environmental projects as the enemy.[11]

This scheme, while never specifically presented as a peacebuilding program, is characteristic of how insensitively applied environmental initiatives can fail while also saddling people and places with whole new challenges. For example, some attempts to engage "problem" countries on environmental issues have merely shone a dangerous spotlight on local partners, as has happened in Iran. Having worked with Western conservationists to try and bolster big-cat protection, the men and women of the Persian Wildlife Heritage Foundation earned the unwanted attention of the security apparatus, which mistrusts contact with foreign scientists. They were all jailed in 2018, one dying soon afterward in suspicious circumstances, and several others withering away in jail until they were released in spring 2024.[12]

Worst of all, as at Jebel Abdelaziz, these schemes have sometimes fueled additional violence, a mark of misguided interference if ever there was one. When ISIS surged through the area in 2013–14, it absorbed an outsized number of residents—about a hundred men, according to a local security source, many seemingly propelled into jihadi ranks by an exaggerated version of the desperation, grievance, and greed that has served the group so well across these lands. Even now, with anti-ISIS forces stationed on the mountain and at checkpoints strung across surrounding roads, the area is reputed to host extremist sleeper cells. After encountering a few overly inquisitive residents, a number of whom panicked my driver by circling back several times to examine us as we conducted interviews along the road, we made ourselves scarce. Ultimately, the takeaway ought to be clear: Bad EP can be worse than no EP at all.

Tempering Expectations

It was a little before 8:00 a.m. on October 7, 2023, when Jerusalem's air-raid sirens sounded to signal incoming rockets. Leaping from the couch to a balcony, I watched as the Iron Dome interceptor system swatted most of the projectiles out of the sky amid loud bangs and wisps of smoke from the detonations high above. At the same time, as reports began to filter through of a massacre in southern Israel, I eagerly scanned social media reports, all while fielding requests for information from observant Jews in neighboring apartments, who on this, a sabbath morning, deemed it religiously impermissible to check the news.

Over the next few hours, my Israeli and Palestinian environmental colleagues and I tried to compute what this meant for the busy week of site visits that we had planned. While ducking in and out of bomb shelters and dodging cars that were going twice the legal limit through the untrafficked streets, a friend and I also marveled at an Old City suddenly emptied of tourists. But as the Israeli checkpoints into the West Bank shuttered and then, a little later, the scale of both the Hamas massacre and the likely scope of Israel's retribution came into focus, we soon realized this was no regular "flare-up" in the conflict. After years of painstaking environmental collaboration, the fruits of these conservationists' collective labors were suddenly in peril, the environment, temporarily at least, fading into irrelevance in the face of the hardest of security issues.[13] When I messaged a normally fast-responding Palestinian environmentalist friend, he replied after a delay: "You don't want to speak to me right now because I'll tell you that this work is useless, even if I don't necessarily believe that."

In the period since then, regional peacebuilders have been confronted by a series of harsh truths, most of which they already knew but which people like me, swept away by the excitement of witnessing EP in action in so many improbable settings, had perhaps conspired to forget: you can detach the environment from a conflict's wider dynamics to a degree, but only to a degree. As Ram Aviram, a former lead Israeli water negotiator and diplomat, found in the 1990s, there is no overcoming certain obstacles. "In 1999, we were close to an all-encompassing water agreement—Israelis, Palestinians, and Jordanians. But the reality of the occupation ultimately got in the way."

You can engineer frequent environmental victories, but without a firm political foundation they can all be horribly fleeting, shattered as easily as good times can be crushed by gunfire at a music festival, as during Hamas's initial October assault, in which they killed myriad environmental and peace activists, or by the subsequent Israeli airstrikes on residential tower blocks across Gaza, which, among many, many others, have also killed some of the Strip's leading environmentalists. In these situations, even "success" can look like anything but success. There is no telling how much worse the security situation in the West Bank and security and humanitarian situations in Gaza might have been without EP efforts. But, amid tremendous suffering, that counterfactual hardly appears persuasive.* As exciting a tool as EP is, there is a limit to its miracle-making.

Hope for Hope

In June 1816, a group of friends, among them Lord Byron, Percy Bysshe Shelley, and Mary Godwin (soon to be Shelley) hunkered down in a Swiss lakeside villa. It was the "year without a summer," a period of temporary cooling brought on by the eruption of Indonesia's Mount Tambora, and the weather was dreadful. Restless, imprisoned inside, and hopped-up on various opiates, Byron challenged the group to a scary-story writing contest. Eighteen-year-old Mary rose spectacularly to the occasion, dreaming up and then quickly putting to paper the first draft of *Frankenstein*. Elsewhere, across a sodden Europe, many others were stirred to similar bursts of creativity. Karl Drais invented an early version of the bicycle, spurred on, it seems, by a pursuit of a horseless means of transport in a land then devoid of oats. Justus Liebig was supposedly disturbed enough by memories of the famine that accompanied the cold to devote his life to agriculture, later becoming the "father of the fertilizer industry."[14] And so on. You get the point. Out of miserable situations can come great things. In a world blighted by climate-related violence, environmental peacebuilding could one day truly come into its own.

Some of this optimism is grounded in technology, a tool which, in peacebuilding terms, has previously promised much but delivered little and which has consequently inspired tremendous cynicism among practitioners. Yet even some of the most skeptical of the skeptics wonder if

---

* This is a problem in EP in general, where practitioners maintain, likely correctly, that they have enjoyed many more successes than is popularly understood. It is just that proving the absence of additional violence can be nigh on impossible.

the future might be different. For example, in the Sahel, organizations are rolling out new tools that are designed to help farmers and herders directly, rather than helping those who are helping farmers and herders, as was largely true of earlier technologies. By cutting out the "middle-man," these schemes are designed to more quickly reach those at the vanguard of climate-conflict vulnerability—and reach them with the kind of information that they need and want.[15] In Mauritania in 2022, I encountered an impressive case in point. A herdsman drew close to the border with Senegal in order to take advantage of a service that, at that time at least, was available in the neighboring country but not his own. Then inserting a Senegalese sim card into his phone, he dialed in to a call center which, for a few cents a minute, provided up-to-date advice from satellite imagery on where he might find suitably rich pasture.

Heartened by how closely some forms of present climate cooperation are mimicking past science diplomacy success, more of this hope derives from great and hostile powers' apparent willingness to detach climate action from their wider relationships. We see this along the Mediter-ranean, where all littoral countries have remained engaged on shared maritime issues despite many hostile inter-state relationships and mul-tiple conflicts along the seaboard.[16] We see this in East Africa, where IGAD, the regional body, has emerged as a leader in applying climate security research, despite frequently tense country-to-country deal-ings.[17] Crucially, we might see it between the United States and China, where officials are trying and possibly succeeding in leveraging the pros-pect of shared climate disaster to keep the relationship on some kind of footing. From the Jordan basin to Ukraine's Donbas region, where peacebuilders brought together scientists from Ukrainian- and Rus-sian-controlled parts of the country in order to prevent more-intense chemical and nuclear contamination following Russia's initial invasion of the area in 2014, we have proof of concept in the most challenging of circumstances.

Above all, there is the very human rationale for relative optimism. Because despite frequent suggestions that only a thin veneer of civilization separates us from a *Lord of the Flies*–style war of all against all, there is a wealth of evidence to the contrary. Very few people actually welcome clashes. It is extraordinary, I have often thought, that there is not more climate-induced violence, given how much circumstances and sometimes officialdom are thrusting people together. Grant communities the means and the mechanisms to temper threats to their stability, and most will leap at them.

Acknowledgments

"Writing a book is a horrible, exhausting struggle, like a long bout of some painful illness," George Orwell insisted in *Why I Write*. For all my tiresome grumbling, though, this process hasn't been too bad. But it hasn't been too bad because of the extraordinary assistance I have received from so many friends, relatives, and colleagues at every step of the way.

First of all, I owe an unpayable debt to the dozens of fixers and interpreters, many superb journalists in their own right, with whom I have worked across so many countries. Without them, I would have struggled to stay safe and produce much of my work, let alone this book. To Mohammed, Raahat, Sohan, Hussam, Rojita, Oumar, Mo, Nosseir, Ahmed, Eremias, and so many others, including a number who would not want to be named given the media climate in their respective countries, a massive thank-you.

An equally big thank-you goes to my colleagues in the climate security world—Lauren Herzer Risi, Frank Femia, Caitlin Werrell, Shiloh Fetzek, Erin Sikorsky, Josh Busby, Daniel Abrahams, Marcus King, Carl Bruch, Lizzie Sellwood, Geoff Dabelko, Aaron Salzberg, Aaron Wolf,

Meaghan Parker, Oli Brown, Wim Zwijnenburg, and so very many others, a number of whom I will kick myself later for not remembering to name-check. Many of you, along with journalist and researcher friends, read chapters, answered endless queries, and provided vital feedback throughout. More importantly, you helped inform my general understanding of climate security risks since early in my career.

Then there are the many people whose work is not mine but which features in this book and has ensured that this is a much more captivating and well-rounded animal than it otherwise would have been. Thank-you to the ten photographer friends who allowed me to use their images. An extra big thank-you to Alexandra Rose Howland, who painstakingly hand-illustrated the maps.

Equally, a thank-you to the Rockefeller Brothers Fund, which gave me a grant to offset some of the last-minute travel I needed to round out some of the gaps in my narrative—and to my editors at various outlets who allowed me to use small excerpts of my earlier work. For saving me some work, as well as improving my features writing in the case of Brian, Rob, Lori, and a range of others at *NatGeo*, I am naturally grateful.

A very necessary note of thanks, too, to both Jessica Papin, my agent, who displayed genuinely unreasonable levels of patience when I took two-plus years to complete my original proposal, and Emily Turner, my editor. She along with the rest of the team at Island Press was a pleasure to work with. It is thanks to her that this became a much more readable book.

To my friends, thank-you for still being my friends after this process. That was by no means a given, the instant-gratification monkey that I am and one who was forced to remain focused on a single task for an extended period for possibly the first time in his life. And to my family and especially my parents, for your constant love and support. My mother, helpfully, an editor, provided invaluable advice on all things book from the beginning. My father posted regular newspaper clips of varying levels of relevance from the US to Greece. Their distinct lettering is always a delight to see in my apartment-building postbox.

Two final expressions of thanks. To John Burbank, who taught me history from the age of eight, and who did more than anyone to instill in me a love of reading, writing, and books in general. And, above all, to my partner Katrin, for her endless words of encouragement and love.

Further Reading

This is a brief list in which I have gone a bit easy on the number of journal papers for the sake of accessibility but have almost invariably omitted a bunch of "must-reads" in the process.

Environment of Peace: Security in a New Era of Risk, Stockholm International Peace Research Institute (SIPRI), May 2022, https://www.sipri.org/research /peace-and-development/environment-peace.
A monster, four-part exploration of all things environment and peace, with a (slightly) shorter summary.

Weathering Risk: Promoting Peace and Resilience in a Changing Climate, Adelphi, June 2023, https://adelphi.de/en/projects/weathering-risk-promoting-peace-and -resilience-in-a-changing-climate.
Similar-ish in its thrust to Environment of Peace but nevertheless covering plenty of different ground, this too is worth reading.

Joshua W. Busby, *States and Nature* (Cambridge, UK: Cambridge University Press, 2022).
Why do climate stresses contribute to severe instability in some places but not in others with similar profiles and equal exposure to the same stresses? Read for a lot of big hints.

Elizabeth Chalecki, *Environmental Security: A Guide to the Issues* (London: Bloomsbury, 2013).
What it says on the tin. A handy primer.

Marwa Daoudy, *The Origins of the Syrian Conflict* (Cambridge, UK: Cambridge University Press, 2020).

Discussion of the extent and nature of climate's contribution to the war in Syria continues to partly animate the climate security field. This is a comprehensive rundown of the debate, which spans Gleick and others who attribute to climate change a significant role, through to de Châtel and company, who largely do not.

Solomon M. Hsiang and Marshall Burke, "Climate, conflict, and social stability: What does the evidence say?" *Climatic Change* 123 (October 17, 2013): 39–55, https://link.springer.com/article/10.1007/s10584-013-0868-3.

From 2013 to 2014, this article triggered a long back-and-forth with other climate- and environmental-security-focused scholars, many of whom disagreed with the manner in which Hsiang and Burke had conducted their analysis and who felt that, as a consequence, they had overstated climate's contribution to conflict. The whole exchange (starting with Halvard Buhaug et al., "One effect to rule them all? A comment on climate and conflict," Climatic Change 127 [October 27, 2014]: 391–97) is well worth reading.

Idean Salehyan and Cullen Hendrix, "Climate shocks and political violence," *Global Environmental Change* 28, no. 1 (September 2014): 239–50, https://www.sciencedirect.com/science/article/abs/pii/S0959378014001344.

These scholars argue that we should fear the security challenges arising out of resource abundance much more than those of scarcity.

Daniel Abrahams, "Conflict in abundance and peacebuilding in scarcity: Challenges and opportunities in addressing climate change and conflict," *World Development* 132 (August 2020), https://www.sciencedirect.com/science/article/abs/pii/S0305750X20301248.

How climate-conflict discourses inform development policy—and why organizations struggle to incorporate these risks into their programming.

Geoffrey D. Dabelko et al., "Backdraft: The Conflict Potential of Climate Change Adaptation and Mitigation," Wilson Center, 2013, https://www.wilsoncenter.org/sites/default/files/media/documents/publication/ECSP_REPORT_14_2_BACKDRAFT.pdf.

A deep exploration of the security perils that could arise from efforts to manage and tackle climate stresses.

"Military Responses to Climate Hazards (MiRCH) Tracker," Council on Strategic Risks, Center for Climate and Security, https://councilonstrategicrisks.org/ccs/mirch/, accessed April 22, 2024.
A useful illustration of the frequency and geographic range within which global militaries are being deployed to combat climate stresses.

"National Intelligence Estimate: Climate Change and International Responses Increasing Challenges to US National Security Through 2040," National Intelligence Council, Office of the Director of National Intelligence, 2021, https://www.dni.gov/files/ODNI/documents/assessments/NIE_Climate_Change_and_National_Security.pdf.
How do US intelligence services assess climate risks to the US? Read.

Adája Stoetman et al., "Military capabilities affected by climate change: An analysis of China, Russia, and the United States," Clingendael, Netherlands Institute of International Relations, January 2023, https://www.clingendael.org/sites/default/files/2023-01/Military_capabilities_affected_by_climate_change.pdf.
A brief-ish rundown of what climate change might mean for leading global militaries.

Sherri Goodman, *Threat Multiplier: Climate, Military Leadership, and the Fight for Global Security* (Washington, DC: Island Press, 2024).
An inside look at how the Pentagon came to see climate change as a threat to US national security—written by one of the field's leading practitioners.

Tobias Ide et al., "The past and future(s) of environmental peacebuilding," *International Affairs* 97, no. 1 (January 2021), https://academic.oup.com/ia/article/97/1/1/6041492.
Written by some of environmental peacebuilding's (EP's) top scholars, a summary of the field's origins and of its possible future directions.

Oli Brown and Giuliana Nicolucci-Altman, "The Future of Environmental Peacebuilding: Nurturing an Ecosystem for Peace," Ecosystem for Peace white paper, 2022, https://static1.squarespace.com/static/61dc05c236d4333322aa36f4/t/61f82d32f94646095e2cd9b4/1643654497051/The+Future+of+Environmental+Peacebuilding+-+A+White+Paper+%282022%29.pdf.
A series of white papers exploring EP across the world.

Notes

Introduction

1. Joshua W. Busby, *States and Nature* (Cambridge, UK: Cambridge University Press, 2022), 71.
2. Kyle Harper, *The Fate of Rome* (Princeton, NJ: Princeton University Press, 2017), 133.
3. Peter Frankopan, *The Earth Transformed* (Knopf, 2023). P 292.
4. Peter Schwartzstein, "Death of the Nile," BBC, October 10, 2017, https://www.bbc.com/news/resources/idt-sh/death_of_the_nile.
5. Peter Schwartzstein, "What Will Happen if the World No Longer Has Water?" *Newsweek*, November 22, 2017, https://www.newsweek.com/2017/12/01/what-happens-world-without-water-jordan-crisis-717365.html.
6. "Number of armed conflicts, World, Uppsala Conflict Data Program, 2023, *Our World in Data*, https://ourworldindata.org/grapher/number-of-armed-conflicts.
7. Bastian Herre, "The World Has Recently Become Less Democratic," *Our World in Data*, September 6, 2022, https://ourworldindata.org/less-democratic.
8. Cullen S. Hendrix, "The streetlight effect in climate change research on Africa," *Global Environmental Change* 43 (March 2017): 137–47, https://www.sciencedirect.com/science/article/abs/pii/S0959378016302412.
9. Solomon M. Hsiang et al., "Quantifying the Impact of Climate on Human Conflict," *Science* 341, no. 6151), August 1, 2013, https://www.science.org/doi/10.1126/science.1235367.
10. Chi Xu et al., "Future of the human climate niche," *PNAS* 117, no. 21 (May 4, 2020): 11350–55, https://www.pnas.org/doi/10.1073/pnas.1910114117.
11. Jay Famiglietti and Jose Ignacio Galindo, "Water shortages must be placed on the climate change agenda. This is why," World Economic Forum (WEF), August 24, 2022, https://www.weforum.org/agenda/2022/08/why-water-shortages-make-water-next-for-industry-reporting/.
12. Jiseon Lee et al., "Water-related disasters and their health impacts: A global review," *Progress*

287

in Disaster Science 8 (December 2020), https://www.sciencedirect.com/science/article/pii/S2590061720300600.

13. Jonathan Franzen, "The Problem of Nature Writing," *New Yorker*, August 12, 2023, https://www.newyorker.com/culture/the-weekend-essay/the-problem-of-nature-writing.

Chapter 1

1. Chapter 1 partly draws off and contains quotes excerpted from this article:

   Peter Schwartzstein, "Climate Change and Water Woes Drove ISIS Recruiting in Iraq," *National Geographic*, November 13, 2017, https://www.nationalgeographic.com/science/article/climate-change-drought-drove-isis-terrorist-recruiting-iraq.

2. Jacqueline Parry et al., "Managing Exits from Conflict in Iraq: A Case Study of Basra and Tel Afar," United Nations University, Centre for Policy Research, August 2022, https://iraq.un.org/sites/default/files/2022-08/MEAC_CaseStudyIraq_1.pdf.

3. Margaret MacMillan, *War: How Conflict Shaped Us* (New York: Random House, 2020), 139.

4. Amy Mackinnon, "Russia Is Sending Its Ethnic Minorities to the Meat Grinder," *Foreign Policy*, September 23, 2022, https://foreignpolicy.com/2022/09/23/russia-partial-military-mobilization-ethnic-minorities/.

5. Peter Schwartzstein, "Climate, Water, and Militias: A Field Study from Southern Iraq," Center for Climate and Security, January 2023, https://climateandsecurity.org/2023/01/briefer-climate-water-and-militias-a-field-study-from-southern-iraq/.

6. Peter Schwartzstein and Wim Zwijnenburg, "'We Fear More War, We Fear More Drought': How Climate and Conflict Are Fragmenting Rural Syria," Pax for Peace, January 2022, https://paxforpeace.nl/wp-content/uploads/sites/2/import/2022-02/PAX_report-Pastoralist_Syria.pdf.

7. Figures for 2022 taken from: World Bank, "Agriculture, forestry, and fishing, valued added (% of GDP)—Iraq," https://data.worldbank.org/indicator/NV.AGR.TOTL.ZS?locations=IQ.

8. World Bank Group, *Iraq Systematic Country Diagnostic*, Report no. 112333-IQ, February 3, 2017, https://documents1.worldbank.org/curated/en/542811487277729890/pdf/IRAQ-SCD-FINAL-cleared-02132017.pdf.

9. Peter Schwartzstein, "Amid Terror Attacks, Iraq Faces Water Crisis," *National Geographic*, November 5, 2014, https://www.nationalgeographic.com/science/article/141104-iraq-water-crisis-turkey-iran-isis.

10. Human Rights Watch, "Basra Is Thirsty: Iraq's Failure to Manage the Water Crisis," July 2019, https://www.hrw.org/report/2019/07/22/basra-thirsty/iraqs-failure-manage-water-crisis.

11. "Human-induced climate change compounded by socio-economic water stressors increased severity of drought in Syria, Iraq and Iran," World Weather Attribution, November 8, 2023, https://www.worldweatherattribution.org/human-induced-climate-change-compounded-by-socio-economic-water-stressors-increased-severity-of-drought-in-syria-iraq-and-iran/.

12. Louisa Loveluck and Mustafa Salim, "Iraq broils in dangerous 120-degree heat as power grid shuts down," *Washington Post*, August 7, 2022, https://www.washingtonpost.com/world/2022/08/07/baghdad-heat-record/.

13. Peter Schwartzstein, "How We Misunderstand the Magnitude of Climate Risks—and Why That Contributes to Controversy," Wilson Center, New Security Beat, January 12, 2021, https://www.newsecuritybeat.org/2021/01/misunderstand-magnitude-climate-risks-contributes-controversy/.

14. Ibid.

15. Ibid.

16. Parry et al., "Managing Exits from Conflict in Iraq."

17. Schwartzstein, "How We Misunderstand the Magnitude of Climate Risks."

18. Ibid.

19. Peter Schwartzstein, "'ISIS Weather' Brings Battles and Bloodshed in Iraq," *Outside* magazine, October 6, 2016, https://www.outsideonline.com/outdoor-adventure/environment/isis-weather-brings-battles-and-bloodshed-iraq/.

20. Schwartzstein, "Amid Terror Attacks, Iraq Faces Water Crisis."

21. Peter Schwartzstein, "The Dangerous State of Iraq's Rivers: A Letter from Abu Ghraib," *Foreign Affairs*, April 7, 2017, https://www.foreignaffairs.com/articles/iraq/2017-04-07/dangerous-state-iraqs-rivers.

22. Peter Schwartzstein, "Cleaning Up after ISIS: How Iraq's New Chemicals Team Is Trying to Undo Years of Pollution," UN Environment Programme, December 5, 2018, https://www.unep.org/news-and-stories/story/cleaning-after-isis-how-iraqs-new-chemicals-team-trying-undo-years-conflict.

23. Peter Schwartzstein, "A Hot Dusty Crossroads: How Waves of Environment-Related Displacement Are Transforming Rural—and Urban—Iraq," *Wilson Quarterly*, Fall 2021, https://www.wilsonquarterly.com/quarterly/_/a-hot-dusty-crossroads.

24. "Iraq Economic Monitor: The Slippery Road to Economic Recovery," World Bank, Fall 2021, https://documents1.worldbank.org/curated/en/981071637593726857/pdf/Iraq-Economic-Monitor-The-Slippery-Road-to-Economic-Recovery.pdf.

25. Peter Schwartzstein, "Iraqi Firefighters Race to Save Last of Middle East's Forests," *National Geographic*, July 22, 2019, https://www.nationalgeographic.com/environment/article/iraq-on-fire-firefighters.

26. Jeff Seldin, "Signs Emerge IS Is Struggling to Keep Up Fight in Iraq, Syria," Voice of America, April 25, 2023, https://www.voanews.com/a/signs-emerge-is-struggling-to-keep-up-fight-in-iraq-syria/7065860.html.

Chapter 2

1. Peter Schwartzstein, "Pirates Are Killing Bengal Tigers," *National Geographic*, November 21, 2018, https://www.nationalgeographic.com/animals/article/pirates-are-killing-tigers.

2. Mohammed Rashed-Un-Nabi and S. M. Monirul Hassan, "Study on Impact of Maritime Piracy and Armed Robbery on Bangladesh Fishers and Their Families," University of Chittagong, ISWAN, Seafarers UK, and The Mission to Seafarers, December 2017.

3. Indian Navy Information Fusion Centre—Indian Ocean Region, February 2023 report, https://www.indiannavy.nic.in/ifc-ior/static/data/reports/monthly/IFC_IOR_MMSU_FEB_2023.pdf.

4. Schwartzstein, "Pirates Are Killing Bengal Tigers."

5. Rashed-Un-Nabi and Hassan, "Study on Impact of Maritime Piracy and Armed Robbery."

6. Ibid.

7. Hemani Bandari, "The reporters who cover the remotest parts of rural India have now reached the Oscars," *The Hindu*, January 8, 2022, https://www.thehindu.com/society/the-reporters-who-cover-the-remotest-parts-of-rural-india-have-now-reached-the-oscars/article38165834.ece.

8. Vice News, "Pirates Are Running Wild off West Africa's Coast," August 21, 2021 https://www.youtube.com/watch?v=6XtuPck0b4U.

9. Willem van Schendel, *A History of Bangladesh* (Cambridge, UK: Cambridge University Press, 2020), 50.

10. Ibid.

11. Amitav Ghosh, *The Great Derangement* (Chicago: University of Chicago Press, 2016), 5.

12. Peter Schwartzstein, "This Vanishing Forest Protects the Coasts—and Lives—of Two Countries," *National Geographic*, June 18, 2019, https://www.nationalgeographic.com/magazine/article/sundarbans-mangrove-forest-in-bangladesh-india-threatened-by-rising-waters-illegal-logging.

13. Philip Gain et al., *Shores of Tear* (Dhaka, Bangladesh: Society for Environment and Human Development, 2013), 56–61.

14. Schwartzstein, "Pirates Are Killing Bengal Tigers."

15. Peter Schwartzstein, "Pirates and Climate Change: A Dispatch from the Bangladeshi Sundarbans," Center for Climate and Security, June 6, 2018, https://climateandsecurity.org/2018/06/pirates-and-climate-change-a-dispatch-from-the-bangladeshi-sundarbans/.

16. Schwartzstein, "Pirates Are Killing Bengal Tigers."

17. Gain et al., *Shores of Tear*, 14.

18. Rashed-Un-Nabi and Hassan, "Study on Impact of Maritime Piracy and Armed Robbery."

19. Schwartzstein, "Pirates Are Killing Bengal Tigers."

20. Gain et al., *Shores of Tear*, 94.

21. M. Monirul and H. Khan, *Tigers in the Mangroves* (Dhaka, Bangladesh: Arannayk Foundation, 2011), 149.

22. Schwartzstein, "Pirates Are Killing Bengal Tigers."

23. Suhasini Raj, "Facing Disastrous Floods, They Turned to Mangrove Trees for Protection," *New York Times*, April 10, 2022, https://www.nytimes.com/2022/04/10/world/asia/sundarbans-mangroves-india-bangladesh.html.

24. Peter Schwartzstein, "Going Under: A Rural Bangladeshi Dilemma," Wilson Center, January 27, 2022, https://www.wilsoncenter.org/article/going-under-rural-bangladeshi-dilemma.

25. Viviane Clement et al., "Groundswell Part 2: Acting on Internal Climate Migration," World Bank, September 13, 2021, https://openknowledge.worldbank.org/entities/publication/2c9150df-52c3-58ed-9075-d78ea56c3267.

26. Syfullah Faruque, "A Look into Journalist Mohsin-ul Hakim's Courageous Story," *Ice Today*, May 3, 2017, https://icetoday.net/2017/05/a-look-into-journalist-mohsin-ul-hakims-courageous-story/.

27. Schwartzstein, "Pirates Are Killing Bengal Tigers."

28. Schwartzstein, "Pirates and Climate Change."

29. Nasir Uddin et al., "Tigers at a crossroads: Shedding light on the role of Bangladesh in the illegal trade of this iconic big cat," *Conservation Science and Practice* 5, no. 7 (March 15, 2023), https://conbio.onlinelibrary.wiley.com/doi/epdf/10.1111/csp2.12952.

30. P. Wester et al., "Water, ice, society, and ecosystems in the Hindu Kush Himalaya: An outlook," International Centre for Integrated Mountain Development (ICIMOD), June 20, 2023, https://hkh.icimod.org/hi-wise/hi-wise-report/.

31. Schwartzstein, "This Vanishing Forest."

32. Schwartzstein, "Pirates and Climate Change."

Chapter 3

1. Chapter 3 partly draws from and includes small excerpts from these articles:

Peter Schwartzstein, "Death of the Nile," BBC, October 10, 2017, https://www.bbc.com/news/resources/idt-sh/death_of_the_nile.

Peter Schwartzstein, "Why the Nile Constitutes a New Kind of Water Dispute," Center for

Climate and Security, July 15, 2020, https://climateandsecurity.org/2020/07/why-the-nile
-constitutes-a-new-kind-of-water-dispute-and-why-thats-dangerous/.

Peter Schwartzstein, "Why Water Conflict Is Rising, Especially on the Local Level," Center
for Climate and Security, February 26, 2021, https://climateandsecurity.org/2021/02
/why-localized-water-violence-is-flourishing-even-as-transboundary-water-wars-are-not/.

2. David Witty, "The US–Egypt Military Relationship: Complexities, Contradictions, and
Challenges," Washington Institute for Near East Policy, May 23, 2022, https://www.wash-
ingtoninstitute.org/policy-analysis/us-egypt-military-relationship-complexities-contra
dictions-and-challenges.

3. Aaron Wolf et al., "Water Can Be a Pathway to Peace, Not War," Wilson Center, July 2006,
https://www.wilsoncenter.org/sites/default/files/media/documents/publication/Navigating
PeaceIssue1.pdf.

4. "Food Price Shocks in Egypt," *Climate Diplomacy*, Adelphi, n.d., https://climate-diplomacy
.org/case-studies/food-price-shocks-egypt.

5. Ahmed Maher, "Egyptian politicians caught in on-air Ethiopia dam gaffe," BBC, June 4,
2013, https://www.bbc.com/news/world-africa-22771563.

6. Al Jazeera / Mohamed Vall, "Trump says Egypt may 'blow up' Ethiopia dam," Al Jazeera,
October 24, 2020, https://www.youtube.com/watch?v=eFpXz-Xbse4.

7. Elias Meseret, "Ethiopia's Nobel-winning leader warns Egypt over dam," Associated Press,
October 22, 2019, https://apnews.com/general-news-9deb28e2af6249198dde54160ff62
c3b.

8. Witty, "The US–Egypt Military Relationship."

9. "Ethiopia bans flights over huge dam 'for security reasons,'" Al Jazeera, October 5, 2020,
https://www.aljazeera.com/news/2020/10/5/ethiopia-bans-flights-over-new-dam-for
-security-reasons.

10. Peter Schwartzstein, "One of Africa's Most Fertile Lands Is Struggling to Feed Its Own
People," *Bloomberg Businessweek*, April 2, 2019, https://www.bloomberg.com/features/2019
-sudan-nile-land-farming/.

11. Jahd Khalil, "Cairo Has a Dangerous Growth Problem—How Can It Be Fixed?" Pulitzer
Center / City Metric, June 26, 2017, https://pulitzercenter.org/stories/cairo-has-dangerous
-growth-problem-how-can-it-be-fixed.

12. Mohamed S. Siam and Elfatih A. B. Eltahir, "Climate change enhances interannual variabil-
ity of the Nile river flow," *Nature Climate Change* 7 (April 24, 2017): 350–54, https://www
.nature.com/articles/nclimate3273.

13. Jessica Barnes, *Staple Security: Bread and Wheat in Egypt* (Durham, NC: Duke University
Press, 2022), 27.

14. Embassy of Egypt, USA, Twitter (X), February 2, 2021, https://twitter.com/EgyptEmbassy
USA/status/1356702143454019584.

15. Peter Schwartzstein, "How a Metastasizing Food Crisis Threatens Sudan's Stability: A
Dispatch from Khartoum," Center for Climate and Security," October 1, 2018, https://
climateandsecurity.org/2018/10/how-a-metastasizing-food-crisis-threatens-sudans-stability
-a-dispatch-from-khartoum/.

16. Peter Schwartzstein and Leyland Cecco, "Sudan's new gold rush: Miners risk their lives in
search of riches," *The Guardian*, December 27, 2015, https://www.theguardian.com/world
/2015/dec/27/sudan-gold-rush-artisanal-miners.

17. Peter Schwartzstein, "Farming the Sahara," Takepart/Participant Media, January 8, 2016,
http://www.takepart.com.s3-website-us-east-1.amazonaws.com/feature/2016/01/08/desert
-farming-egypt/.

18. Terje Tvedt, *The River Nile in the Age of the British* (Cairo: American University in Cairo Press, 2006), 110.

19. Ibid., 303.

20. Schwartzstein, "One of Africa's Most Fertile Lands."

21. Mesenbet Assefa, Twitter (X), June 18, 2020, https://twitter.com/messiassefa/status/127352 4055438700544.

22. Daniel Yergin, *The Prize: The Epic Quest for Oil, Money, and Power* (New York: Simon & Schuster, 1990), 482.

23. Tvedt, *The River Nile in the Age of the British*, 162.

24. David D. Kirkpatrick, "Secret Recordings Reveal Mubarak's Frank Views," *New York Times*, September 22, 2013, https://www.nytimes.com/2013/09/23/world/middleeast/secret -recordings-reveal-mubaraks-frank-views-on-a-range-of-subjects.html.

25. Youm7, "السيسي: ال يوجد أزمة.. ومصر والسودان وإثيوبيا دولة واحدة," ("Sisi: There is no crisis. Egypt, Sudan, and Ethiopia are one country"), January 29, 2018, https://www .youtube.com/watch?v=5TqWssX7nMg&t=100s.

26. Haggag Salama, "23 killed in feud between families in south Egypt," Associated Press, April 5, 2014, https://apnews.com/article/673550ad5f16494f87dc086d8e52a54c.

Chapter 4

1. Chapter 4 is an expansion and extension of this article, which I have excerpted throughout: Peter Schwartzstein, "The Merchants of Thirst," *New York Times*, January 11, 2020, https:// www.nytimes.com/2020/01/11/business/drought-increasing-worldwide.html.

2. Guoqing Zhang, "Underestimated mass loss from lake-terminating glaciers in the greater Himalaya," *Nature Geoscience* 16 (April 3, 2023): 333–38, https://www.nature.com/articles /s41561-023-01150-1.

3. Abrar Mattoo, "Explained: Climate change, earthquakes, and hydropower in the Himalayas," *The Third Pole*, May 11, 2023, https://www.thethirdpole.net/en/climate/explained -climate-change-earthquakes-and-hydropower-in-the-himalayas/.

4. Damir Cosic, "Climbing Higher: Toward a Middle-Income Nepal," World Bank, May 23, 2017, https://www.worldbank.org/en/region/sar/publication/climbing-higher-toward-a -middle-income-country.

5. Diana Mitlin et al., "Unaffordable and Undrinkable: Rethinking Urban Water Access in the Global South," World Resources Institute, August 13, 2019, https://files.wri.org/d8/s3fs -public/unaffordable-and-undrinkable_0.pdf.

6. "World Urbanization Prospects: The 2018 Revision," United Nations Department of Economic and Social Affairs, 2019, https://population.un.org/wup/Publications/Files/WUP 2018-Report.pdf.

7. Ibid.

8. Sudan Bikash Maharjan et al., "The Melamchi flood disaster: Cascading hazard and the need for multihazard risk management," International Centre for Integrated Mountain Development (ICIMOD), August 2021, https://lib.icimod.org/record/35284.

9. Jack D. Ives et al., "Formation of Glacial Lakes in the Hindu Kush–Himalayas and GLOF Risk Assessment," ICIMOD, May 2010, https://www.unisdr.org/files/14048_ICIMODG LOF.pdf.

10. Gabriele Spilker et al., "Attitudes of urban residents towards environmental migration in Kenya and Vietnam," *Nature Climate Change* 10 (June 22, 2020): 622–27, https://www .nature.com/articles/s41558-020-0805-1.

11. P. Wester et al., "Water, ice, society, and ecosystems in the Hindu Kush Himalaya: An outlook," ICIMOD, June 20, 2023, https://hkh.icimod.org/hi-wise/hi-wise-report/.

Chapter 5

1. Chapter 5 is partly drawn from and contains excerpts from this article:
   Peter Schwartzstein, "Out of Place, Out of Time: The Experience of Senegal's Migratory Pastoralists," Wilson Center, January 27, 2023, https://www.wilsoncenter.org/article/out-place-out-time-experience-senegals-migratory-pastoralists.

2. Leif Brottem, "The Growing Complexity of Farmer–Herder Conflict in West and Central Africa," Africa Center for Strategic Studies, July 12, 2021, https://africacenter.org/publication/growing-complexity-farmer-herder-conflict-west-central-africa/.

3. Tor A. Benjaminsen and Boubacar Ba, "Fulani–Dogon Killings in Mali: Farmer–Herder Conflicts as Insurgency and Counterinsurgency," *African Security* 14, no. 1 (May 13, 2021), https://www.tandfonline.com/doi/full/10.1080/19392206.2021.1925035.

4. "Stopping Nigeria's Spiralling Farmer–Herder Violence," International Crisis Group, July 26, 2018, https://www.crisisgroup.org/africa/west-africa/nigeria/262-stopping-nigerias-spiralling-farmer-herder-violence.

5. Alex Thurston, "The Hollowness of 'Governance Talk' in and about the Sahel," Italian Institute for International Political Studies (ISPI), April 12, 2021, https://www.ispionline.it/en/publication/hollowness-governance-talk-and-about-sahel-30026.

6. Giuseppe Tomasi di Lampedusa, *The Leopard* (London: Harvill Press, 1986), 147.

7. Peter Frankopan, *The Earth Transformed* (New York: Knopf, 2023), 23, 164.

8. Faisal H. Husain, *Rivers of the Sultan* (New York: Oxford University Press, 2021), 80.

9. Matt Luizza, "Urban Elites' Livestock Exacerbate Herder–Farmer Tensions in Africa's Sudano-Sahel," *Climate Diplomacy*, Adelphi, June 14, 2019, https://climate-diplomacy.org/magazine/conflict/urban-elites-livestock-exacerbate-herder-farmer-tensions--sudano-sahel.

10. "Global Terrorism Index 2023," Institute for Economics and Peace, March 14, 2023, https://reliefweb.int/report/world/global-terrorism-index-2023.

11. Michael Nwankpa, "The North–South Divide: Nigerian Discourses on Boko Haram, the Fulani, and Islamization," Hudson Institute, October 26, 2021, https://www.hudson.org/national-security-defense/the-north-south-divide-nigerian-discourses-on-boko-haram-the-fulani-and-islamization.

12. James Courtright, Twitter (X), July 16, 2023, https://twitter.com/JCourtright08/status/1680565466081775617.

13. Kristina Petrova, "Floods, communal conflict, and the role of local state institutions in Sub-Saharan Africa," *Political Geography* 92 (January 2022), https://www.sciencedirect.com/science/article/pii/S0962629821001712?via%3Dihub.

14. Stefan Döring and Jonathan Hall, "Drought exposure decreases altruism with salient group identities as key moderator," *Nature Climate Change* 13 (July 24, 2023): 856–61, https://www.nature.com/articles/s41558-023-01732-2.

15. Idayat Hassan, "Disinformation Is Undermining Democracy in West Africa," Centre for International Governance Innovation (CIGI), July 4, 2022, https://www.cigionline.org/articles/disinformation-is-undermining-democracy-in-west-africa/.

16. Richard W. Franke and Barbara H. Chasin, *Seeds of Famine* (Montclair, NJ: Allanheld Osum, 1980), 6.

17. Peter Schwartzstein, "Indigenous Farming Practices Failing as Climate Change Disrupts Seasons," *National Geographic*, October 14, 2019, https://www.nationalgeographic.com/science/article/climate-change-killing-thousands-of-years-indigenous-wisdom.

18. Peter Schwartzstein, "The Extraordinary Benefits of a House Made from Mud," *National Geographic*, January 19, 2023, https://www.nationalgeographic.com/environment/article/why-these-west-african-architects-choose-mud-over-concrete.

19. C. J. Chivers, *The Gun* (New York: Simon & Schuster, 2011), 13.

Chapter 6

1. Chapter 6 is partly based on and includes excerpts from these articles:

    Peter Schwartzstein, "How Jordan's Climate and Water Crisis Threatens Its Fragile Peace," Center for Climate and Security, September 9, 2019, https://climateandsecurity.org/2019/09/climate-water-security-and-jordans-fragile-peace/.

    Peter Schwartzstein, "What Will Happen if the World No Longer Has Water?" Newsweek, November 11, 2022, https://www.newsweek.com/2017/12/01/what-happens-world-without-water-jordan-crisis-717365.html.

2. Sean Yom, "US Security Assistance in Jordan: Militarized Politics and Elusive Metrics," chap. 11 in *Security Assistance in the Middle East*, ed. Hicham Alaoui and Robert Springborg (Boulder, CO: Lynne Rienner, 2023).

3. Deepthi Rajsekhar, "Increasing drought in Jordan: Climate change and cascading Syrian land-use impacts on reducing transboundary flow," *Science Advances* 3, no. 8 (August 30, 2017), https://www.science.org/doi/10.1126/sciadv.1700581.

4. Jillian Schwedler, *Protesting Jordan: Geographies of Power and Dissent* (Palo Alto, CA: Stanford University Press, 2022), 19.

5. Jim Yoon et al., "A coupled human–natural system analysis of freshwater security under climate and population change," *Proceedings of the National Academy of Sciences* (*PNAS*) 118, no. 14 (March 29, 2021), https://www.pnas.org/doi/10.1073/pnas.2020431118.

6. Schwedler, *Protesting Jordan*, 101.

7. Ibid., 4.

8. Katrina Sammour, "Jordan's Nativists Thrive Online—And Might Exacerbate the Country's Divisions," Century Foundation, November 2, 2022, https://tcf.org/content/commentary/jordans-nativists-thrive-online-and-might-exacerbate-the-countrys-divisions/.

9. Henrikas Bartusevičius and Florian van Leeuwen, "Poor Prospects—Not Inequality—Motivate Political Violence," *Journal of Conflict Resolution* 66, no. 7-8 (May 30, 2022), https://journals.sagepub.com/doi/full/10.1177/00220027221074647.

10. "Data Analysis Tool," Arab Barometer, https://www.arabbarometer.org/survey-data/data-analysis-tool/.

11. Taim Alhajj, "The Al-Assad Regime's Captagon Trade," Carnegie Endowment for International Peace, October 6, 2022, https://carnegieendowment.org/sada/88109.

12. George Orwell, *Down and Out in Paris and London* (Boston: Mariner Books, 1933), 14.

13. Jon B. Alterman, "Ties That Bind: Family, Tribe, Nation, and the Rise of Arab Individualism," Center for Strategic and International Studies (CSIS), December 2, 2019, https://csis-website-prod.s3.amazonaws.com/s3fs-public/publication/Alterman_Loyalty_interior_v8_WEB_FULL.pdf.

14. Marc Gelkopf et al., "Protective factors and predictors of vulnerability to chronic stress: A comparative study of 4 communities after 7 years of continuous rocket fire," *Social Science & Medicine* 74, no. 5 (March 2012), https://www.sciencedirect.com/science/article/abs/pii/S0277953611006654?via%3Dihub.

15. Hana Namrouqa, "Water supply to be disrupted as alleged sabotage hits Disi project," *Jordan Times*, August 22, 2019, https://www.jordantimes.com/news/local/water-supply-be-disrupted-alleged-sabotage-hits-disi-project.

16. "Implementation Completion and Results Report on IRBD Loans," World Bank, December 31, 2018, https://documents1.worldbank.org/curated/en/222301546546705732/pdf/icr00004657-12282018-636818041906584165.pdf.

17. Yoon et al., "A coupled human–natural system analysis of freshwater security."

18. "Jordan announces compulsory military service for jobless men as unemployment surges," *Al-Monitor*, September 10, 2020, https://www.al-monitor.com/originals/2020/09/jordan-military-service-unemployment-coronavirus-tourism.html.

19. Zoltan Barany, "Foreign Contract Soldiers in the Gulf," Carnegie Middle East Center, February 5, 2020, https://carnegie-mec.org/2020/02/05/foreign-contract-soldiers-in-gulf-pub-80979.

20. Eckart Woertz, *Oil for Food: The Global Food Crisis and the Middle East* (Oxford, UK: Oxford University Press, 2013), 51.

21. Yom, "US Security Assistance in Jordan: Militarized Politics and Elusive Metrics," chap. 11.

Chapter 7

1. Chapter 7 is an expansion of and includes excerpts from this article:

   Peter Schwartzstein, "One of Africa's Most Fertile Lands Is Struggling to Feed Its Own People," *Bloomberg Businessweek*, April 2, 2019, https://www.bloomberg.com/features/2019-sudan-nile-land-farming/.

2. Deepa Babington, "Foreign groups snap up South Sudan farmland: Report," Reuters, March 23, 2011, https://www.reuters.com/article/idUSJOE72M0NK/.

3. "How Saudi Arabia Is Investing to Transform Its Economy," Goldman Sachs, October 13, 2023, https://www.goldmansachs.com/intelligence/pages/how-saudi-arabia-is-investing-to-transform-its-economy.html.

4. Elizabeth Dickinson, "The Korean company stuck in the middle of Madagascar's unrest," *Foreign Policy*, February 10, 2009, https://foreignpolicy.com/2009/02/10/the-korean-company-stuck-in-the-middle-of-madagascars-unrest/.

5. "Ethiopia: Army Commits Torture, Rape," Human Rights Watch, August 28, 2012, https://www.hrw.org/news/2012/08/28/ethiopia-army-commits-torture-rape.

6. Klaus Deininger et al., *Rising Global Interest in Farmland: Can It Yield Sustainable and Equitable Benefits?*, World Bank, 2011, https://documents1.worldbank.org/curated/en/998581468184149953/pdf/594630PUB0ID1810Box358282B01PUBLIC1.pdf.

7. Muhammad Atiq Ur Rehman Tariq, "A detailed perspective of water resource management in a dry and water scarce country: The case in Kuwait," *Frontiers in Environmental Science* 10 (December 1, 2022), https://www.frontiersin.org/articles/10.3389/fenvs.2022.1073834/full.

8. Daniel Yergin, *The Prize: The Epic Quest for Oil, Money, and Power* (New York: Simon & Schuster, 1990), 281.

9. Peter Ball, "World Cup 2022: How did water-stressed Qatar find enough for pitches?," BBC, December 15, 2022, https://www.bbc.com/news/world-63988887.

10. Eckart Woertz, *Oil for Food: The Global Food Crisis and the Middle East* (Oxford, UK: Oxford University Press, 2013), 115.

11. Ibid., 77.

12. Peter Schwartzstein, "Gulf Countries Look to Farm Abroad as Aquifer Dries Up," *National Geographic*, April 26, 2016, https://www.nationalgeographic.com/culture/article/gulf-countries-look-to-farm-abroad-as-aquifer-dries-up.

13. Lawrence Wright, *The Looming Tower* (New York: Knopf, 2007), 190.

14. Woertz, *Oil for Food*, 188.

15. Wright, *The Looming Tower*, 190.
16. Eckart Woertz, "Virtual water, international relations, and the new geopolitics of food," *Water International* 47, no. 7 (November 17, 2022), https://www.tandfonline.com/doi/full/10.1080/02508060.2022.2134516.
17. Woertz, *Oil for Food*, 47.
18. Schwartzstein, "Gulf Countries Look to Farm Abroad."
19. Anwar Ahmad, "Police warn motorists not to leave these items in their car during summer," *Gulf News*, June 14, 2020, https://gulfnews.com/uae/police-warn-motorists-not-to-leave-these-items-in-their-car-during-summer-1.72037308.
20. Schwartzstein, "Gulf Countries Look to Farm Abroad."
21. Martin Keulertz, "Drivers and impacts of farmland investment in Sudan: Water and the range of choice in Jordan and Qatar" (master's thesis, King's College, London), 2014, https://kclpure.kcl.ac.uk/portal/en/studentTheses/drivers-and-impacts-of-farmland-investment-in-sudan.
22. "Understanding Land Investment Deals in Africa: Nile Trading and Development, Inc., in South Sudan," Land Deal Brief, Oakland Institute, June 2011, https://www.oaklandinstitute.org/sites/oaklandinstitute.org/files/OI_Nile_Brief_0.pdf.
23. Roman Olearchyk and Henry Foy, "Saudi Arabia's Salic strikes deal to boost Ukraine farming," *Financial Times*, September 12, 2018, https://www.ft.com/content/49fff8b8-b664-11e8-bbc3-ccd7de085ffe.
24. Christopher Flavelle and Jack Healy, "Arizona Limits Construction around Phoenix as Its Water Supply Dwindles," *New York Times*, June 1, 2023, https://www.nytimes.com/2023/06/01/climate/arizona-phoenix-permits-housing-water.html.
25. Rob O'Dell and Ian James, "Arizona provides sweet deal to Saudi farm to pump water from Phoenix's backup supply," *Arizona Republic*, June 9, 2022, https://eu.azcentral.com/in-depth/news/local/arizona-environment/2022/06/09/arizona-gives-sweet-deal-saudi-farm-pumping-water-state-land/8225377002/.
26. Alex Weiner, "Arizona revokes water permits for Saudi Arabia–owned alfalfa farm," KTAR News, April 23, 2023, https://ktar.com/story/5487088/arizona-revokes-water-permits-for-saudi-arabia-owned-alfalfa-farm/.
27. Jean-Baptiste Gallopin, "Bad Company: How Dark Money Threatens Sudan's Transition," European Council on Foreign Relations, June 9, 2020, https://ecfr.eu/publication/bad_company_how_dark_money_threatens_sudans_transition/.
28. "WFP warns that hunger catastrophe looms in conflict-hit Sudan without urgent food assistance," UN World Food Programme, December 13, 2023, https://www.wfp.org/news/wfp-warns-hunger-catastrophe-looms-conflict-hit-sudan-without-urgent-food-assistance.
29. Jess Middleton and Will Nichols, "Heat stress to threaten over 70% of global agriculture by 2045," Verisk Maplecroft, September 7, 2022, https://www.maplecroft.com/insights/analysis/heat-stress-to-threaten-over-70-of-global-agriculture-by-2045/.
30. Daishi Chiba et al., "Chinese companies coralling land around world," *Nikkei Asia*, July 13, 2021, https://asia.nikkei.com/Spotlight/Datawatch/Chinese-companies-corralling-land-around-world.
31. Zongyuan Zoe Liu, "China's Farmland Is in Serious Trouble," *Foreign Policy*, February 27, 2023, https://foreignpolicy.com/2023/02/27/china-xi-agriculture-tax/.
32. Peter Schwartzstein, "African farmers say they can feed the world, and we might soon need them to," *Quartz*, July 17, 2016, https://qz.com/africa/736626/african-farmers-say-they-can-feed-the-world-and-we-might-soon-need-them-to.

Chapter 8

1. "Interplay of climate change–exacerbated rainfall, exposure, and vulnerability led to widespread impacts in the Mediterranean region," World Weather Attribution, September 19, 2023, https://www.worldweatherattribution.org/interplay-of-climate-change-exacerbated -rainfall-exposure-and-vulnerability-led-to-widespread-impacts-in-the-mediterranean -region/.

2. William J. Broad, "Inside the C.I.A., She Became a Spy for Planet Earth," *New York Times*, January 5, 2021, https://www.nytimes.com/2021/01/05/science/linda-zall-cia.html.

3. Caroline Houck, "Half of the US Military's Sites Are Vulnerable to Climate Change. Now What?" *Defense One*, January 31, 2018, https://www.defenseone.com/threats/2018/01 /half-us-militarys-sites-are-vulnerable-climate-change-now-what/145629/.

4. Nicholas Kusnetz, "Rising Seas Are Flooding Norfolk Naval Base, and There's No Plan to Fix It," *Inside Climate News*, October 25, 2017, https://insideclimatenews.org/news/2510 2017/military-norfolk-naval-base-flooding-climate-change-sea-level-global-warming -virginia/.

5. "Where are the hosepipe bans in place across the UK," ITV, June 26, 2023, https://www.itv .com/news/2023-04-25/where-are-hosepipe-bans-in-place-across-the-uk.

6. Alison Hird, "Farmers in drought-stricken southwest France invoke Saint-Gaudérique for rain," Radio France Internationale, March 19, 2023, https://www.rfi.fr/en/france/20230319 -farmers-in-drought-stricken-southwest-france-invoke-saint-gaud%C3%A9rique-for-rain -perpignan-national-rally.

7. Jen Christensen, "It's so hot in Arizona, doctors are treating a spike of patients who were burned by falling on the ground," CNN, July 24, 2023, https://edition.cnn.com/2023/07 /24/health/arizona-heat-burns-er/index.html.

8. "Firefighters battle California fires in conditions so harsh some water evaporates before it hits the ground," Associated Press, July 10, 2021, https://www.cbc.ca/news/world/california -wildfires-heath-wave-west-coast-1.6097963.

9. Avi Asher-Schapiro, "As California sizzles, Amazon drivers feel the heat over metrics," Reuters, September 13, 2022, https://www.reuters.com/article/idUSL8N30G46P/.

10. Zygmunt Bauman, *Liquid Fear* (Jersey City, NJ: Wiley, 2006), 130.

11. "Glocal Climate Change," European Data Journalism Network, https://climatechange.euro peandatajournalism.eu/en/.

12. Douglas Kenrick and Steven W. Macfarlane, "Ambient temperature and horn honking: A Field Study of the Heat/Aggression Relationship," *Environment and Behavior* 18, no. 2 (March 1986), https://journals.sagepub.com/doi/10.1177/0013916586182002.

13. Austin Troy et al., "The relationship between tree canopy and crime rates across an urban– rural gradient in the greater Baltimore region," *Landscape and Urban Planning* 106, no. 3 (June 15, 2012), https://www.sciencedirect.com/science/article/abs/pii/S0169204612000 977.

14. "Mass Shootings in 2022," Gun Violence Archive, https://www.gunviolencearchive.org /reports/mass-shooting?year=2022.

15. Josh Busby, "Why Do Climate Changes Lead to Conflict? Provocative New Study Leaves Questions," *New Security Beat*, September 12, 2013, https://www.newsecuritybeat.org/2013 /09/climate-lead-conflict-provocative-study-leaves-questions/.

16. Courrier International, "La Grèce enregistre la plus forte hausse du nombre de féminicides en Europe," *Courrier International*, February 28, 2023, https://www.courrierinternational .com/article/rapport-la-grece-enregistre-la-plus-forte-hausse-du-nombre-de-feminicides-en -europe.

17. Somini Sengupta, "This Is Inequity at the Boiling Point," *New York Times*, August 7, 2020, https://www.nytimes.com/interactive/2020/08/06/climate/climate-change-inequality-heat.html.

18. Anita Mukherjee and Nicholas Sanders, "The Causal Effect of Heat on Violence: Social Implications of Unmitigated Heat Among the Incarcerated," National Brueau of Economic Research, July 2021, https://www.nber.org/papers/w28987.

19. "Spanish police seize 74 tonnes of stolen olives amid soaring prices," Reuters, October 6, 2023, https://www.reuters.com/world/europe/spanish-police-seize-74-tonnes-stolen-olives-amid-soaring-prices-2023-10-06/.

20. Meredith Deliso and Edward Szekeres, "Dozens injured in violent clash between French police, demonstrators at anti-reservoir protest," ABC News, March 25, 2023, https://abcnews.go.com/International/dozens-injured-violent-clash-french-police-demonstrators-anti/story?id=98125426.

21. Natalie Kitroeff, "'This is a War': Cross-border Fight Over Water Erupts in Mexico," *New York Times*, October 14, 2020, https://www.nytimes.com/2020/10/14/world/americas/mexico-water-boquilla-dam.html.

22. Valentina Di Donato and Tim Lister, "The Mafia is poised to exploit coronavirus, and not just in Italy," CNN, April 19, 2020, https://edition.cnn.com/2020/04/19/europe/italy-mafia-exploiting-coronavirus-crisis-aid-intl/index.html.

23. Ciarán O'Connor, "The Conspiracy Consortium," Institute for Strategic Dialogue, December 17, 2021, https://www.isdglobal.org/isd-publications/the-conspiracy-consortium-examining-discussions-of-covid-19-among-right-wing-extremist-telegram-channel/.

24. Andreas Malm, *How to Blow Up a Pipeline: Learning to Fight in a World on Fire* (London: Verso, 2021), 67.

25. Peter Frankopan, *The Earth Transformed* (New York: Knopf 2023), 414.

26. Eric Chaney, "Revolt on the Nile: Economic Shocks, Religion, and Institutional Change," *Econometrica* 81, no. 5 (September 2013), https://www.jstor.org/stable/23524311.

27. Adam Yeeles, "Heat and Hotheads: The Effect of Rising Temperatures on Urban Unrest," New Security Beat, Wilson Center, March 23, 2015, https://www.newsecuritybeat.org/2015/03/heat-hotheads-effect-rising-temperatures-urban-unrest.

28. Lucy Gilder, "Climate change: Rise in Google searches around 'anxiety,'" BBC, November 22, 2023, https://www.bbc.com/news/science-environment-67473829.

29. Shaun Walker, "Beatings, dog bites, and barbed wire: Life and death on the Poland–Belarus border," *The Guardian*, October 2, 2023, https://www.theguardian.com/world/2023/oct/02/beatings-dog-bites-and-barbed-wire-life-and-death-on-the-poland-belarus-border.

30. Alex Smith, "Wild Country: Militia Activity along the Southern Border and Their Relationship with the USG," *Pardee Atlas Journal of Global Affairs*, https://sites.bu.edu/pardeeatlas/advancing-human-progress-initiative/back2school/wild-country-militia-activity-along-the-southern-border-and-their-relationship-with-the-usg/.

31. Frankopan, *The Earth Transformed*, 8.

32. Keely Brewer, "The Mississippi River is reaching historic highs and lows—forcing the shipping industry to adapt," KCUR, October 2, 2023, https://www.kcur.org/2023-10-02/mississippi-river-historic-lows-forcing-shipping-industry-adapt.

33. Michelle Fleury, "Can the Panama Canal Save Itself?" BBC, March 6, 2024, https://www.bbc.com/news/business-68467529.

34. Holly Ellyatt, "A critical shipping lane in Europe's economic heart is drying up in the searing heat," CNBC, July 20, 2022, https://www.cnbc.com/2022/07/20/germanys-rhine-river-levels-running-low-putting-economy-at-risk.html.

35. Hao Guo et al., "Rice drought risk assessment under climate change: Based on physical vulnerability, a quantitative assessment method," *Science of the Total Environment* 751 (January 10, 2021), https://www.sciencedirect.com/science/article/abs/pii/S0048969720350105.

36. Aled Jones et al., "Scoping Potential Routes to UK Civil Unrest via the Food System: Results of a Structured Expert Elicitation," *Sustainability* 15, no. 20 (October 12, 2023), https://www.mdpi.com/2071-1050/15/20/14783.

37. Julia Kollewe, "EDF cuts output at nuclear power plants as French rivers get too warm," The Guardian, August 3, 2022, https://www.theguardian.com/business/2022/aug/03/edf-to-reduce-nuclear-power-output-as-french-river-temperatures-rise.

38. Ben Christopher and Grace Gedye, "State Farm won't sell new home insurance in California. Can the state shore up the market?" CalMatters, May 31, 2023, https://calmatters.org/housing/2023/05/state-farm-california-insurance/.

39. Kathy Baughman McLeod, "Heat is killing us—and the economy too," Atlantic Council, September 7, 2021, https://www.atlanticcouncil.org/content-series/the-big-story/heat-is-killing-us-and-the-economy-too/.

40. Graham Caswell, "IMF Staff Warn of Climate 'Minsky Moment,'" Green Central Banking, June 24, 2022, https://greencentralbanking.com/2022/06/24/imf-staff-warn-of-climate-minsky-moment/.

41. "Lesbos keen to woo back tourists after migration crisis," Agence France-Presse, May 24, 2019, https://www.france24.com/en/20190524-lesbos-keen-woo-back-tourists-after-migration-crisis.

42. Peter Schwartzstein and Alexander Clapp, "Greece's Popular Islands Are Crowded—With Plastic," *Bloomberg*, November 10, 2021, https://www.bloomberg.com/news/features/2021-11-10/greece-s-popular-islands-are-crowded-with-plastic.

43. Peter Schwartzstein, "Water and Sabotage in Paradise: Greece's Hidden Climate Conflict," Center for Climate and Security, August 17, 2022, https://climateandsecurity.org/2022/08/water-and-sabotage-in-paradise-greeces-hidden-climate-conflict/.

44. Eurydice Bersi, "Too Much of a Good Thing? Wind Power and the Battle for Greece's Wild Heart," Reporters United, October 7, 2021, https://www.reportersunited.gr/en/6557/too-much-of-a-good-thing-wind-power-and-the-battle-for-greeces-wild-heart/.

45. Paul Tullis, "Nitrogen Wars: The Dutch Farmers' Revolt That Turned a Nation Upside Down," *The Guardian*, November 16, 2023, https://www.theguardian.com/environment/2023/nov/16/nitrogen-wars-the-dutch-farmers-revolt-that-turned-a-nation-upside-down.

46. Alexia Kalaitzi, "How Greece's Coal-Mining Heartland Won a Brief Reprieve after the War in Ukraine," *Balkan Insight*, February 21, 2023, https://balkaninsight.com/2023/02/21/how-greeces-coal-mining-heartland-won-a-brief-reprieve-after-the-war-in-ukraine/.

47. John Bluedorn and Niels-Jakob Hanse, "The Right Labor Market Policies Can Ease the Green Jobs Transition," International Monetary Fund, April 13, 2022, https://www.imf.org/en/Blogs/Articles/2022/04/13/blog041322-sm2022-weo-ch3.

48. Saijel Kishan et al., "Red States Will Reap the Biggest Rewards from Biden's Climate Package," *Bloomberg*, April 25, 2023, https://www.bloomberg.com/graphics/2023-red-states-will-reap-the-biggest-rewards-from-biden-s-climate-package/.

49. Patrick Coate and Kyle Mangum, "Recent Trends in U.S. Labor Mobility: Not So Fast," Federal Reserve Bank of Philadelphia, December 8, 2020, https://www.philadelphiafed.org/the-economy/regional-economics/recent-trends-in-u-s-labor-mobility-not-so-fast.

50. Neela Banerjee et al., "Exxon: The Road Not Taken," *Inside Climate News*, 2015, https://insideclimatenews.org/book/exxon-the-road-not-taken/.

51. "Big Oil's Trade Group Allies Outspent Clean Energy Groups by a Whopping 27 Times,"

February 15, 2023, https://www.desmog.com/2023/02/15/big-oil-trade-groups-american -petroleum-institute-outspent-clean-energy/.

52. "Dutch farmer protests create uproar in the Netherlands," *Tucker Carlson Tonight*, Fox News, July 10, 2022, https://www.foxnews.com/video/6309351715112.

53. Antonia Juhasz, "Iraq Gas Flaring Tied to Cancer Surge," Human Rights Watch, May 3, 2023, https://www.hrw.org/news/2023/05/03/iraq-gas-flaring-tied-cancer-surge.

54. Monica Mark, "Life Inside the South African Gangs Risking Everything for Copper," *Financial Times*, May 11, 2023, https://www.ft.com/content/19973223-cda7-43c0-8ba5 -ddd329fc9ff9.

55. "Because of the war, 90% of the wind energy capacities have been decommissioned— Galuschenko," *Fakty*, October 23, 2022, https://fakty.com.ua/en/ukraine/ekonomika/2022 1023-cherez-vijnu-90-potuzhnostej-vitrovoyi-energetyky-vyvedeni-z-ekspluatacziyi -galushhenko/.

56. Alejandro de la Garza, "We need geoengineering to stop out of control warming, warns climate scientist James Hansen," *Time* magazine, November 2, 2023, https://time.com /6330957/james-hansen-climate-warning-geoengineering-study/.

57. Cassandra Garrison, "Insight: How two weather balloons led Mexico to ban solar geoengi- neering," Reuters, March 27, 2023, https://www.reuters.com/business/environment/how -two-weather-balloons-led-mexico-ban-solar-geoengineering-2023-03-27.

58. "Iran's Climate Changes Are Suspicious," Iran Students' News Agency (ISNA), July 11, 2017, https://www.isna.ir/news/97041106044.

59. Aime Williams and Alice Hancock, "Climate engineering: A quick fix or a risky distraction?" *Financial Times*, September 1, 2023, https://www.ft.com/content/da1c7642-3d88-40f5 -a4c2-682455194b21.

60. "China Burned More Fossil Fuels in 2023 Despite Green Push," *Bloomberg News*, February 29, 2024, https://www.bloomberg.com/news/articles/2024-02-29/china-burned-more -fossil-fuels-in-2023-despitegreen-push.

61. National Intelligence Council, "National Intelligence Estimate: Climate Change and International Responses Increasing Challenges to US National Security through 2040" (NIC-NIE-2021-10030-A), Office of the Director of National Intelligence, 2021, https:// www.dni.gov/files/ODNI/documents/assessments/NIE_Climate_Change_and_National _Security.pdf.

62. David Wallace-Wells, "Beyond Catastrophe, A New Climate Change Reality Is Coming into View," *New York Times*, October 26, 2022, https://www.nytimes.com/interactive/2022 /10/26/magazine/climate-change-warming-world.html.

63. Quil Lawrence, "Hotter climate means a never-ending fire season for the National Guard," National Public Radio, August 23, 2023, https://www.npr.org/2023/08/23/1194434368 /fire-season-national-guard-climate-change.

64. Cecile Mantovani and Denis Balibouse, "Swiss army airlifts water to thirsty animals in Alpine meadows," Reuters, August 11, 2022, https://www.reuters.com/world/europe/swiss -army-airlifts-water-thirsty-animals-alpine-meadows-2022-08-11/.

65. Michael Birnbaum, "As wildfires grow, militaries are torn between combat, climate change," *Washington Post*, September 26, 2022, https://www.washingtonpost.com/climate-environ ment/2022/09/26/europe-military-wildfires-warming-slovenia/.

66. Kylie Mizokami, "Sweden dropped a laser-guided bomb on a forest fire," *Popular Mechanics*, July 25, 2018, https://www.popularmechanics.com/military/aviation/a22550688/sweden -dropped-a-laser-guided-bomb-on-a-forest-fire/.

67. Andrew Freedman, "Scientists Fear Ukraine War Will Worsen Siberian Wildfires," *Axios*, April 22, 2022, https://www.axios.com/2022/04/22/siberia-wildfires-war-ukraine.

68. Birnbaum, "As wildfires grow, militaries are torn."

69. National Intelligence Council, "National Intelligence Estimate: Climate Change and International Responses Increasing Challenges to US National Security."

70. Peter Schwartzstein, "Mediterranean fishermen face perfect storm as tensions and temperatures rise," *Politico*, February 8, 2021, https://www.politico.eu/article/mediterranean-fishermen-struggles-tensions-temperatures-rise/.

71. "Offutt AFB PMO Timeline [for Flood Rebuild]," Offutt Air Force Base Project Management Office, https://www.offutt.af.mil/Home/Flood-Rebuild/.

72. Marc Kodack, "Climate change adversely affecting aircraft performance in Greece: Implications for militaries?" Center for Climate and Security, October 12, 2020, https://climateandsecurity.org/2020/10/climate-change-adversely-affecting-aircraft-performance-in-greece-implications-for-militaries/.

73. Armed Forces Health Surveillance Branch, "Update: Heat Illness, Active Component, U.S. Armed Forces, 2018," *Health.mil* (official website of the Military Health System), April 1, 2019, https://health.mil/News/Articles/2019/04/01/Update-Heat-Illness.

74. Munir Muniruzzaman, email message to author, January 2024.

75. "Former President Trump Holds Rally in Durham, New Hampshire," C-SPAN, December 16, 2023, https://www.c-span.org/video/?532231-1/president-trump-holds-rally-durham-hampshire.

Chapter 9

1. Chapter 9 is partly based on and includes excerpts from this article:
Peter Schwartzstein, "How Climate Change Can Help Heal Conflicts—Not Just Fuel Them," National Geographic, November 10, 2022, https://www.nationalgeographic.com/environment/article/climate-change-can-help-heal-conflicts-environmental-peacebuilding.

2. Tobias Ide et al., "The past and future(s) of environmental peacebuilding," *International Affairs* 97, no. 1 (January 11, 2021), https://academic.oup.com/ia/article/97/1/1/6041492.

3. Peter Schwartzstein, "Biblical Waters: Can the Jordan River Be Saved?" *National Geographic*, 22, 2014, https://www.nationalgeographic.com/science/article/140222-jordan-river-syrian-refugees-water-environment.

4. Erica Gaston et al., "Climate-Security and Peacebuilding: Thematic Review," United Nations report, April 2023, https://www.un.org/peacebuilding/content/thematic-review-climate-security-and-peacebuilding-2023.

5. Gidon Bromberg et al., "A Green Blue Deal for the Middle East," EcoPeace Middle East, December 2020, https://ecopeaceme.org/wp-content/uploads/2021/03/A-Green-Blue-Deal-for-the-Middle-East-EcoPeace.pdf.

6. Hamid Pouran et al., "Dust storms: A shared security challenge for the Middle East," Chatham House, July 11, 2023, https://www.chathamhouse.org/2023/07/dust-storms-shared-security-challenge-middle-east.

7. Gaston et al., "Climate-Security and Peacebuilding."

8. "Water catchment project is expanded to aid peace and economic recovery in North Darfur," UN Environment Programme (UNEP), November 27, 2018, https://www.unep.org/news-and-stories/story/water-catchment-project-expanded-aid-peace-and-economic-recovery-north.

9. Peter Schwartzstein, "A Recipe for Perpetual Insecurity? The Case of a Syrian Protected Area," Center for Climate and Security, November 5, 2021, https://climateandsecurity.org/2021/11/a-recipe-for-perpetual-insecurity-the-case-of-a-syrian-protected-area/.

10. Geraldine Chatelard, "Jebel Abdel Aziz, socioeconomic assessment," United Nations

Development Programme (UNDP), 2009, https://shs.hal.science/halshs-00356885/file /Jebel_Abdel_Aziz_socioeconomic.pdf.

11. Tobias Ide, "The Dark Side of Environmental Peacebuilding," *World Development* 127 (March 2020), https://www.sciencedirect.com/science/article/abs/pii/S0305750X19304267.

12. Peter Schwartzstein, "How Iran Is Destroying Its Once-Thriving Environmental Movement," *National Geographic*, November 12, 2020, https://www.nationalgeographic .com/environment/article/how-iran-destroying-once-thriving-environmental-movement.

13. Peter Schwartzstein, "A Reminder from Israel and Gaza on the Importance and Limitations of Environmental Peacebuilding," Wilson Center, October 13, 2023, https://www.new securitybeat.org/2023/10/reminder-israel-gaza-importance-limitations-environmental -peacebuilding/.

14. Ian Ritchie, "How the year without summer gave us dark masterpieces," *The Guardian*, June 16, 2016, https://www.theguardian.com/music/2016/jun/16/1816-year-without-summer -dark-masterpieces-beethoven-schubert-shelley.

15. Hannah Rae Armstrong, "The tech that helps these herders navigate drought, war, and extremists," *MIT Technology Review*, March 1, 2024, https://www.technologyreview.com /2024/03/01/1089006/high-tech-solutions-garbal-call-centers-herding-conflict-africa-sahel/.

16. Peter Schwartzstein, 'History's Greatest Sea Is Dying," *The Atlantic*, December 14, 2019, https://www.theatlantic.com/international/archive/2019/12/mediterranean-sea-pollution -un-climate/603442/.

17. Florian Krampe et al., "Responses to Climate-Related Security Risks: Regional Organizations in Asia and Africa," Stockholm International Peace Research Institute (SIPRI), August 2018, https://www.sipri.org/sites/default/files/2018-08/sipriinsight1808_igos_and_climate _change.pdf.

Index

About the Author

Peter Schwartzstein is an award-winning British American environmental journalist and researcher who has reported on water, food security, and particularly the conflict–violence nexus across more than thirty countries in the Middle East, Africa, and further afield. Since 2013, he has mostly written for *National Geographic*, but his work has also appeared in the *New York Times*, the BBC, *Bloomberg Businessweek*, and many other outlets. He is a Global Fellow with the Wilson Center's Environmental Change and  Security Program, a TED fellow, and a fellow at the Center for Climate and Security. Based in Athens, Greece, he consults for the UN Development Programme, the UN Environment Programme, and Amnesty International, among other organizations, and regularly speaks at climate security conferences and other environmental symposiums. This is his first book.